BEAGLES
TODAY

Andrew H. Brace

Howell Book House

HOWELL
BOOK
HOUSE

New York

Beagles Today

This book is dedicated to Ada,
otherwise known as Ch. Too Darn Hot for Tragband,
whose prowess in the show ring was only eclipsed
by her years of devotion and loyalty
as the best friend I have ever had.

HOWELL BOOK HOUSE
A Simon & Schuster / Macmillan Company
1633 Broadway
New York, NY 10019

MACMILLAN is a registered trademark of Macmillan, Inc.

Library of Congress Cataloging-in-Publication data
available on request.

ISBN 0–87605–086–0

Manufactured in Singapore

10 9 8 7 6 5 4 3 2 1

CONTENTS

ACKNOWLEDGEMENTS

This book would not have been possible without the great help and assistance of several people to whom the Beagle breed is as dear as it is to me. I would like to place on record my thanks to all the following people:

To the many Beagle breeders, both at home and overseas, who have supplied me with detailed information on their kennels, and accompanying photographs.

To Barbara and Peter Roderick, on behalf of the Beagle Club, who have allowed me to borrow some important photographs from its collection for inclusion.

To Marion Spavin for sharing with me many of her "secrets" which have been incorporated into the chapter dealing with breeding.

To Jesper Eades for supplying invaluable information on the drag hunting scene.

To Andrew Smalley for producing illustrations of the lesser-known hound colours, and for providing further details of Beagle packs.

To Viv Rainsbury for her excellent line drawings.

To Eleanor Bothwell for her presentation of breed points, and also her fascinating contribution on Infertility Syndrome.

To Sylvia Tutchener for sharing with me her knowledge of the Australian Quarantine Detector Dogs programme.

To Marcos Adler (South America), Richard Gilmore (USA), Shirley Winslow (Canada), Steven Seymour (Australia), Noelene Hughes (New Zealand), Ros Glaysher (South Africa), Jesper Pedersen (Denmark), Catharina Linde-Forsberg (Scandinavia) and Jochen Eberhardt (Europe) for providing detailed analyses of the breed in their respective countries, enabling me to cover the global picture of the Beagle in considerably more detail than would ever have otherwise been possible. Catharina has also given me the benefit of her specialist knowledge in the fields of artificial insemination and hereditary defects.

My thanks also to the many photographers whose pictures have been used in the book, and to Sylvia Evans, my former secretary, Les and Anne Davis, my wonderful neighbours, and, of course, my parents, who have all been invaluable Beagle-sitters when I have been away from home.

FOREWORD

I wish I could say that I have owned Beagles for all of my life, but that would be a lie. My childhood companion was a Boxer dog who kindled in me a passion for the whole dog world which has never dwindled. It was in 1971, when I was showing my Pekingese around the small Open Shows in my native South Wales, that I saw a Beagle bitch whom I will never forget. I had seen Beagles before but they had struck me as quite ordinary. However, this little tricolour bitch had such quality and smartness, such exquisite balance and a lovely expression, that I felt I would have to find out more about her. Her name was Imdee Aimee and she was a daughter of the American import, Appeline Validay Happy Feller. She was later to have a half-brother, Ch. Dialynne Gamble, who would revolutionise the breed in Britain.

My new-found interest in Beagles caused me to seek out Beagle breeders in the area and I soon struck up a friendship with Veronica Bradley, who owned the Dufosee Beagles, her then husband David, and their family. My first Beagle was Dufosee Gatsby of Tragband, litter brother to the famous Ch. Dufosee Harris Tweed, a son of Gamble and Veronica's exceptional producer, Ch. Dufosee Bonnie Girl. My subsequent success in Beagles has been largely due to friendships formed through the breed – the one with the Bradley family led to my co-owning several Dufosee Beagles with their daughter Sue. These included Ch. Dufosee Radleigh of Tragband, Ch. Dufosee Quaker Girl of Tragband and Ch. Dufosee Aria of Tragband.

My friendship with Di and Carl Johnson of the Dicarl Great Danes, at the time when I owned Aria, led to them buying a Beagle, a younger sister of Aria, called Dufosee Geisha. She in turn was mated to Ch. Dialynne Blueboy and produced a litter which contained a bitch called Dicarl Gay's The Word. My friendship with Ken Sinclair and Adrian Edwards resulted in my buying Gay's The Word and giving her to them as a housewarming present, on the understanding that I could have a puppy back from her in due course when I had found the right stud dog for her. I judged the American import Ch. Am. Ch. Graadtres Hot Pursuit of Rossut at his second British show, gave him the Challenge Certificate and Best of Breed, and told Ken and Adrian that I had found "the right stud dog" to breed me that special puppy. That puppy turned out to be Ch. Too Darn Hot for Tragband, known as Ada, who not only became the breed record holder, but the best friend I have ever had.

My friendship with Marion Spavin led to her taking an Ada daughter, Tragband Sweet Bird of Youth, on breeding terms. She bred my latest Champion, Dialynne Tolliver of Tragband, otherwise known as Mikey, by Ch. Soloman of Dialynne.

So, a highly successful involvement with the breed I hold dearest has only been possible through the kindness of friends. *But the best friends of all are the Beagles.*

1 ORIGINS OF THE BEAGLE

Few puppies can match the chocolate-box appeal of an eight-week old Beagle, as anyone involved with manufacturing and marketing will bear out. Probably no other breed has been featured more on greetings cards, posters and all manner of saleable items. It is indeed a hard heart which will not melt at the sight of the "mild appealing expression" which is so very much the breed's trademark. Yet behind that "cute" image which, unlike so many other breeds, lasts through adulthood, lie centuries of history and a breed which has been developed by humans to work alongside them in one of their most basic pursuits – hunting.

EARLY DEVELOPMENT

To understand fully, and to appreciate the Beagle breed with all its subtleties and complexities, it is essential that any prospective owner knows at least a little of the breed's origins, for many of its most primitive instincts have stood the test of time and remain with it to the present day. The Beagle was originally developed from various types of primitive hound to follow the scent of small game, specifically hare. As early as the time of the Roman invasion, it seems likely that hounds, similar in many ways to early Beagles, were being used to hunt in Britain. Some were probably larger, and others smaller, than what is now perceived as being a typical Beagle, and they would have exhibited marked regional differences, but there can be little doubt that they were the progenitors of the contemporary Beagle. Across the Irish Sea, as far back as the eighteenth century, the Kerry Beagle could be found, a breed which exists to this day. This breed, however, now bears few similarities to the modern Beagle, as it is a much taller and more racy hound altogether, and is believed to have been instrumental in the development of the American Black and Tan Coonhound, to which it bears more than a striking resemblance.

It has been suggested – erroneously, it should be stressed – that Beagles were bred down from Foxhounds. While they may have shared common ancestors, it should be pointed out that Beagling was extremely popular as a sport long before foxhunting gained a foothold in the eighteenth century, heralding the conscious development of the Foxhound as a separate entity, whereas, previously, Beagles had been used extensively in hunting fox. As foxhunting and Foxhounds increased in

The Beagle as depicted on a cigarette card, produced by W.D. and H.O. Wills, and issued in 1914.
The painting is by the famous canine artist Arthur Wardle.

Courtesy: Patrick Vaughan.

popularity, many Beagle packs were disbanded, and it was not for another century that Beagling enjoyed something of a revival. The countless literary references to the Beagles of the nineteenth century and before, all of which have been well documented in previously published works on the breed, are consistent in pointing out that one of the characteristics of the Beagle was its relative smallness. Bear in mind that the prime function of these hounds was actively to hunt and follow a scent, and yet smallness was an essential feature, as the humans had to keep up with these dogs on foot. I stress this point because, in recent years, the British show fraternity has witnessed some rather large hounds winning top honours. The owners of said hounds invariably claim that excessive size is a direct throw-back to the authentic Beagle. In fact, nothing could be further from the truth, and to suggest so shows a lack of understanding of the breed's history.

RECOGNITION OF THE BREED
The Beagle was recognised by the British Kennel Club as far back as 1873, eight years before the Association of Masters of Harriers and Beagles was formed. The Beagle Club had, interestingly, been formed in 1890 and held its first show in 1896. It celebrated its centenary show in 1996. While it is popularly believed that early Beagles in Britain were lighter in build, more rangey, and sharper-muzzled than the modern specimen, in truth it would appear that in the nineteenth century there were also to be found Beagles which were far heavier-headed than the modern Beagle – almost to the point of appearing somewhat 'bully' – and correspondingly thicker built. Similarly, other hounds, which were also grouped under the Beagle name, tended to be rather bow-fronted, long and low, with more than a passing resemblance to a primitive Basset type.

The modern Beagle has undoubtedly been developed by blending together certain regional types within the breed (some of which would have contained Harrier or Foxhound blood) until the overall type became more even, whereupon certain breed points were refined through selective breeding. It has been stated quite categorically that terrier blood was at one time introduced in an attempt to reduce the size of larger hounds, and some photographs of early Beagles would seem to give credibility to this theory. The Beagle packs which supplied the foundation stock from which the present-day exhibition Beagle has been bred were mainly formed in the late nineteenth or early twentieth century.

STABILISING TYPE

During the early part of the twentieth century great advances had been made in stabilising type in Beagles. While size still varied, most Beagle fanciers and breeders were in agreement about the important breed characteristics and the "look" which was desirable. Mr F.B. Lord, who was not only a keen sportsman around the turn of the century but also a successful exhibitor of Beagles, wrote: "Type was most lamentably neglected till the Beagle Club took Beagles in hand, but since then, year by year, type has been bred for as well as working power and Beagle lovers must certainly be satisfied with the results. A few years ago the best Beagles exhibited were

very poor, ordinary specimens, while now it is quite the exception to see a bad Beagle on the bench. I was once exceedingly doubtful as to the good of dog shows, but I now think they promote type and quality as well as work."

THE DIFFICULT WAR YEARS

Just as Beagles were beginning to establish themselves on the show bench, the First World War saw an end to all dog showing activities. Virtually all breeding was abandoned, and many kennels were either totally disbanded or drastically reduced in size. Food was a luxury and dogs came low on the list of most people's priorities. Dog shows resumed again in the 1920s, but few Beagles were to be seen taking part. Some of the pre-war fanciers had managed to keep the breed alive on a limited scale, but quality breeding-stock was hard to find and the masters of hounds no longer sent Beagles along to dog shows, as had previously been the case. By 1927 only two names had been added to the Kennel Club's Beagle register.

It could be said that the saviour of the breed was Mrs Nina Elms, a great devotee of hound breeds who kept a kennel not only of Beagles but also of Bloodhounds

The Crowder Beagle Pack, photographed in 1935. The heads of these hounds would be considered rather plain by modern standards, but note the width of forequarters and the excellent spring of rib.   *Photo courtesy: Basil J. Waterton.*

and Basset Hounds. Her Reynalton kennel was no small concern, and it is reported that at one Crufts Dog Show Mrs Elms made no fewer than sixty entries with her three breeds. It has previously been suggested that without Mrs Elms' boundless enthusiasm for the breed, and readiness to introduce and encourage new Beagle exhibitors, the Beagle might have become as rare a sight in the show ring as the Foxhound is today. Many breeders of the time acquired Reynalton foundation stock on which they built their own kennels – but many of these were to be halted in their progress with the coming of the Second World War.

EARLY BREEDERS

In 1945 just one Beagle was registered with the Kennel Club, but the following year the figure rose to eighteen. Of the pre-war exhibitors, only Mrs Stockley (who owned the famous Grappler, a hound who achieved immortality through the trophies which carry his name and are presented annually by the Beagle Club) resumed her interest. Her post-war Ch. Limbourne Violet is acclaimed as being a "superlative hound about fourteen inches in height". Other leading lights in the breed at the time were Mrs and Miss Wilmshurst who had the Stanhurst affix, carried by several significant hounds such as Ch. Solomon of Stanhurst. Making an impact on the breed during the same period were Miss Joan Whitton, who owned the Tavernmews Beagles, and Miss Ruth Brucker, whose affix was Twinrivers. A major force in Beagles was Douglas Appleton, one time Secretary of the Beagle Club, and owner of the Appeline affix which he shared with his wife Carol. The Appletons owned some of the most outstanding hounds of the era and in later years were to elevate the breed to a new level of quality through the

judicious importation of top-class American Beagles.

As recently as the 1940s (which is, let's face it, just fifty years ago) many of the Beagles entered in the Kennel Club Stud Book came from parents which were either "unregistered" or of "pedigree unknown". Early breeders who were interested in competing in the show ring with their Beagles were working very much in the dark as regards their basic breeding stock's ancestry, and the breed owes a great deal to their ability to select the best, based on form and function. Today's breeders are lucky in that they can study pedigrees going back many generations, and form a picture of the type of dogs which figure in those pedigrees, thus gaining much valuable information before they effect a proposed mating. In the early days breeders did not have that luxury. However, no matter how much breeders will tell you that they can plan a mating on paper, it all boils down to what the late Elizabeth Somerfield, the great Boxer breeder, said: "To breed good-looking puppies, you breed a good-looking bitch to a good-looking dog ... and if the pedigree looks good, then that's a bonus."

BASIC INSTINCTS

Many of the early exhibitors in the breed also worked their Beagles, so it would follow that they would only keep dogs which could perform the task for which the breed was originally developed. Thus few show Beagles would have been selected purely for beauty; they would need the mental capacity to follow a scent, and also the overall construction and stamina. Such hounds may well have excelled in the basic breed attributes, but could easily have lacked some of the minor cosmetic or aesthetic qualities which have today, perhaps, taken priority. With the development of the Beagle as a companion,

Even the most domesticated of Beagles will instinctively follow a scent. Here Ch. Too Darn Hot for Tragband is in hot pursuit of a rabbit.   Photo: Panther Photographic.

the basic mentality of the breed has gradually changed, to a certain degree. Beagle puppies bred today tend to be less wilful and disobedient than their forebears. Some will actually come when they are called! I know that many present-day breeders maintain that we should preserve the breed's natural scent-following ability, and to that end many still engage themselves in working trials. That is their privilege. Personally I feel that, as the vast majority of puppies bred are destined to end up as companions, the less likely they are to go off at the slightest whiff of a rabbit, the better. Nowadays Beagles fit in

much more comfortably into a home environment, are less destructive and much more obedient. Had these attributes not improved over the years, I fear we would have a far greater rescue problem in the breed, with pet puppies being returned because their owners "couldn't do a thing with them".

No matter how much we may "humanise" this breed, no matter how trainable they become, and how generally social, there is no getting away from the fact that those basic instincts are there. Deep-seated they may be, but they are there nonetheless. Let me tell you a story. I

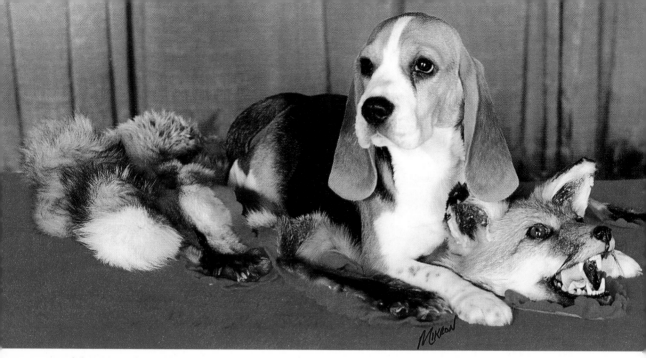

Memories of a foxhunting past: A highly individual portrait of Shirley Winslow's Can. Ch. Lenwins Kummin Up Klover, pictured here at four and a half months.   Photo: Mikron.

have never, ever, worked any of my Beagles. They are, first and foremost, my companions, and I like to think that when they are exercising free, they will come when they are called.

One day I had taken Ada – Ch. Too Darn Hot for Tragband – for an early morning photography session with Sally Anne Thompson, the legendary animal photographer, at her home in Gloucestershire. She had suggested taking pictures at around 7 a.m. because the marvellous cloud formations would give us a perfect background. We walked to a nearby golf-course, with Ada off the leash as was quite usual, took some wonderful photographs, and then began to walk home to Sally's cottage. Suddenly, like a bullet from a gun, Ada took off, baying that unique Beagle bark, which I had never, ever heard from her before. She was three weeks in whelp at the time with her first litter to Ch. Dufosee Influence, and later that day she was being shown at The Hound Show,

her last show ring appearance before maternity leave. I was panic-stricken and, call as I might, there was no sign of Ada.

Following the sound of her incessant baying I made my way through the bracken and undergrowth until I came across a rather weary Beagle bitch, sitting astride two tiny fox cubs, a very puzzled look on her face. It was as if something had triggered a mechanism in her brain, she had reacted spontaneously, not knowing why, and just followed that "basic instinct". Thank heavens, there was no vixen in sight. We returned to the car – Ada on the leash, my knees still knocking, gave her a quick wash and brush up and set off for the Hound Show where she duly won the Challenge Certificate and Best of Breed. It was with great pride that I related the story of the morning's events to some of the "hunting" fraternity within the breed, and the looks on their faces suggested that I might as well have been telling them the story of Hansel and Gretel!

DEVELOPMENT OF THE SHOW DOG

By the mid-1950s the breed had become quite well established in the show ring, but, for example, in 1955, there were just ten sets of Kennel Club Challenge Certificates available. The Appeline kennel tended to dominate the Beagle ring, but the breed had by then attracted newer exhibitors who were to make their mark on the British Beagle, such as Gladys Clayton and her daughter Patricia (Barvae), Dolly Macro (Deaconfield) and Dorothy Crowther-Davies (Cannybuff). Interestingly, exhibiting Beagles at the time were Yvonne Oldman (better known for her Barsheen Bloodhounds) and Joyce Caddy (whose Ouaine Cocker Spaniels achieved fame). By the end of the decade great strides were being made by two other lady breeders, namely Thelma Gray, whose Rozavel affix achieved the highest accolades in several breeds, and Joan Beck, of the Letton kennel, which was also successful in a variety of different breeds. Both Rozavel and Letton kennels worked hard with American imports, and their efforts in helping to create the "modern" Beagle should never be under-emphasised.

The 1960 Kennel Club Stud Book contains entries of two Derawuda bitches, bred by Fred Watson who owned the legendary Best in Show winner, Ch. Barvae Statute, and shown by relatively new exhibitors to the breed. Derawuda Vanity was a daughter of Ch. Statute and her owner was none other than Marion Spavin, the leading Beagle breeder in the UK for many years. Vanity proved a marvellous foundation bitch and virtually all of the present-day Dialynnes can be traced back to

LEFT: This photograph was used as a Christmas card sent by Gladys Clayton and her daughter Patricia in the 1950s. Mrs Clayton founded the Barvae kennel which, in turn, supplied foundation stock to many other breeders. The featured dogs are: Barvae Varner, Ch. Barvae Paigan and Barvae Ponder.

Photo courtesy: Marion Spavin.

RIGHT: The modern Beagle owes much to Ch. Dialynne Gamble. Sired by the Appleton's American import, Appeline Validay Happy Feller out of Ch. Dialynne Nettle (a double grand-daughter of Ch. Dialynne Huntsman), Gamble was a great winner in the show ring, but excelled as a sire. He produced an unprecedented 26 British Champions, and most of today's top winners are closely line-bred to him.
Photo: Diane Pearce.

The Barvae Beagles are behind virtually all of today's show kennels. Ch. Barvae Paigan (pictured left), born 1954, illustrates a smartness of outline and 'style' rather ahead of his time.

The important import, Barvae Benroe Wrinkles, brought into Britain by Gladys Clayton. Wrinkles proved a very successful stud dog.
Photo courtesy: David Nicholson.

her in direct line. The other Derawuda bitch, Wheatear, was owned by Leonard and Heather Priestley, whose Pinewood affix was to be carried by many top-class hounds in the years to come.

Through the sixties the breed attracted many more exhibitors and breeders and by 1970 there were no fewer than twenty-eight sets of Challenge Certificates on offer through the year. Many of these enthusiasts are still active in the breed so I shall refrain from mentioning them here as they will appear in a later chapter. However, kennels which made an impact at the time include:

Annasline, Judith Ireland's very American-minded kennel which brought invaluable blood into the country, notably from the Page Mill kennel, and exported significant dogs to several countries; **Cornevon**, owned by Alice Gibson and her enthusiastic daughters Penny Jeffries and Janice Roberts, whose kennel went on to

be even more successful in Irish Setters; **Ditchmere**, owned by Thelma Hosking, who had been the judge of the breed at the Hound Show before which Ada had gone AWOL!; **Easthazel**, the Scottish-based kennel of David McKay, which produced Beagles which were incorporated into several other significant kennels' breeding programmes; **Grattondown**, Don Lester's kennel from which stock went to several newer breeders to help establish their kennels; **Harque**, the affix of Ann Argyle who, while going on to achieve greater prominence in Whippets, always bred a very good type of Beagle – Ann was one of several Beagle aficionados who went on to have the honour of judging Best in Show at Crufts; **Oudenarde**, the kennel of Ferelith Somerfield's mother and aunt, Diana and Helen Hamilton, who never campaigned the breed heavily but produced some significant quality Beagles which were

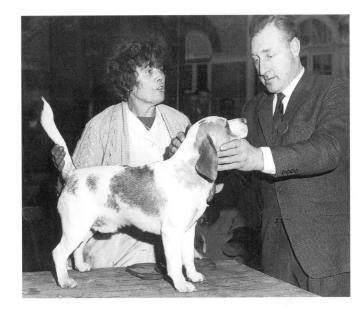

One of the British Beagle world's best-loved and most-missed characters was Dolly Macro, seen here exhibiting one of her beloved Deaconfield Beagles. The judge is the late Peter Tarry, husband of Sheila Tarry who enjoyed great success in the 1960s with Ch. Penwarne Jonavere Apple Blossom. The Deaconfield affix continues in the ownership of Dolly's grand-daughter, Debbie Taylor.

Photo: C.M. Cooke.

shown by other kennels, notably Dialynne and Rossut; **Sylvahue**, Hubert Foster's kennel from where came sound stock which was sought after by other breeders of the time; **Trewint**, owned by Judith Ireland's mother, 'Stevie', who produced excellent type and size, yet never campaigned dogs owing to her geographical location deep in the English West Country – nonetheless several Trewints won well for other owners at home and overseas; **Wendover**, the kennel of famous all-rounder judge, L.C. 'Jimmy' James and his wife 'Jay' – their affix was synonymous with all that is best in

Irish Setters, yet its contribution to Beagles was enormous, Ch. Wendover Billy achieving immortality in the form of the Beswick Beagle model.

Despite rather chequered and varied origins, the Beagle was by now established as a smart and willing quality show dog, with a certain consistency of type and an amiable disposition which made the breed an ideal companion as well. The pioneer breeders had done a great job, and had laid solid foundations on which the Beagle fanciers of the future would be able to build still further.

2 CHOOSING YOUR BEAGLE

First of all, are you really sure that the Beagle is the breed for you? Most dog breeders will tell you that their breed is the ideal all-purpose companion, but sometimes they tend to gloss over the breed's shortcomings – and all breeds have them.

CHARACTERISTICS

The Beagle's pack ancestry, while to a large degree very much diluted these days, is a factor which must always be considered by any prospective owner. The breed has a keen nose and will follow a scent at the drop of a hat. They can turn a deaf ear to the most forceful of commands, even when apparently well trained, and they need above average exercise if they are to be kept fit. Beagles do not do well if kennelled alone – in fact no breed does – and a solitary Beagle will become bored and consequently destructive. If you are seriously thinking of becoming a Beagle owner, there should be someone at home all day so that the dog has constant companionship. Should circumstances be such that your Beagle will have to spend long periods of time without human company, then you will be better off keeping two, so that they will provide entertainment and companionship for each other.

Your home should have a dog-proof garden – Beagles can be great escapologists – and if you are contemplating a couple of hounds, then a kennel and large run are essential, so that they can be kept securely when you are out of the house. Given that there is someone at home all day, and several long walks are part of the daily routine, there is no reason why a single Beagle will not fit in as part of an apartment home with no garden. Company and exercise are the Beagle's two major requirements. That apart, they are relatively maintenance-free. They need little grooming, will eat virtually anything – as you will discover if you leave an expensive pair of shoes lying around unattended! – and are fairly easy to housetrain. The Beagle tends to be quite long-lived, with fifteen being an average age, so if you are planning on sharing your life with the breed, this is a long-term commitment.

DECIDING ON TYPE

After having considered all the pros and cons, and decided that the Beagle is the breed for you, you will then have to decide whether you want a puppy or an adult, a

The Beagle is rated by many as the ideal all-purpose companion. Ch. Southcourt Wembury Merryboy, owned by Heather and Leonard Priestley of the Pinewood Beagles, sums up the breed's appeal.

Photo: Anne Roslin-Williams.

dog or a bitch. Most buyers assume that a baby puppy is the only option if they want to be able to mould the dog's personality and develop the dog's character around their own lifestyle. To some extent that may be true, but often there is much to be said for giving a home to a dog which has, through no fault of its own, come into Rescue but is still young and healthy. Also, breeders will occasionally have a young adult, or older puppy, which they may have been "running on" as a potential show dog, but which has now developed some minor blemish which may spoil the chances of the dog becoming a great winner. Such defects in no way prevent the dog from being a happy, healthy and attractive companion, one whom the breeder will be happy to place in a pet home. If this is the case, however, the breeder's wishes should always be respected and in the UK most breeders of such a dog will have the registration papers endorsed "Not Eligible for Exhibition".

As regards sex, there are advantages and disadvantages with either. Dogs can, when mature, develop the urge to do what comes naturally and may take to practising on your velvet scatter cushions or an elderly aunt's ankle! Bitches, on the other hand, come into season twice yearly on average and, if you live in a neighbourhood where

Even if you are being offered one particular puppy by the breeder, it is always advisable to see the whole litter together so that you can see your puppy in context. These three puppies bred by the Dufosee kennel are remarkably even.

Photo: Thomas Fall.

there are roaming dogs, you could find yourself with many unwelcome biannual visitors. Temperamentally dogs and bitches differ very slightly. Some will say that bitches are more affectionate, but I have known many male hounds who are real "softies" and very much people-dogs. You should also think about colour. Some people will only consider a blanketed tricolour. Others prefer the softer colours of the tan or lemon and white hounds.

CHOOSING A BREEDER

Decide on what you want – age, sex and colour – and contact a reputable breeder. The best way of finding conscientious Beagle breeders in your area is to visit several dog shows where you will have the chance to meet exhibitors, many of whom will be breeders. Look at the dogs these people are showing, and see which of them have hounds which particularly appeal to you. When they have finished showing – never before – approach them and tell them what you are looking for. You will probably be interrogated in some detail if they are responsible breeders with a genuine interest in the welfare of their dogs, and you should not object to this. Beware of the breeder

who claims to have just the right dog for you and asks nothing of your circumstances or situation. The breeders who invite you to visit them to see their dogs and talk about what you want are far more promising.

Make an appointment to visit the breeder, and be punctual. Dog breeders live hectic lives and time is precious. Look at their adult dogs and visualise one of these living with you. Discuss your needs in detail with the breeder, and if you are set on a tricolour bitch puppy, don't allow yourself to be talked into an adult lemon male! If you do, you'll always regret it. Buying a dog is not like shopping at a supermarket, and puppies do not come to order. You may have to wait months for what you want, but be patient. That wait will be far better than rushing into an impulse-buy when you could end up with something other than what you have your heart set on.

If you want a pet puppy, and say so, you will be offered a pet puppy. If you feel you might like to dip your toe in the water of showing, then be honest with the breeder and say that is your intention. Nothing is more irritating for a breeder than to sell, in good faith, a pet puppy, not of top show

ABOVE: If you are buying a puppy with a view to showing, it needs to be examined thoroughly with the points of the Breed Standard in mind.

LEFT: Paolo Dondina, the great Italian Beagle fancier and all-rounder judge, pictured with a home-bred seven-week-old puppy, Viola del Pesco.
Photo courtesy: Hermione Bruton.

quality, only to find at a later date that the owner is showing the dog. This is not fair on the breeder, the owner or the dog.

PRICE AND TERMS

Breeders vary as to how they price their puppies. Buying at eight weeks, it is difficult to guarantee anything about a puppy, and I find it surprising that some breeders will charge one price for a 'pet puppy', and considerably more for a 'show puppy'. I prefer to charge the same for all my puppies at that age, pointing out to the buyers that what they are buying is a healthy, well-bred puppy of quality. If that puppy subsequently develops into a dog with show potential, then that's a bonus.

   Some breeders who may not have large kennels themselves may, if you are buying a bitch puppy, suggest to you that you may wish to consider 'breeding terms'. Initially this may sound attractive as, essentially, this arrangement involves paying much less (or even nothing at all) for the original purchase, but then giving back to the

breeder several puppies when your bitch is bred from. My advice is – don't! More people have fallen out over breeding terms than you can imagine. It is far better to buy your bitch outright. She is then yours and no-one else has control over her future.

ASSESSING YOUR PUPPY

Once you have put your trust in a breeder, and possibly paid a deposit as a gesture of goodwill, you should wait until the breeder comes back to you with news of a possible puppy. The breeder already knows your requirements as regards sex and colour, so will be able to sort out a puppy for you. You may be offered a choice, if there are sufficient puppies in a litter, or you may be offered one particular puppy. Whatever, when you visit, ask to see the whole litter together – even though the others are not available – as this will be a good way of seeing your puppy in a relative sense. Is your puppy smaller or larger than the siblings? Does your puppy seem outgoing, or somewhat overpowered by the others?

19

The head is a very important aspect of the Beagle, and puppies should always show plenty of fullness in the muzzle at eight weeks. These three dog puppies, sired by Danish Ch. Tragband In Hot Water out of Danish Ch. Gold Line's Better Be Fame, show excellent head type. Some Beagle puppies may take longer than others for the nose pigment to fill in, as seen in the puppy on the left.
Photo courtesy: Jesper and Annette Pedersen.

Your puppy should be plump, without being pot-bellied or "wormy", well-boned and sweet-smelling. Watching how puppies interact with their littermates is very important. A puppy who seems shy and retiring may need a lot of hard work in order to build up confidence through puberty. One who is downright nervous should be avoided, no matter how much you may feel sorry for the puppy. This temperament is not typical for the breed and will always prove a substantial drawback.

If you are buying a puppy with showing in mind, you will have to rely on the breeder's integrity to a large degree, as your novice eye will lack sufficient experience to assess quality from an exhibition standpoint. However, there are some basic guidelines which should help you be able to evaluate such a puppy. A promising show-quality Beagle puppy of eight weeks should have solid, round bone of quality, with definite "knuckles" into which they will grow. The front should be straight, the forelegs dropping parallel, but there will always be a certain amount of looseness and play at that age. The feet should be tight and cat-like. Beagle head-type varies to some extent, depending on bloodlines, but I like to see a puppy of eight weeks having a definite occipital peak, clean cheeks and a

Even as puppies, there should be a noticeable difference between the Beagle dog (right)) and bitch (left).
Photo: Paul Jones.

really full foreface, with a "budgerigar bump" on the bridge of the nose when viewed in profile. The mouth should suggest that, when the second teeth come through, there will be a scissor bite, with the upper incisors closing over the lower. The eyes should be dark enough to give a soft expression, and ideally there should not be prominent haw (the third eyelid), especially if the membrane is unpigmented. The puppy should have good length of neck, a short level back, a deep ribcage and a high-set tail which should be carried happily but not too gaily over the back, nor inclined forward at the root. The hindquarters should have sufficient bend of stifle, and short, low hocks. The puppy trotting around, even at this age, should appear to move steadily without forelegs plaiting, or hocks too close.

TAKING YOUR PUPPY HOME

When you have decided on your puppy, and paid for him, the breeder should give you the registration papers, a diet sheet, and enough food for the first few days. You should always follow the breeder's suggestion as regards feeding, as to change diet drastically will result in an upset tummy and instant loss of condition. When buying a young puppy, the chances are that no inoculations will have been

administered. Once you have got your puppy home, telephone your local vet and ask for advice on a vaccination programme. Until fully immunised, the puppy should not leave your property.

I am a great believer in dog crates. They are a marvellous invention and a great boon in so many ways. When you go to collect your puppy, I strongly recommend that you buy in advance a dog crate large enough for an adult Beagle to stand up in. That crate can be used for travelling, sleeping and house-training, and, although apparently quite expensive, will prove a very worthwhile investment. For the journey home, put layers of newspaper in the bottom of the crate, and an old blanket. Maybe the breeder will let you take one of the puppy's toys, which will carry familiar smells. The puppy will cry a little, and may be car-sick. Talk comfortingly, but leave the puppy in the crate and try not get into the habit of picking up and cuddling your new baby as soon as there is any crying, or you will be laying the foundations for a rather spoilt Beagle.

Once home, put your puppy in the garden in a spot which you are quite happy to be used as a toilet area. Clean up the crate if necessary and put more permanent bedding in it. These days there are lots of fleecy-type dog bedding available which

A dog crate will prove invaluable for travelling, house-training, and for sleeping.

Photo: Andrew H. Brace.

Children should be taught to respect puppies and handle them gently. Melanie Spavin, pictured right with her mother, Dianna, grew up to be a leading Beagle breeder in her own right.

Photo courtesy: Marion Spavin.

keep puppies warm and dry. A piece of this can be put on top of newspaper and if it does get soiled, any fluids will drain through on to the paper. Follow the breeder's suggestions regarding feeding to the letter, and do not be influenced by vets, or other well-meaning "experts". The breeder knows best. On the first night after you have collected your puppy, get into the recommended feeding regime immediately. After the last meal in the evening, both of you go into the garden and both stay there until the puppy's bladder and bowel have been emptied. Praise the puppy, then return indoors and shut the puppy in the crate which is to be the permanent sleeping place, and be sure to provide some toys for

the puppy to chew on. When you retire, the puppy will doubtless cry a little, but you have to be a little hard-hearted if you are going to train your Beagle sensibly. If you come down and make a big fuss every time there is a whimper, the puppy will soon learn that this is the way to get your attention. If you ignore it, the puppy will soon realise that objecting noisily has no effect, and will settle down and go to sleep. One great advantage of having a dog sleep in a crate is that puppies are reluctant to soil the area where they sleep, and if you use a crate, you will find that your puppy will be clean through the night in no time at all.

3 CARING FOR YOUR BEAGLE

The Beagle is, as I have said, a low-maintenance breed which will thrive given good food, adequate company and physical and mental stimulation. Caring for your Beagle involves common sense more than anything else, and up-bringing will require firmness combined with affection. If you are about to acquire your first Beagle, it is most likely that you will be buying a puppy which will be a house-pet. From the outset you and your puppy need to know where you stand. It is essential to establish, from day one, that you are the boss and that

there are certain house rules which must be obeyed. Far too many inexperienced owners find disobedience and natural puppy waywardness "cute" and amusing; but allowing even the youngest of puppies to get away with transgression unreprimanded will cause unnecessary problems in the future.

BASIC RULES
As mentioned in an earlier chapter, you must decide where your puppy is going to sleep, and from the start that should be

It will not be long before your Beagle becomes an integral member of the family.

Photo: Andrew H. Brace.

your Beagle's own space. I will repeat myself by saying that a large dog crate kept in a kitchen or utility room is ideal. It can contain the appropriate dog bedding, acts as a wonderful aid to housebreaking, and can double as a travelling box when needed. Dogs should always have access to clean, fresh drinking water. Always make sure that you leave a heavy, spill-proof water-dish in the kitchen, or somewhere which is easily accessible, and that the puppy, after having a drink, is put into the garden, or whatever toilet area you have chosen, and you must wait until the puppy's bladder empties.

FEEDING YOUR BEAGLE

Feeding dogs used to be a complicated business, but gone are the days when breeders collected unwashed green tripe from the local abattoir, boiled up various vegetables, then added kibble and various extras. The day of the complete feeds has arrived with a vengeance. I must confess, I used to be rather old-fashioned in thinking that dogs had to eat meat of some description. However, I am now totally converted to a complete feed regime which is simply that – complete. Feeding a complete diet takes the guesswork out of rearing, there is no need for additives of any description, and it is so easy to monitor

a dog's weight and condition.

Thanks to the research and development initiatives of the modern petfood industry there is now a huge variety of complete feeds on the market. Your puppy's breeder will probably recommend the brand he or she has been using and, if it is easily obtainable, you would be well-advised to stick with that. One brand which I find excellent includes specially formulated feeds for puppies, active adults, and pensioners. If you choose to use a complete feed, follow the manufacturer's instructions – and remember: the food you are using has been designed by skilled and professional dieticians who have been careful to include all the necessary minerals and vitamins. So many people feed a complete feed, then add some meat to "make it taste better" and also throw in some extra vitamin pills for good luck! This is courting disaster. There is no need for any extras if you feed a complete formulation.

EARLY TRAINING

From the start, you will need to spend time getting to know your puppy. This means "quality time" together, combined with opportunities for rest and relaxation. It also involves basic training. Whenever you put a meal down for your puppy, it is a good idea to remove it immediately for a few

Who said Beagles were disobedient? This incredible photograph shows 15 well-trained Beagles at the True Lines kennel, owned by Silke and Jochen Eberhardt in Germany.

Photo courtesy: Heather Priestley

It is important to establish some house rules, such as whether your Beagle is allowed on the furniture. No such rules exist for the Riversong Beagles, who live in the lap of luxury!

Photo courtesy: Basil J. Waterton.

moments, then replace the dish and let the pup begin eating. This helps to prevent dogs from becoming possessive over food. Beagles are naturally mild-mannered, but sometimes can be a little fractious where food is concerned. When they are, they should never be allowed to get away with it. Similarly, when playing puppy games with toys, your puppy should be taught that when you give the command Drop or Leave, you expect whatever is in the puppy's mouth to be released. You must insist that the puppy acquiesces at all times – and having done so, can be praised and rewarded accordingly. Never let the puppy get one up on you, as you will live to regret it. Beagles are natural gluttons and will do anything for food. When you are beginning your basic training and teaching simple commands such as Come, Heel, Stand, Sit etc., a little tidbit after a successful exercise works wonders. Make training sessions short but frequent, as puppies have a very low boredom threshold.

Establish your house rules as soon as possible. If your house has "no go" areas such as upstairs, or a "best" room, the puppy should never be allowed to trespass. It is pointless carrying a baby Beagle out-of-bounds for a cuddle then, a few months later, chastising the slightly older dog for venturing into the same place. If your Beagle is to be allowed on the furniture, all well and good, but don't expect a dog to differentiate between your dilapidated old sofa and the man of the house's brand new leather armchair! My advice is, train your Beagle not to jump on the furniture. In my experience a comfortable dog bed, placed at the side of the fireplace, will prove inviting enough, especially if it contains a few interesting toys. On the subject of toys, be sensible about what you give your Beagle to play with. Buy purpose-built doggy toys which are strong and fairly indestructible. Avoid bones unless they are the really huge marrowbones which will not splinter. Doggy chews can soften and get stuck in the throat, baked cow-hooves can shatter and cause great damage, so stick with toys of strong man-made material. Don't be tempted to throw a worn-out old shoe into the toy box. Beagles will find it hard to distinguish brand new Gucci loafers from ageing slippers.

After your puppy has had all the necessary inoculations, you should start lead-training as soon as possible. Begin at home in the garden or in an enclosed park. I believe in starting even young puppies

Diana Brown's Ch. Raimex Kracker enjoying life away from the rigours of the show ring. Beagles love the beach – and the sea!

Photo courtesy: Diana Brown.

with a fairly large-linked slip or choke chain. They soon get the hang of it and it breaks them of pulling quite quickly. Beagles should never be allowed to pull on the lead – nothing is guaranteed to widen a front more than constant pulling. When they do, a sharp check on the chain will get them back in line.

Coming when called is an essential in Beagle training, and far from easy, as so many are conveniently deaf at times. The best way of training obedience of this kind is to use one of the extending flexible leads which will enable you to "reel in" your Beagle as you call your dog's name. This exercise needs to be repeated at least twice daily until your Beagle comes immediately on being called. Only when you are absolutely sure that your dog will return when called should you consider allowing any free running in a public place.

EXERCISE
Exercise is vitally important to the well-being of any Beagle who is to remain fit and healthy, but it should be exercise of the right sort. Up until twelve months of age I believe that free running in the garden, or local park, two or three times a day, is sufficient for a puppy, combined with small walks to teach lead-manners. A dog who is over a year old should have regular, controlled exercise, ideally trotting at a steady pace, for half an hour, twice daily. Unless you are a keen jogger, the ideal way of giving your dog this kind of sustained exercise is by cycling with the dog alongside. This is not terribly practical in some areas, however. Either way, an adult Beagle, to be kept in peak physical muscular tone, will need around four miles a day of steady trotting. This may not be considered important if your dog is merely a companion, but remember that an under-exercised dog will have excess energy to use up and also be given to obesity, a major problem with the breed. You should always keep an eye on your Beagle's weight, as it is all too easy for the waistline to disappear! If you feel your dog is broadening, reduce food and increase exercise.

GROOMING
Grooming the Beagle is very straightforward, especially if yours is not a show dog. A weekly rub-down with a rubber grooming pad or rubber brush is all that should be necessary, but always keep an eye on your dog's nails. Normal wear-and-tear with average roadwork should keep them worn well down, but I find some lines seem to produce Beagles with more rapid nail growth than others. If you are inexperienced, trimming nails should be left to your dog's breeder or the vet, and it is advisable to have a puppy's nails clipped for the first time when they are quite young (three months of age), just to get them used to it. An adult Beagle having nails cut for the first time can find the experience horribly traumatic. I have found that many Beagles take much more readily to having their nails filed, and I use a large carpenter's file, obtainable from most hardware stores. Hounds which object violently to the clippers will invariably lie back and enjoy this alternative manicure. Many people do not bath Beagles very often. If yours is to be a house-pet, then I suggest a bath every two weeks to keep the dog smelling sweet. Beagles can have quite oily coats and do develop a not unpleasant, but nonetheless "doggy", odour. A routine bath with a mild insecticidal shampoo is also a good way of ensuring that no unwanted visitors have come to stay!

SOCIALISATION
Do get your Beagle used to travelling in the car. Nothing is more exasperating than a car-sick dog who just will not relax, even on the longest of journeys. From an early age your Beagle should get used to it, initially with short journeys, and always in a crate, or travelling box, for safety's sake. A well-adjusted Beagle will only come about through careful socialisation, and your puppy, when old enough to be taken out, should be exposed to as many sights and sounds as possible and taken to shopping malls, lorry parks, funfairs, school playgrounds – anything where there will be something new to see. Accompanied by you, the dog will feel secure and soon get accustomed to the unfamiliar. One of the joys of owning a Beagle as a companion is that this is a go-anywhere, do-anything kind of dog who should be able to share

your life as widely as possible. I frequently argue with kennel-owners who say that pet dogs never make great show dogs because they are so spoilt. I disagree totally. All my show dogs have been first and foremost pets, and I know their characters inside out. I can go to a show and know exactly how they will react to a backfiring car or a screaming child. This gives the pet dog an advantage in my estimation. Having a "pet life" gives the companion show dog a great advantage over the kennelled show dog, whose experience of the big wide world outside may be limited.

If you are not at home for a large part of the day I have already suggested that you will be better off with more than one Beagle. Keeping a single dog alone will cause frustration, neuroses and – the Devil makes work for idle paws! In this case you will really need a kennel and run so that your Beagles can have some degree of freedom when you are away from home. There are many ready-made kennels available, some with adjoining runs, but frequently these runs are too small. It is often a far better idea to buy a cheaper garden shed which can have a pop-hole cut out of one side, and site it in a large chain-link run, with the chain link buried at least six inches into the ground and then concreted in – Beagles can be great diggers. If you have to kennel your Beagles, they should still spend as much time as possible in the house with the family, and be appropriately housetrained, as this will make them much more socially acceptable and nicer to know.

THE VETERAN BEAGLE

Your Beagle heading towards old age will begin to slow down generally and you may have to adjust the exercise and feeding regimes – less food, more often, and less exercise – but many Beagles can be kept trim, hale and hearty until they are twelve or more. The well-filled Veteran classes at Beagle shows prove that they are a long-lived breed and often dogs continue to win top honours when they are past retirement age. There is nothing more heart-warming than an elderly Beagle with a greying face. The soft expression becomes even softer and old Beagles have a calmness about them which I have never found in any other breed. They become more dependent and more clinging, and it is tragic that owners seem to get closer than ever to their Beagles when they are in their twilight years.

We all hope and pray that our Beagles will pass away naturally, as human beings are dreadful cowards and no-one wants to have to make "that" decision. Should your Beagle become infirm to such an extent that quality of life and dignity has been taken away, you must consider making that decision, no matter how heartbreaking it may be. Can you really bear to see your best friend existing, rather than living life to the full? Try not to be selfish if your Beagle gets to this stage. It may be the best thing to let your dog pass away peacefully. After all, you know that you are going to meet up in the hereafter, as I have every confidence that all Beagles go to Heaven.

4 YOUR BEAGLE'S HEALTH

The Beagle is a naturally healthy breed, free from major hereditary problems, and tends to be long-lived, provided that the dog has adequate exercise and a sensible diet. Beagles are gluttons, and one of the main problems in the breed is obesity, so do please refrain from giving tidbits, other than when training. Beagles will soon pile weight on given the chance to over-indulge. Here are some hints on first aid, but if any condition persists, veterinary attention should always be sought.

FIRST AID FOR COMMON AILMENTS

BEAGLE TAIL
This is a condition seen in various breeds and is otherwise known as "wet tail", "dead tail" and other names, depending on the breed. The symptom is that the end of the tail appears quite limp, almost as if it is broken, and there is considerable difference of opinion as to the cause, nothing ever having been proved conclusively. The condition is probably due to inflammation which occurs in the third or fourth coccygeal vertebra from the root of the tail, this inflammation giving rise to heat which, in turn, causes pain and discomfort. It is not unlike a rheumatic symptom. It has been suggested that Beagle Tail can result after bathing, when water or shampoo finds its way through the anus and causes irritation. Personally I believe that a more likely cause is that a wet Beagle, after bathing, is put into a crate with lots of towels to help the drying process. Any dog when wet will shake vigorously, and in so doing can very easily knock his tail on the sides of the crate. As a precaution, it is best not to bath a dog the day before a show; better to do so two days in advance, just in case there is a risk of Beagle Tail. If your dog does get the condition, there is a not a lot you can do about it other than sit and wait, and invariably it will right itself after two or three days, maybe even less. Mild pain-killers can be given, and have been known to help if a dog is dosed a few hours before being shown.

BITES
Should your Beagle be bitten by another dog, or any animal, the severity of the wound should be assessed immediately. Antibiotic powder should always be kept in the first aid kit, the wound should be washed and a mild antiseptic applied, and then a coating of the powder. Obviously if

Ch. Too Darn Hot For Tragband: A well-cared-for Beagle should experience few health problems.

Photo: Panther Photographic.

there is a deep wound, and bleeding is copious, a visit to the vet is essential.

BURNS & SCALDS
Burns and scalds can be treated with an ice pack to bring down the temperature, or, as a substitute, a large packet of frozen peas wrapped in a towel will suffice. Proprietary sprays can be easily obtained from any pharmacist and used accordingly. Obviously treatment will depend on the affected area, and a badly scalded head, for example, should be dealt with by the vet after a cold compress has been applied.

CHERRY EYE
This condition involves the gland underneath the haw which becomes very swollen and inflamed, and can hang out of the eye, having become enlarged to the size of a pea. Occasionally this will right itself, but more often than not it will recur. The gland can be lanced and removed in a simple operation, with no after-effects, but your vet will advise.

CHOKING
The utmost care should be exercised when giving your Beagle any kind of toys, edible or otherwise, and items which are so small that they may be swallowed should always be avoided. Sometimes the popular hide chews can become very soft and be swallowed, causing a blockage. Immediate

examination should reveal whether or not the obstruction can be retrieved manually. If it is too far down the throat, it is advisable to try to push it even further down, and then follow this with a large piece of dry bread. The dog should swallow this automatically and hopefully the chew will then gradually be digested.

COUGHING
What is commonly referred to as "kennel cough" should really be re-named "canine cough" as it is by no means restricted to kennel dogs. One dog can easily contract a contagious cough simply by meeting another in the local park. The symptoms are a rasping cough often accompanied by the impression of choking or retching, resulting in a little froth being brought up. Unless the dog is noticeably poorly, refusing food and much more lethargic than usual, a human expectorant can be administered using a syringe, and this will aid speedy recovery. If the condition persists, and there is no improvement after two weeks, veterinary advice should be sought.

CUTS
Depending on the size and severity of such wounds, these should be treated as above for bites. If a cut is sufficiently deep that flesh is visibly hanging, stitching will probably be necessary.

DIARRHOEA
There are various causes of diarrhoea:
1) Over-eating.
2) Bacterial infection.
3) Sudden change of diet or water.
4) Stress.
If your Beagle has very loose motions, food should not be given for twenty-four hours, just fluid – ideally boiled water with added glucose. Also arrowroot can be stirred in to speed recovery.

EAR MITES
You may notice that your Beagle is scratching at his ears constantly, and examination of the ears may reveal a brown discharge around the inner ear. This should be treated with one of the many proprietary cures available from vets or pet shops, either drops or powder.

FITS
Beagles rarely suffer from fits, but occasionally they may occur, the symptoms being frothing at the mouth and convulsions. Leave the dog in a quiet, darkened room and obtain some bromide tablets from the pharmacist. These will help to sedate the dog. If the fits recur, obviously your vet must be consulted.

FLEAS & LICE
Dogs will from time to time pick up fleas from other animals. Fleas do not lay eggs actually on their host, but in surrounding areas, such as carpets or furniture. Fleas can be detected by brushing the hand against the lay of the coat and examining close to the skin. There will invariably be signs of flea-dirt, usually at the base of the tail or on the neck. A strong insecticidal shampoo should be used as directed, and treatment repeated one week later. Also it is important to spray the home environment with a specially-made product. Lice may be easier to treat, as the eggs are laid on the dog, usually behind the ears, but they can be found all over the body area. They should be treated similarly.

HEATSTROKE
If a dog is suffering from heatstroke he will appear somewhat dazed, with a glassy look about the eyes, and may stagger around with a distinct lack of co-ordination. In such a case, the dog should be immersed in a bath of cold water, ideally with ice packs

added, so that the temperature is reduced as quickly as possible.

LACK OF APPETITE

Beagles are generally enthusiastic doers, but when a puppy is teething, he may well go off his food. As this is a vital growing age, puppies should never be allowed to lose too much weight as they will seldom get it back and will, more importantly, lose bone. Many puppies of that age will sooner eat a dried food which will relieve the soreness of the gums and help the new teeth through, rather like the human baby and his rusk. Plenty of hard chewable biscuits should be available, otherwise your teething puppy may resort to chewing the furniture!

LAMENESS

Often puppies who play rough can sustain mild injury to the shoulder which will result in slight lameness. Do not panic and rush off to the vet, who may try to convince you that your young dog has some dreadful hereditary condition which is the result of "in-breeding". The dog should be rested and given the minimum of exercise until he is again sound. Also, lameness may be the result of a cut pad. Examine the pads closely and, if a cut is detected, treat as a normal cut, as above. If the pad has a hair-line cut, a product such as "New Skin" can be painted over it which will give external protection while the cut heals.

MISMATING

In the unlikely event of your in-season bitch getting mated by an intruder, it is essential that you take her to the vet for an injection which will prevent conception, but will prolong the season. You will, however, be extra vigilant this time, and ensure that the same thing does not happen again.

NAIL CUTS & RIPS

If you cut your dog's nails too close to the quick, they may bleed profusely and cause great pain. To assist drying up and healing, a styptic pencil, or a proprietary powder manufactured especially for this situation can be used in lesser cases, but if there is excessive bleeding you may have to resort to applying potassium permanganate. This will be effective but you will be prevented from showing a dog with brown feet for a week or so! Sometimes a dog will catch his nail in a fence or crate and I have to admit that, marvellous as they are, permanent car-crates can easily rip out a nail if a dog is allowed to jump up into the back of the car and happens to catch his foot on the edge, so it is best to lift the dog up into the crate. A hound can also rip a nail when playing, if it happens to turn quickly and catch it. If the nail is badly damaged but still attached to the toe, it may be best to have it removed, as it can be very painful. If the nail is ripped right out, there will be great distress initially, but gradually it will begin to grow back.

STINGS

Beagles are naturally inquisitive and will find wasps and bees very interesting. If your dog should be stung by a bee, the sting should be removed and antiseptic applied. When the sting is in the mouth, it can prove dangerous if swelling is detected, and veterinary help should be sought as soon as possible.

VOMITING

Dogs frequently eat grass and will vomit as a result, though this may be mainly froth and the consumed grass. It is a natural process and cleansing agent, and will not result in any harm. However, if the dog should have consumed a toxic plant, it can be more serious. The dog will try to vomit and may appear to go off his legs. In this case pour strong salt water down the dog's throat and encourage him to vomit further. If the symptoms persist, veterinary assistance is essential.

HEREDITARY CONDITIONS

As I said at the beginning of this chapter, the Beagle as a breed is generally quite healthy, not least in comparison with many other popular breeds of dog, but there is no sense in denying that, in addition to the common defects that occur in many breeds such as overshot and undershot bites, umbilical and inguinal hernias, knee ligament problems due to straight stifles, and cryptorchidism, there are also other conditions which have been found in the Beagle. Some breeders tend to shut their eyes to these problems, but unless we accumulate information on abnormal conditions as they appear, and act upon it, they will surely become more common in the breed. It is important to be aware of any problems which may occur when using any particular bloodline, especially when outcrossing into a "new" line. The attitude towards hereditary diseases also varies greatly from country to country. Whereas Scandinavia and Europe are very conscious of monitoring hereditary conditions, in the USA, for instance, hereditary abnormalities which are not life-threatening and can be treated using lifelong medication, are seen by some, less diligent, breeders as inconsequential. Others will find it unethical to breed from dogs which themselves cannot survive without treatment. The following are some of the conditions which have been identified in Beagles frequently enough to warrant concern.

EPILEPSY

Epilepsy is a dysfunction of the brain, causing seizures of varying degree and frequency. There is a difference of opinion as to whether or not epilepsy can actually be inherited, and there appears to be no conclusive genetic mode of inheritance, but it can also be caused by external factors such as trauma to the head, a brain tumour or metabolic disease, for instance. In Beagles, the hereditary form can be seen to occur as early as three months of age or as late as nine years. In cases with more sporadic seizures, no therapy is usually given. If the Beagle has seizures at least every week, he will need treatment. Most cases can be successfully treated, and it is seldom necessary to euthanise the affected dog, but medication continues for life. It is probably wise to assume that all cases of epilepsy in Beagles have a hereditary factor, unless categorically proven otherwise, and refrain from breeding from affected animals and their close relatives.

DRY EYE

This is a condition first identified in American Beagles, and a few cases have appeared in Scandinavia in offspring of an American dog. Dry eye (or keratoconjunctivitis sicca) is a malfunction of the tear gland, resulting in a dry cornea, keratitis and conjunctivitis. It is very painful for the dog and untreated cases can eventually result in blindness. Spontaneous cases are considered to be autoimmune-mediated. It can also be seen as a consequence of other diseases such as hypothyroidism, distemper, or of treatment with some of the sulphonamides. Therapy usually consists of eye-drops as replacement for the missing tear production, combined with cyclosporin therapy as an immuno-suppressant. Therapy is life-long, but because the amount of tear production can vary with time, the treatment can be given periodically. Another approach is to surgically move the salivary ducts so that they drain into the eye.

HYPOTHYROIDISM

This is a metabolic disease resulting in hypofunction of the thyroid gland, causing the affected dog to become lethargic, fat, and often to have skin and reproductive problems. It may also cause dry eye. It has been shown to be hereditary in 90 per cent of the cases occurring in Beagles, and is said to be on the increase, so the condition should be taken seriously. Its manifestation is often the result of an auto-immune reaction, and it usually occurs in the middle-aged dog. The diagnosis is made by a blood test, and therapy is successful but continues through the dog's life. Like so many other diseases in Beagles, hypothyroidism was first described in American research Beagles, probably due to the fact that they were closely bred and this revealed previously hidden defects. Today the diagnosis is made in most countries.

INTER-VERTEBRAL DISC DISEASE

The vertebrae of the spine are joined by elastic discs. In some breeds these have a tendency to break, whereby the disc mass prolapses and causes pressure on the spinal cord. This tendency is especially common in the chondrodystrophic breeds, to which some of the Beagle's ancestors belong. The slipped disc may appear in the neck region, often first noticed as the dog appears to have difficulty in bending down to his food or water bowl, or in the back region where it may cause varying degrees of pain or paralysis. In many cases the condition can be relieved by confining the dog in a crate somewhere warm, and maybe administering corticosteroids for a period of three weeks. Severe cases may have to undergo surgery if veterinary attention is not sought until the acute stages of the disease.

HIP DYSPLASIA

Hip dysplasia is an abnormal formation of the hip socket or the relaxation of some of its ligaments. It is caused by a combination of hereditary and environmental factors. In some countries it occurs in a high proportion of Beagles and in Germany, for example, Beagles have to be X-rayed before being bred from. In Sweden, compulsory X-raying for hip dysplasia was introduced some ten years ago, because some dogs imported from the USA and UK had been found to be affected. This caused initial alarm, but the measures taken turned out to be adequate and today only around 7 per cent of the Beagles that are examined actually have hip dysplasia, and then only to a very mild degree. During the first years, however, more severe cases were found and some dogs were actually euthanised because of the pain caused by the severity of the condition.

DYSTOCIA (Abnormal labour)

The Beagle is a very "normally" constructed breed, with no exaggerated breed-specific details. There should consequently be no reason for bitches to experience difficulties delivering puppies. Yet some lines exhibit frequent dystocias, resulting in the puppies being delivered by Caesarean section. In the USA it is said that as many as 40 per cent of Beagle bitches that are bred from need to have a Caesarean performed. This certainly should not be necessary in this kind of breed and, as uterine inertia and a narrow pelvis are inherited traits, those bitches should not be given a second chance to breed and perpetuate those undesirable faults. Obviously some cases of dystocia are caused by factors that are not due directly to the shortcomings of the bitch, like the "one puppy syndrome" where a very small litter does not trigger a strong enough hormonal response to uterine contractions in the bitch, thus delaying the production of pituitrin which is necessary to begin the whelping process; or the very large litter which exhausts the uterine wall by overstretching, the resultant distension rendering the uterus unable to contract. Malpresentations of pups, or pups that are too big or malformed, can also cause problems. When a bitch-related factor is involved, the bitches in question should not be bred from again.

STERILITY

Many diseases, including prostatitis, may cause a dog to become sterile, but over the years some male Beagles have become sterile without any obvious reason. Sometimes their testicles can be seen to have degenerated, becoming small and hard, or softer than normal, but in many cases the testicles appear to be perfectly normal. Yet the dog does not produce sperm. Sometimes these dogs have produced some litters before becoming sterile, but that is not always the case. In one family of Beagles, this tendency in the males has been connected to a tendency for the bitches to suffer uterine inertia, indicating that the central hormonal system may be involved. The problem on the male side eventually will prove self-eliminating, but this again emphasises the importance of selecting breeding stock from healthy, self-whelping lines.

INFERTILITY SYNDROME

Many breeders have problems from time to time with bitches "missing", i.e. failing to conceive having been mated. Sometimes the problem can be due to a deep-rooted infection within the kennel. This is known as BHS, Beta-haemolytic streptococcal (Lancefield type G and L), and the problems caused by these bacteria are

encountered in show dogs in many countries of the world. The following information has been supplied to me by Eleanor Bothwell (Norcis Beagles) and is an account of her experiences over a period of nearly thirty years breeding dogs. Eleanor originally wrote it with the intent to inform and help breeders, such as herself, who had experienced the heartbreak of Infertility Syndrome in their kennels. She felt that breeders tend to keep problems of this nature hush hush, but realised that it is only when you are faced with a problem of this magnitude, with no forewarning, that you realise the importance of sharing experiences and knowledge. Subsequently she has delivered the information as a paper to various breed clubs.

BETA-HAEMOLYTIC STREPTOCOCCAL (Lancefield Type G and L) INFECTION IN THE BITCH AND DOG

The obstacles and problems the seriously dedicated dog breeder can face in the pursuit of the ideal are many. Anyone who has bred dogs over a number of years will have had their setbacks. Breeders being a resilient lot, most of the seemingly awesome obstacles are overcome. However, it matters not whether you have the best dogs and bitches in the world, or merely 'also rans', if the ugly problem of infertility arises and your bitches are not producing puppies, it is absolutely heartbreaking. All of your carefully planned breeding programmes can be seriously set back or even brought to a halt.

Infertility can be permanent or temporary. The former cannot be aided, the latter can usually be cured if diagnosed speedily and corrective treatment given. The problem of infertility does not happen overnight. It creeps up over some time.

One bitch misses – how easy it is to find a convenient reason for that to happen. Another bitch misses. Still philosophical, you accept the setback and make more excuses. By this time a third bitch may have been mated to no avail, and only now that niggling thought in the back of your mind has to be accepted: "Perhaps there is something wrong with the bitches." Even to begin to reach this conclusion three bitches have missed and some 18 months may have passed. This, before investigations have begun. By now the infection has had plenty of time to become deep-rooted.

The most common cause of failure to conceive, abortion, foetal absorption, stillbirths and early puppy mortality, is a uterine infection caused by the bacteria Beta-Haemolytic Streptococcal Lancefield Type G and L, sometimes called BHS infection or fading puppy syndrome. The infection can occur in both sexes but is most common in bitches. Rarely does it affect the testicular tissue of the dog. Other forms of Streptococci found in the bitch's genital area have little or no pathological significance.

SYMPTOMS AND DIAGNOSIS OF THE DISEASE IN THE BITCH

ABNORMAL SEASONS
Infected bitches often have irregularly timed seasons. Instead of the six or seven month cycle, she may have seasons with two to 12 month gaps. Others may show seasonal activity every few weeks; some just don't come into season for one or two years. Young infected bitches may have a very late first season, sometimes missing the first season entirely. The season itself varies from the normal 21 days – in some cases two to five days, or as long as four to six weeks. The discharge is also different from normal – profuse or scant, heavy or pale

throughout the entire season. If the bitch is having abnormal seasons, then BHS should be suspected. Another symptom is a lack of sexual interest shown by the stud dog for mating the bitch.

STERILITY SYNDROME
Failure to conceive is a common result of BHS infection. It may be due to ovarian infection and inflammation which may cause non-development of the ova, production of misshapen or infertile ova, or a failure to ovulate; or the ripe ova are shed at abnormal times, too early or too late in the season. If there is inflammation of the fallopian tubes this makes it nigh impossible for the ova to travel down. Inflammation of the uterine walls retards or stops the embryonic process of implantation. Also, the secretions from the inflamed uterus are often lethal to live sperm. So BHS should be suspected when successful matings do not produce results, especially after repeated attempts.

ABSORPTION – ABORTION SYNDROME
In spite of having BHS the bitch does conceive and a seemingly normal pregnancy ensues for about four to five weeks. Abortion happens when the foetus can no longer maintain its attachment to the uterine wall. If this happens before 21 days, then the only symptoms the bitch will exhibit are those of being slightly off-colour and having a profuse dark, bloody discharge. Later on in the pregnancy the symptoms are similar but more dramatic. Dead foeti can be seen in the discharge. Bitches can show mild or severe distress. Foetal absorption happens when the blood supply from the mother to the foetus is lost. Those foetuses become detached from the uterine wall. Instead of aborting, they remain in situ. Mummification occurs,

followed by re-absorption. It most cases these bitches show little or no discharge or distress. Sometimes there can be a rise in temperature, loss of appetite and a general feeling of being off colour. Such bitches recover in a week or so. Occasionally the bitch can develop severe symptomatic reactions. Therefore BHS should be suspected when bitches who seem to be pregnant and then fail to complete the pregnancy, when bitches have abnormal discharge at any stage of pregnancy, and when bitches have periods of general malaise along with a rise in temperature during pregnancy.

FADING PUPPY SYNDROME

This is the most common and the most heartbreaking result of BHS infection. There is a normal pregnancy, normal whelping and healthy new-born puppies. Puppy deaths start to happen at about four or five days. The puppies weaken from about three days old and lose the desire to suckle. They develop a bluish/purplish colouring on the belly, they dehydrate, lose weight and cry incessantly. Unless remedial action is taken immediately they will die very quickly. The bitch who has been perfectly healthy at first becomes emotionally distressed by the crying of the pups. Her mammary glands become engorged as the pups stop feeding, leading to discomfort and pain. That requires remedial treatment to ensure that she does not develop a systemic infection.

It is important to realise that puppies born of bitches infected with BHS are healthy and normal at the time of birth. The puppies become infected by suckling the infected milk from the bitch. It is the milk that contains the BHS. The ingestion of this infected milk causes severe generalised disease usually resulting in death. If the puppies from the infected bitch are removed quickly and fostered or hand-reared, they do not develop the disease. If Fading Puppy Syndrome is suspected, and immediate removal of the pups from the bitch plus treatment with antibiotics is carried out, they stand a fair chance of survival. They should be hand-reared or fostered. The important thing is early diagnosis and treatment. So, if puppies whine and weaken, seek immediate veterinary advice.

Confirmation of BHS can be made by growing a sample of the bitch's vaginal discharge in culture and identifying the bacteria. A suitable antibiotic can be prescribed. This can take a few days, which can be too long for the survival of the pups. A broad spectrum antibiotic could be given, thus saving valuable time while the culture is growing. The presence of BHS can also be confirmed by a post-mortem examination of any dead pups in the litter and by bacteriological testing of the bitch's milk.

INFECTION CONTACT: The most common way for a bitch to pick up this BHS infection is by direct contact of the external genital organs, particularly during her seasons, when the cervix is dilated. As she sits to urinate or defecate, the vulva lips come into contact with the ground. If the bacteria are present, infection can take place. It is also thought possible for infection to take place when the bitch licks her genital area, thus ingesting the bacteria, if present. The stud dog can act as a carrier of the disease. If he has mated an infected bitch, the BHS infection can survive on his penis and genital area for some 48 hours, and it is possible for him to infect the next bitch. Only rarely does the infection in dogs affect the testicular tissue, but when it does, the ejaculate of such dogs contains BHS organisms. These dogs should not be used at stud until completely recovered.

TREATMENT: Unfortunately sensitivity in BHS strains varies from one patient to another. If time is available it is important to use specific drugs on specific patients after laboratory testing. The vet should advise you on this. Antibiotic treatment is effective, which can be given by injection or orally. The bitch and her puppies are usually treated for five to seven days, after which the pups could, theoretically, go back to the bitch. During treatment careful nursing, and high-quality feeding to both bitch and pups is essential. In order to clear up infection in the breeding kennel, each bitch, whether she is to be mated or not, must be swabbed and treated with antibiotics as soon as she comes into season. She should be swabbed on the first day of each season and this is to be carried out until she proves clear of infection for two successive seasons. The antibiotic treatment is given orally and has been found to be successful only if started when the bitch is in season. When the bitch is not in season the treatment is useless. For the first five days of her season, the bitch has 500 mg Ampicillin Trihydrate in two daily doses of 250mg – the dosage suitable for Beagle-size animals. Obviously the dosage varies, depending on the size of the breed. The treatment is repeated four-and-a-half weeks later, and again just about five days before whelping is due.

There is another method of treating BHS and that is by the use of autogenous vaccines, which have proved to be successful in some kennels, but they can only be prepared under licence, when requested by a vet. The procedure is that all dogs and bitches in the kennel are swabbed. The swabs are sent off to the laboratory for culture, where the micro-organisms are identified and sufficient vaccine is prepared to treat the whole kennel. It is a lengthy, difficult and complicated process, but it is an alternative if antibiotics have failed.

PREVENTION: Floors of kennels and exercise runs should be of impervious material which is easy to disinfect. All bitches, as they come into season, should be kept isolated for the full season period. Infected bitches should be isolated and the kennel and run sterilised before any other animal is housed there. A stud dog should not be used on different bitches within a five day period, unless it is known that they are free of infection. In this way the male's role of passive vector is minimised. Bitches should not be taken to dog shows during their seasons. And a breeder should not ignore any small indication that all is not right – *never* ignore 'gut feelings'. A brood bitch's breeding years are few, and seasons are usually only twice yearly. So time is of the essence when there is the least suspicion of BHS infection, and you and your vet need to work together fast to counteract it.

5 BREEDING BEAGLES

Few people deliberately set out to start a kennel of any breed. More usually they acquire their first pet, go along to a dog show where they manage to win a modest prize, and their enthusiasm is immediately fired to go on to bigger and better things. Many novice owners decide to breed their bitch for the wrong reasons – it will do the bitch good; having a litter of puppies will help the children understand "the miracle of life"; breeding from her will improve her temperament – and the list goes on.

Speaking frankly, there should be only one valid reason for contemplating breeding a litter of Beagles, and that is that your bitch has something to offer the breed. Many successful breeders of today started with very indifferent stock and have gradually managed to improve with each generation. For example, Marion Spavin's original bitch was Derawuda Vanity – what an uphill struggle it must have been for Marion to bring the Dialynnes up to the unrivalled level of quality which they boast today.

Stocking fillers: Ten beautiful puppies bred at the Gold Line kennel in Denmark sired by Danish Ch. Tragband In Hot Water.   *Photo courtesy: Jesper and Annette Pedersen.*

Like mother, like daughter! Ch. Too Darn Hot for Tragband (right) and her daughter by Ch. Dialynne Nimrod of Ramlacim, the CC winning Tragband Sweet Bird of Youth, in turn dam of Ch. Dialynne Tolliver of Tragband.

Photo: Sally Anne Thompson.

APPRAISING YOUR BITCH

If you are serious about breeding Beagles, do try to appraise your bitch as objectively as possible. Ideally she should be sound in mind and body, and be free of any major faults. It is not a major disaster if she is not a top-class show bitch, but she should be essentially typical and come from proven breeding stock. Often the really glamorous bitches, who win everything in the show ring, do not go on to produce as well as their Plain-Jane sisters. I remember a Boxer breeder once saying "The best sort of brood bitch is one that has the body of a charwoman and the face of a lady"! Furthermore your bitch *must* have excellent temperament. If she is nervous or aggressive she should never be bred from. Giving birth will do nothing to change her disposition – it will simply release on to an unsuspecting public a litter of puppies which risk ruining the good name of our breed. I cannot stress strongly enough the importance of breeding for and maintaining absolutely correct

temperament in the Beagle. Assessing your bitch's breeding will not be easy if you are new to the breed. With time and experience you will learn to be able to "read" a pedigree, but this takes years of research and asking questions. In any event, you should still research everything you can about all the dogs on your bitch's pedigree, at least for four generations. Find out by asking the senior breeders, who will remember them if they were shown. Ask about their type, temperament, movement and so on, and find out if they had brothers and sisters which went on to produce. Some top winners are just "one-offs" and never produce as good as themselves. Invariably they come from a fairly open pedigree which is a mish-mash of different strains and bloodlines, with no dominating line or ancestor. If you feel your bitch is not really good enough, or has breeding which is less than promising, it might be better to forget any idea of mating her, and look around for a bitch specifically as a brood bitch.

THE PRACTICAL ASPECTS OF BREEDING

You also need to consider very thoroughly the practical aspects of breeding. Introducing a new litter of puppies into the world demands time, money, dedication and responsibility. It is not something to be undertaken lightly as, for at least two months, you will be virtually housebound.

Do you have somewhere for the bitch to whelp and then rear her family in peace? If and when puppies arrive, can you guarantee that you will be able to sell them? You really need to have some potential homes waiting before you mate your bitch, as, if you are a novice breeder, it is unlikely that puppy-buyers will be beating a path to your door, because you will not yet have acquired a reputation. Being stuck with six puppies of eight weeks which are eating you out of house and home is not a very happy prospect, is it? You will need to be sure you have caring owners lined up for your new babies. Happily these days Beagle breeders do not have the same degree of worry as we did some years ago, when research establishments often bought puppies through "middle men" who posed as respectable pet buyers. But still you can't be too careful. You want your puppies to go to responsible permanent homes, but if circumstances should alter, and the new owners cannot keep the puppy through no fault of their own, are you in a position to take him back until you can re-home him? Far too many breeders refuse to accept any responsibility for their puppies once they have sold them, and happily allow them to become just another Beagle Welfare statistic. This is not good breeding practice, and hardly the behaviour of a dog lover.

Even though you might live on a very large property, it is not a good idea to consider that a remote shed with an adjoining run is an ideal maternity wing.

Beagle mums and their babies need reassurance and human contact through confinement and weaning, so the best plan is to use a utility room or conservatory as the nursery – somewhere which is near to all the family's comings and goings, but spacious enough for the bitch and puppies to be left in peace.

SELECTING THE STUD DOG

You will need to decide on a stud dog for your bitch, and that is going to take a lot of careful thought. In the first place you should establish in which respects your bitch could be improved. Maybe she could do with a better head? Maybe she is a little long in back? Perhaps she is slightly flat-footed? Ruthlessly analyse her failings, and then look for a selection of available dogs which excel in the points where she fails. You should never fall into the trap of thinking that you should breed from extremes and mate opposites, because that doesn't work. In other words, if your bitch has a rather fine head, don't use a dog because he is overdone in skull. You should be looking for a dog with a correct head.

Once you have arrived at several possibilities, look at the breeding of the prospective suitors and compare their pedigrees with that of your bitch. If there are any dogs common to both pedigrees, you need to discover as much as possible about these dogs as, if you go ahead with that mating, you will be line-breeding to that particular ancestor and he or she will probably have a marked influence on your litter.

TYPES OF BREEDING

Basically there are three types of breeding. Outcrossing is where you mate a dog and bitch which have no common ancestors for at least five generations. This type of mating will probably produce a very varied litter where the puppies are rather uneven. There may be one "flyer" but the chances are that the litter will lack consistency. Line-breeding is where you mate a dog and bitch which have one or more common ancestors quite close up on the pedigree. This type of breeding should produce relative consistency and endorse both the virtues and faults of the dogs which repeatedly appear in the puppies' pedigree. In-breeding is where you mate very close relatives, e.g. mother to son, grandsire to grand-daughter, brother to sister, etc. This should only be undertaken with great caution and a lot of knowledge. It is one way of discovering rapidly if you have any skeletons in your pedigree closet, as if there are faults lurking in the background, you will get them. While close in-breeding may prove a rapid way of discovering what faults may be in your line, it can also produce outstanding virtues which can be strongly emphasised in the resulting stock. Such dogs can subsequently be outcrossed with safety.

Do not rush off to use a dog just because you like the look of him and he is winning everything in sight. You would be better off considering a dog which is of the basic type you need, and which has even better dogs behind him which also appear in your bitch's pedigree. But at the end of the day the decision is yours and breeding dogs is a continuous learning curve. We all make mistakes, and it is those mistakes which, hopefully, teach us a lesson and make us better prepared for the future.

You will have decided on a stud dog, and confirmed with the stud dog's owner that he will accept your bitch. Not all dogs are "at public stud" and many discerning owners will refuse to accept a bitch if they feel she lacks quality, or alternatively if they feel that she is of breeding which will prove incompatible.

TIMING THE MATING

Most bitches come in season every six months, but dogs are individuals and this period can vary dramatically from bitch to bitch. Six months will generally be the minimum period between normal seasons, so six months after the previous season you should watch your bitch closely for the first signs. Generally the vulva will swell and there will be a consequent heavy, bloody discharge. This should gradually pale to a much pinker colour at around the eleventh day of the season, but this is not always the case and some bitches have been mated successfully while still showing heavy colour.

The best guide as to when a bitch is most likely to conceive is when she will stand eagerly for the stud dog. However, there are again the exceptions. I have known of bitches which would happily receive a stud dog for as long as ten days – some Beagle bitches are just tarts! By "stand" I mean that the bitch will, having flirted with the dog, stand rock-solid and flag her tail to one side. Indeed, when a bitch is ready, and there is no available male, just tickling her around the tail area will often give the same result.

THE MATING

It is considered good manners to contact the stud dog owner to advise when your bitch first starts her season so that an estimated date of mating can be arranged. Kennel owners are very busy people and do not appreciate last-minute visitors with no prior appointment. On arrival, the stud dog owner will probably wish to examine your bitch internally, to ascertain that there is no stricture or other physical abnormality which may prevent an easy mating. If he should find a problem and advise against mating, then please accept his word – after all, he will be the one losing out on the stud fee! If the mating is to go ahead, allow your bitch to relieve herself before she is introduced to the stud dog. Flirting is very important, as dogs enjoy a ritual courtship in the wild, and domesticated animals are no different. This foreplay is a valuable aid to mental and physical preparation for the mating. Stud dog owners vary considerably in their attitude to stud work, and, indeed, their management of the stud dog. There are those who insist that their stud's prowess is such that he only needs to look at a bitch to get her pregnant, and advocate a rather regimented and clinical kind of mating, while others prefer to let dog and bitch indulge in some harmless foreplay, during which they will get well acquainted.

Personally I feel that a free mating is always the ideal, but by free I do not mean letting dog and bitch loose to frolic at the bottom of the garden; rather that they are allowed some freedom in a confined space where they are totally under control. Given that the bitch is ready and the dog keen, the dog should soon mount the bitch and she will be happy to have him do so. He will grab her quite firmly with his forelegs, bringing her closer to him, and begin a rhythmic thrusting until such time as he penetrates the bitch. This is the time when the bitch should be held firmly, ideally by means of a thick leather collar, as there may be a minimal degree of discomfort caused by the initial penetration, and there is always the danger that the bitch may panic and turn on the dog, possibly doing irreparable damage to both herself and her paramour.

Some stud dog owners will insist that bitches be muzzled from the outset if they show the slightest sign of anxiety at first, which may develop into aggression. Oftentimes pet bitches, who may be rather spoilt by their owners, can be difficult to mate, and if you fall into this category, you would best be guided by the stud dog owner, who may prefer to take the bitch away from you and effect the mating with the help of more experienced hands. This in no way suggests any attempt at malpractice, and any responsible stud owner will be happy for you to witness the "tie" after the mating – if only to assure you that your bitch has been mated to the stud dog for whom you are paying. The tie involves the male swelling up considerably inside the bitch, preventing him from breaking loose for anything up to an hour, but generally twenty minutes would be average. Once the pair are tied, and relaxed, invariably the stud's owner will lift one of the male's back legs over the bitch's rear, so that the dog and bitch can both stand comfortably, in a "back to back" position. The "tie" is effected when the bulbous base of the engorged penis of the male is held by the strong constricting muscles of the bitch's vagina. When her muscles relax, the dog is released. The reason for dogs tying in this way is that the dog ejaculates slowly and in three stages: firstly a clear fluid, containing no semen, flushes and disinfects the bitch's passage; secondly comes fluid which is rich with semen; thirdly further clear fluid from the prostrate flushes the semen forward into the bitch's womb.

DIFFICULT MATINGS

As regards difficult matings, I personally believe that if a healthy dog and a healthy bitch, who is at the optimum stage of her season, will not mate readily, there may be a very good reason for it and I would never advocate a forced mating. The chances are that the lack of enthusiasm stems from a clinical problem, and furthermore I am sufficiently old-fashioned to believe that Mother Nature knows best and could be trying to tell us something. Also, I find it hard to justify what is tantamount to rape being perpetrated. Occasionally, and again it is normally pet bitches that cause the problems, an above-average level of control is necessary, but few responsible stud owners will force a mating; indeed a totally forced mating is very difficult to effect.

STUD FEES

Having secured a successful mating, you will need to pay the agreed stud fee. Please remember that a stud fee covers the actual service, and not any resulting puppies, as is popularly believed. It is true that most breeders will offer a repeat service should your bitch fail to conceive, but this is a courtesy on their part, and not your right. I rather favour the Scandinavian practice of charging a nominal fee for the actual mating, and then a set fee per puppy born. This is a logical and satisfactory arrangement for both parties. When I first became involved in dogs, traditionally a stud fee was the equivalent of the price of a pick-of-litter puppy. While puppy prices have steadily increased, stud fees have not done so proportionately and, consequently, you can now use a quality stud dog for half of the price of the average pet puppy. In the UK when you have paid your stud fee, the dog's owner should give you a signed Kennel Club form, verifying the mating. Without this you will be unable to register your puppies, so insist on having this when you have paid.

CARING FOR THE PREGNANT BITCH

Do not make the mistake of pumping your hopefully pregnant bitch full of every additive under the sun as soon as you get her home. Until she is into the seventh week of her pregnancy, and showing some signs that she is in whelp (increased girth, pinkness of the teats, lack of appetite and a more sedate demeanour being some of the possible signs), she should be fed and exercised as normal. Thereafter, if the bitch is particularly large, her food should be increased very slightly and her daily ration be split into two smaller meals. There is still no need for supplements of any description, given that your bitch has always enjoyed a balanced diet. Far too many people cause problems for their bitch by over-compensating and adding nutrients which are adequately covered by the majority of today's complete feeds. Bitches which are overweight, carrying puppies which may be overdeveloped, will be less likely to have an easy whelping than a fit bitch whose puppies are of normal size.

PREPARATIONS FOR WHELPING

You will have already decided on the whelping area, and by the eighth week you should have a whelping box set up, ideally a specially-built model which incorporates a pig-rail, to lessen the likelihood of puppies being crushed by an over-zealous mother. The box should also have a hinged lid, to afford easy access and yet retain warmth. At this stage your bitch should be encouraged to sleep in the whelping box. She will probably be feeling less than agile, and be happy to retire to such a secluded spot. While the average gestation period in the dog is 63 days, bitches have been known to whelp up to four days early, or four days late with no problems.

Close to the whelping box you will need some basic equipment, including an ample supply of towels for rubbing puppies dry and stimulating circulation; sterile scissors for cutting any umbilical cords which the bitch herself may not have severed; strong cotton for tying any umbilical cords which may still be bleeding; brandy – no, not for you, but a drop can be applied to the tongue of a puppy which may appear lifeless, and often performs miracles; a plentiful supply of newspaper for the floor of the box; and several sheets of the fleecy-type dog bedding which is readily available, as a sheet should be put on top of the newspapers to keep the pups warm and allow any fluids to drain through to the papers below. Be sure to have your vet's telephone number right by the whelping box, and advise him beforehand of your bitch's expected date of whelping.

THE WHELPING

Keep an eye on your bitch from the 58th day after mating, and if she begins to refuse food, she may be close to the first stages. She will become very restless and begin scratching up her bed, possibly moving about the house exploring all alternatives, so watch her closely. If your bitch is determined to whelp in another part of the house, and seems reluctant to use the whelping box, then, rather than force her into the box, let her have the first puppy in her chosen spot. Then you can move her and her firstborn into the box when she will be so preoccupied with the new baby that she will soon settle and deliver the other puppies in the appropriate place.

Before the actual birth, the bitch will often pass a blackish membrane, or this may be only partially discharged. If no puppy appears within the hour, telephone your vet, as a shot of pituitrin may be necessary to advance the whelping. Should the bitch be visibly bearing down during this period, with no signs of any result, veterinary help should also be enlisted. Puppies will generally be presented head first. In the event of a head being visible, yet delivery does not then advance, you can help by gently but firmly holding the head in a towel, and each time the bitch contracts, you can slowly try to move the puppy further out, using a side-to-side motion. This will normally succeed. In the event of

a puppy's feet being presented first – a breech-birth – you should again resort to the "towel method" mentioned above and gently try to ease the puppy away.

Normally the bitch will open the enclosing bag herself and proceed to eat the afterbirth and sever the umbilical cord. This may be distasteful to you, but it is perfectly natural and will aid cleansing the bitch's system and help the entire whelping process. However, if you have removed a puppy manually, the bitch may be less inclined to open the bag, so you will have to assist – and quickly. Tear open the bag near the head using your fingers, otherwise the puppy will drown. You will probably need to cut the umbilical cord on such a puppy, and do so about two inches away from the tummy, tying with cotton to avoid any haemorrhaging.

Should a puppy be born which appears rather lifeless, use your finger to place a drop of brandy on its tongue. This may help the puppy to rally. If it does not, hold the puppy firmly in your hand, with the head poking out between your thumb and forefinger, and swing it downwards several times. This may well cause the puppy to gasp and help it to start breathing. You should try this for ten minutes or more before giving up.

Bitches vary but can go up to twenty minutes between puppies, yet some turn out a family like shelling the proverbial peas. If your bitch proves one of the latter, you are lucky. If the bitch appears to still be straining but no further puppies arrive after an interval of one hour, the vet should be called, as there may be a puppy stuck, which could necessitate a Caesarean section, or further administration of pituitrin.

POST-WHELPING CARE
If there are no such problems, and your

A sheet of fleecy dog bedding screwed to the floor of the whelping box, with newspapers underneath it, will keep the puppies warm and dry, and help them to get a firm grip when they get up on their feet.

Photo courtesy: Brenda Haslam.

bitch appears to be contented with her puppies, licking and nuzzling them close to her, the chances are that she has no further puppies left. She will be reluctant to leave her new clutch, but at this stage she should be taken outside and encouraged to relieve herself totally. Meanwhile, you will have the opportunity to clean the whelping box and replace both papers and fleecy bedding. It can be a help actually to fix the bedding in place, using large-headed screws which can be easily removed. This will prevent one or more of the puppies from getting underneath it and the bitch accidentally lying on them, and when the puppies get older and are on their feet it will give them much better grip than a bedding sheet, which slips and slides underneath them.

Offer the bitch a drink of warm milk when she returns, and now that the new family is safely delivered, this is the time for you to think about increasing the quantity of her food. At one time many breeders would have administered extra calcium to the bitch, and maybe cod-liver oil etc.; however, today's advanced feeding regimes are such that any quality complete feed makes this unnecessary.

Beagle puppies are born with dewclaws on their forelegs and occasionally on the hind legs too. These should always be removed as they can cause injury if torn in later life. Generally, if the puppies are strong and healthy, the dewclaws should be removed at around three days of age. Either an experienced breeder or your vet will carry out this simple operation, which causes minimal distress.

Your bitch should, for the first week after labour, be given two normal meals daily; afterwards the meals can be increased in size but the total daily intake depends very much on the size of the litter. Obviously a bitch nursing eight puppies is having to give much more of herself than a bitch nursing three, so here again use common sense – the most valuable tool of the successful dog breeder.

WEANING
The puppies will be quite happy with mother's milk for the first three weeks of their lives, but then you should begin weaning. This should initially involve

offering the puppies an appropriate complete puppy meal, such as the recently introduced Puppy Porridge marketed by the major petfood manufacturers. This is easy to administer and highly palatable and most puppies take to it instantly. When beginning weaning, take the bitch away from the puppies for about two hours so that they get hungry but have no milk bar to turn to. Offer a little of the porridge by gently pushing the puppies' noses into a dish. They will soon get both the taste and the idea, and will generally start lapping without any further encouragement. On the second day of weaning, give them two such feeds and by the end of a week – when they are now four weeks old – they should be on three meals daily. At this stage a proprietary puppy meal – either canned or dried – can be introduced. If a canned food is being used, it should be very slightly warmed as this will intensify the appetising odour. If a dried food is the choice, this should always be soaked in warm water or gravy for at least an hour before feeding.

Puppies should be checked for worms and wormed once they begin to accept solid food. Today there are various worming preparations available and it is always essential that the manufacturers' recommendations are followed as regards age and dosage.

When the puppies are five weeks old and eating happily their regular meals, they should gradually be weaned off their mother. Up until this age, it is recommended that the bitch still sleeps with them; however, beyond this age the bitch should be taken away at night. If she still has an obvious quantity of milk, she should be allowed to visit them at least three times a day until she begins to dry up. At six weeks she should be completely off the puppies and her milk should then dry up completely.

LEAVING HOME

By the time the puppies are seven weeks old, they should be eating four hearty meals a day. Their mother should be happy to leave them alone, and they should be running around, getting into all sorts of mischief and ready for their new homes. Most Beagles are ready to adapt to a new home at this age, and the earlier they go, the more readily they settle into a new routine. You will obviously advise new owners of the puppy's diet, and it is advisable to always give them a quantity of that food so that there is no dramatic change in their feeding habits at this stressful time. Should the new owners choose to change the puppy's diet, it should be done very gradually.

Hopefully your puppies' new owners will have been carefully vetted, as you will want to be as sure as is possible that they are going to give their adopted families as much pleasure as your bitch has. Do ask them to keep in touch, and each Christmas when you receive those festive cards with photographs of what was once your baby playing with his new family, you will be so proud and happy. I also suspect that, if you really are hooked, you are already planning that next litter.

ARTIFICIAL INSEMINATION

The showing and breeding of pedigree dogs becomes a more and more international hobby with each passing year. Judges travel worldwide to officiate at major shows, while breeders increasingly visit such shows, notably national breed Specialty events, and thereby get the opportunity to see many of the best dogs in the world. This is invaluable to breeders as they can then gauge the level of quality found in a breed from country to country, and can identify where certain virtues and weaknesses prevail. Sometimes outstanding dogs are located and may be for sale, but usually they are not. In such cases, the technique of artificial insemination (AI) can be a successful alternative, so that instead of buying the dog, some doses of semen are collected and shipped. Also, for countries which still have strict quarantine regulations, the possibility of AI is of great importance as a method of increasing what may be a restricted gene pool. Should you ever consider embarking on the AI route to breeding, it is vital that you consult both the relevant government Ministry and also your national Kennel Club, which may have certain restrictions regarding the registration of puppies resulting from AI – and do so well in advance.

To obtain good results with AI it is important to use semen of the best possible quality, to handle the semen properly, and to inseminate the bitch at the optimum time during her season, using adequate techniques for the actual insemination. Only dogs and bitches with normal fertility should be used for AI because it is not a method of improving fertility; rather it should be expected to result in a pregnancy rate slightly below that obtained by a natural mating, especially when using thawed frozen semen.

Dog semen can be used freshly collected if both dog and bitch are present and it is used immediately. It may also be chilled, extended, or frozen, if it is to be shipped or stored for any length of time. From countries not too far away, chilled, extended semen (which can retain its fertilising capacity for 12-48 hours or even longer) can be used. From more distant countries, the semen must be frozen and stored in liquid nitrogen at –197C. This is also convenient in case semen enough for several bitches is required. Frozen dog semen can be stored practically forever (1-2,000 years).

Should you decide to import a particular dog, or even semen from it, it is of fundamental importance that you get as much information as possible about the dog and, if possible, his forebears. To make such decisions, which will have far-reaching effects on your breeding programme, based solely on photographs of a dog, may result in your getting some unpleasant surprises. Such things as temperament, bites, testicles, movement and eye colour, to mention just a few, may be looked upon in totally different ways in different countries. What may be acceptable in the country from which you are thinking of importing, may be totally taboo in your own. In these days of amazingly inexpensive air travel, flying to see a dog in the flesh is infinitely preferable to a very costly mistake.

Most artificial inseminations are performed with fresh, or chilled, extended semen. Fresh semen is used when both dog and bitch are present, but for some reason cannot, or are not permitted to, mate naturally. To collect semen from a dog is quite simple, and to inseminate a bitch with fresh or chilled, extended semen is not that complicated, as long as the inseminator has a good knowledge of the genital anatomy of the bitch. The semen is usually deposited in the cranial vagina, and the bitch held with elevated hindquarters for ten minutes or so to facilitate the transport of sperm through the cervix and uterus to the ovarian tubes, where fertilisation takes place. Care has to be taken, however, not to cause damage to the bitch and not to use semen contaminated by bacteria – for instance, from a dog with prostatic infection (which may well be the reason for his refusing to mate naturally in the first place). Semen quality should always be checked before using it for AI, which is why contact with a veterinarian specialising in canine reproduction is advisable.

If the semen is to be shipped, it should always be diluted with an extender to provide nourishment, and to protect the sperm membranes from the shock of shaking during transport, and the semen should be chilled to slow down the sperms' metabolism and thus encourage them to retain their fertilising capacity for longer. Dog semen treated in this way can often be successfully used after two days or more. It can be shipped in an ordinary vacuum flask, which is cheap to buy and does not have to be returned. Shipments of chilled, extended dog semen between Europe and the USA have been successful.

If the transport takes more than two days, or if semen for several bitches is to be sent, the semen should be frozen. The freezing of dog semen also makes it possible to store it in a semen bank, to be used at some stage in the future. This technique is rather more complicated and is best left to the experts. A special freezing extender has to be used, and the semen cooled at a certain rate, then finally frozen in liquid nitrogen at a temperature of –197C. The semen has to be shipped in a liquid nitrogen container, a costly piece of equipment which will have to be returned.

There are various ways to freeze dog semen, and considerable commercialisation has developed in this field, notably in the USA. Unfortunately, many companies are very secretive about both the methods they use and, more importantly, the results they obtain. The breeders have not put enough pressure on them to come forward with their success rates, but hopefully this will change as the use of AI becomes more commonplace.

The Swedish Kennel Klub has decided that, for a litter to be eligible for registration, the AI has to be reported to them within two weeks, i.e. some time before it can be established whether or not the bitch has conceived. Only veterinarians with special training in canine AI may perform the inseminations; the results of such breeding are reported each year, and are available for breeders to study. This system has been in operation since 1990, and, during the ensuing six years, approximately 1,500 AI breedings have been recorded with the SKK. A large number of veterinarians have performed the inseminations and/or collected and preserved the semen. The average success rate, using both fresh and frozen semen, is around 50 per cent. Whelping rate after natural mating has been reported as between 80 and 90 per cent in the dog. This discrepancy in results after AI and natural mating depends partly on the fact that a number of AIs are performed on dogs with problems, and also that sometimes the semen is of poor quality, or the bitch has not been inseminated at the optimal time of her season. If only semen of high quality is used, and on bitches at the right time of their season, the results are around 80 per cent with fresh semen.

Frozen dog semen should be deposited directly into the uterus of the bitch, because this can also result in an 80 per cent whelping rate when using high quality semen, as opposed to only 40-45 per cent when semen is deposited in the cranial vagina. In the Scandinavian countries a method of non-surgical intrauterine AI by catheterisation of the cervix was developed during the early 1970s and has been used routinely since. The bitch is not sedated, and the technique is neither painful nor dangerous. It takes some time, and dedication, to learn, which is why in many countries the intrauterine AI of frozen semen still involves full abdominal surgery. Again, the breeders should put pressure on those performing AI in dogs to apply the more modern, less invasive techniques.

6 THE BREED STANDARD DISCUSSED

When dog showing began to develop as a popular pastime, it became necessary for every recognised breed to have a formulated, written description of the ideal specimen – a blueprint against which competing dogs could be evaluated in the show ring. Such blueprints were termed Breed Standards and to this day all judges are obliged to judge dogs in the show ring against the relevant Breed Standard for their breed. In the United Kingdom the Kennel Club controls the Breed Standards, as do the governing bodies in several other countries. In the United States, however, the Breed Standards remain the property of the parent breed clubs and it is they who maintain ultimate control. Which system is preferable remains a debatable point.

In this chapter it is my intention to look at the Beagle Breed Standard which is in force in the United Kingdom (this Standard also applies in all countries affiliated to the co-ordinating body, Federation Cynologique Internationale, as they adopt the Breed Standard from a breed's country of origin) and also the Breed Standard which is in force in the United States, and examine any subtle differences which may be apparent. Many of the original Breed Standards which were

drawn up in the United Kingdom were based on a scale of points, the various component parts of the dog bearing a certain value in points, and their sum totalling one hundred. This is no longer the case with any British Breed Standard, but the American Standard still carries a scale of points. It has been said that by "dissecting" a dog in this way, appraisal does not take into consideration such intangibles as quality, style or balance, and for this reason many people find the points system quite unsatisfactory and rather clinical.

GENERAL APPEARANCE
UK A sturdy, compactly-built hound, conveying the impression of quality without coarseness.
USA A miniature Foxhound, solid and big for his inches, with the wear-and-tear look of a hound that can last in the chase and follow his quarry to the death.

When the British Breed Standards were last updated and "streamlined" (some would say "sterilised"!) it was decided that any references in a Breed Standard to another breed, in whatever context, should be removed. Whether or not the Americans' maintaining of the Foxhound reference is of value is debatable. In the first place, the USA recognises two separate breeds of Foxhound – the American Foxhound and the English Foxhound. I would respectfully suggest that I have seldom seen a Beagle in the American show ring which remotely resembles a miniature version of either. In my opinion the British clause serves the breed better. It stresses that the Beagle should be sturdy, which suggests well-boned and firm-bodied, it mentions compactness which is a breed essential, and it also refers to the need for quality without coarseness. Thus the reader instantly knows that the Beagle should not be a common-looking animal, neither should he be flimsy or in any way underdone.

CHARACTERISTICS AND TEMPERAMENT
UK **A merry hound whose essential function is to hunt, primarily hare, by following a scent. Bold, with great activity, stamina and determination. Alert, intelligent and of even temperament. Amiable and alert, showing no aggression or timidity.**

USA Regrettably the American Standard contains no reference to characteristics or temperament.

I say "regrettably" because the Beagle's even temper is one of its greatest assets, and students of the Standard should really be left in no doubt that viciousness or nervousness are totally alien and therefore unacceptable in the breed. The fact that the American Standard makes no mention of temperament may give some readers the wrong impression that disposition is of no consequence. It is a major characteristic of the breed, and on no account should quarrelsome, aggressive Beagles be tolerated. Certainly, in a pack situation, such hounds would be short-lived. In the present day, when so much anti-dog feeling exists amongst the general public, Beagles which display untypical temperament should be humanely destroyed for the sake of the breed's reputation, which has hitherto been exemplary.

HEAD AND SKULL
UK **Fair length, powerful without being coarse, finer in the bitch, free from frown or wrinkle. Skull slightly domed,**

A most engaging head study of Ch. Millmar Beeswax, owned and bred by Isobel Miller, from her two Champions Mistylaw Chuckle of Millmar and Millmar Brevity. Beeswax won Best in Show at the Beagle Club Championship show under judges Patricia Sutton and Marion Watson.

Photo courtesy: Isobel J.M. Miller.

A delightful head study of the 1993 World Ch. Harrowill's Alien, a son of Argen. Ch. Blackspot Zany. *Photo courtesy: Marcos Adler.*

moderately wide, with slight peak. Stop well defined and dividing length, between occiput and tip of nose, as equally as possible. Muzzle not snipy, lips reasonably well flewed. Nose broad, preferably black, but less pigmentation permissible in lighter coloured hounds. Nostrils wide. Eyes: dark brown or hazel, fairly large, not deep set or prominent, set well apart with mild appealing expression. Ears: long, with rounded tip, reaching nearly to end of nose when drawn out. Set on low, fine in texture and hanging gracefully close to the cheeks. Mouth: the jaws should be strong, with a perfect, regular and complete scissor bite, i.e. the upper teeth closely overlapping the lower teeth and set square to the jaws.

USA The skull should be fairly long, slightly domed at the occiput, with cranium broad and full. Ears: set on moderately low, long, reaching when drawn out nearly, if not quite, to the end of the nose; fine in texture, fairly broad – with almost entire absence of erectile power – setting close to the head, with the forward edge slightly inturning to the cheek – rounded at tip. Eyes: large, set well apart – soft and houndlike – expression gentle and pleading; of a brown or hazel color.

Muzzle: of medium length – straight and square cut – the stop moderately defined. Jaws: level. Lips free from flews; nostrils large and open. Defects: a very flat skull, narrow across the top; excess of dome, eyes small, sharp or terrierlike, or prominent and protruding; muzzle long, snipy or cut away decidedly below the eyes, or very short. Roman-nosed, or upturned, giving a dish-face expression. Ears short, set on high or with a tendency to rise above the point of origin.

In principle the descriptions of the head in both Standards are very close, but there are perhaps shortcomings in both. Both stress that the Beagle head should be of fair length but, while the British version points out that the skull should be powerful yet free from coarseness, the American Standard requires a broad and full cranium, which may lead to that being interpreted as allowing a degree of coarseness. Both point out that there should be a slight occipital peak, but the American Standard goes on to list excessive dome as a defect. (N.B. No British Breed Standard lists specific faults, as each Standard is appended with the following clause: **Any departure from the foregoing points should be considered a fault and the seriousness with which the fault should be regarded should be in exact proportion to its degree.** That, in my opinion, is preferable to listing individual faults and disqualifications, as a judge is then at liberty to evaluate all shortcomings according to his or her own personal priorities and, perhaps, it leaves a little more room for personal interpretation.)

The British Standard stresses that the head should be free from frown or wrinkle, wisely so, in my opinion, as a wrinkled head in a Beagle can create, at best, a very worried,

and not at all "appealing" expression or, at worst, a rather menacing one.

Both Standards call for moderate stop and this is one aspect of the Beagle head which does vary considerably. In some hounds the stop will be minimal, creating a rather plain, bland expression. In others the stop may be a little too deep and this, coupled with the often present dish-face, can give an almost Pointer-like head, which thus becomes wholly untypical. Only the British Standard points out that the stop should divide the head into two equal halves; the American simply calls for both skull and muzzle to be fairly long. The American Standard requires the muzzle to be straight and square-cut, rather an ambiguous expression maybe, as from which angle is the muzzle seen as straight? In fact, this refers to the line from the base of the stop to the nose. The square-cut requirement in this Standard equates well with the "not snipy, lips reasonably well flewed" in the British version, both suggesting sufficient "drop of lip" as to give a smoothly squared-off foreface. A snipy muzzle lacking this finish will appear sharp, hard and detrimental to the essential softness of the characteristic Beagle expression. Any scenthound should have large open nostrils for obvious reasons. Note that the American Standard makes no reference to the colour of the nose leather, whereas the British asks for the nose to be preferably black, with the rider that less pigmentation is permissible in lighter coloured hounds. In fact you will seldom find a dark nose in a light-coloured hound, and it is surprising how many judges prove their ignorance when they dismiss lemon Beagles because they have "off-coloured noses"! Furthermore, a black nose on a lemon or tan hound looks quite incongruous and out of place. For your own interest, if you have a lemon Beagle, colour the nose with "black chalk" and see how it changes the expression (at home, of course, not for the show ring!). The head will look quite strange and the expression hard and stark.

We are told that the Beagle's eyes should be set well apart, large (according to the American Standard) or fairly large (according to the British). In colour, both agree they should be hazel or brown, but the British Standard suggests dark brown. I have always had a problem, particularly with people in other breeds where the darker the eyes are, the better, when I try to explain that in Beagles you can have an eye which is *too* dark. If the eye is such a dark brown that it tends towards black, you will get a hardening of expression and lose that mild, appealing look which is so essential to the breed, and which can only be achieved with a medium-brown eye. Another interesting aspect of the Beagle eye and the Standard is that neither Standard actually mentions shape. Now if you were to ask most Beagle breeders what shape a Beagle eye should be, the majority will say "round". Basically they are right, but a Beagle eye which is perfectly round usually results in a slightly open, vacant expression. In reality, the ideal Beagle eye is one that I would describe as being round with the slightest tendency towards almond shape.

Neither Standard mentions the fact that the Beagle's eye-rims should be fairly tight, but not so much so as to create a mean "slant eye". However, often Beagles can be found with rather loose, drooping lower eyelids which creates a somewhat "hang dog" expression. Another aspect of the eye totally neglected by the Breed Standards is the haw, or third eyelid. Ideally both haws should be darkly pigmented, as this enhances the softness of expression. One, or both, haws are frequently unpigmented.

In a correctly shaped, sufficiently tight eye, the haws will be barely noticeable, and when unpigmented they will not affect the expression at all. However, with one or both unpigmented haws and a rather loose eye, the expression can be rather wild and not at all appealing.

Both Standards agree on the set of the ears and their length and, though worded slightly differently, both convey the need for the inner edge of the ear to hang closely to the cheek. Rounded tips are essential to creating the overall Beagle expression, as any suggestion of a point will destroy the softness to a degree. While both Standards say that ears should be fine in texture, this is misleading. Some readers may assume that the fineness refers to the actual leather, whereas in fact the breed's original purpose was such that a fine leather would prove disastrous when following a scent. The fineness rather refers to the quality of hair on the ears, which is altogether softer and finer than on any other part of the body. The ear leather itself is actually quite thick and serviceable.

As regards the mouth, the American Standard requires that the jaws be level, but makes no mention of the actual bite. The British Standard is more specific in requiring a standard scissor bite. Mouths have not been a problem in the breed, and it is to be hoped that judges will continue to insist on a correct scissor bite. Occasionally one finds a Beagle mouth which is slightly overshot or, indeed, slightly undershot (the latter being the more obvious), and both should be avoided. As for one crooked tooth in an otherwise even bite, that is up to individual judges to deal with as they themselves see fit.

Only the British Standard points out that the bitch's head will be finer than the male's. This is so true, and any Beagle bitch should have a sweetness of expression which instantly conveys her gender. It should never be necessary to look at the other end of a Beagle to tell whether it is a dog or a bitch. Overall, the quality and balance of the Beagle head, the eye set, shape and colour, and the set and shape of the ears, all help to create the soft, appealing expression which is very much part of the breed. A Beagle without that mild expression just isn't a Beagle.

NECK

UK **Sufficiently long to enable a hound to come down easily to scent, slightly arched and showing little dewlap.**
USA **Neck rising free and light from the shoulders, strong in substance yet not loaded, of medium length. The throat clean and free from folds of skin; a slight wrinkle below the angle of the jaw, however, may be allowable. Defects: a thick, short, cloddy neck carried on a line with the top of the shoulders. Throat showing dewlap and folds of skin to a degree termed "throatiness".**

In essence both Standards ask for a fairly long neck which is free of dewlap. I find it strange that only the British Standard draws attention to the slightly arched neck, as it is in their elegant crest of neck that so many American Beagles score. There is also a tendency for hounds which excel in arch of neck to have a definite indentation behind the skull, where the head and neck merge, which gives a certain nobility and smartness to the outline. Only the American Standard makes any reference to carriage of the neck, and then that is only under "defects". In the show Beagle, it is often assumed that the correct carriage of the head is on a neck held upright and proud. However, the natural carriage of the Beagle is such that, when he is moving at a reasonable speed, he will lower his head and the neck will be

rather more outstretched forward than upright. Often a well-constructed Beagle will be moved on a tightly-strung leash, the result being that he throws his front around alarmingly because it is out of balance. Moved at fair speed on a loose leash, the well-constructed Beagle will naturally move with his head lowered somewhat, though this may well be at odds with what is popularly perceived to be the desirable show ring deportment.

BODY

UK **Forequarters: shoulders well laid back, not loaded. Forelegs straight and upright well under the hound, good substance, and round in bone, not tapering off to feet. Pasterns short. Elbows firm, turning neither in nor out. Height to elbow about half height to withers. Feet: tight and firm. Well knuckled up and strongly padded. Not hare-footed. Nails short.**
USA **Shoulders: Sloping – clean, muscular, not heavy or loaded – conveying the idea of freedom of action with activity and strength. Forelegs: straight, with plenty of bone in proportion to size of hound. Pasterns short and straight. Feet: close, round and firm. Pad full and hard. Defects: straight, upright shoulders. Out at elbows. Knees knuckled over forward, or bent backward. Forelegs crooked or Dachshund-like. Feet long, open or spreading.**

Considering that the Beagle is such a moderate and unexaggerated breed in all respects, and the desired front assembly is as "normal" as one is likely to find in any breed of dog, I have found it very difficult to understand why extremely good fronts are so hard to find in the breed. Both the British and American Standards summarise the front assembly well. What is required is

Points of the Beagle.

Line drawings by Viv Rainsbury.

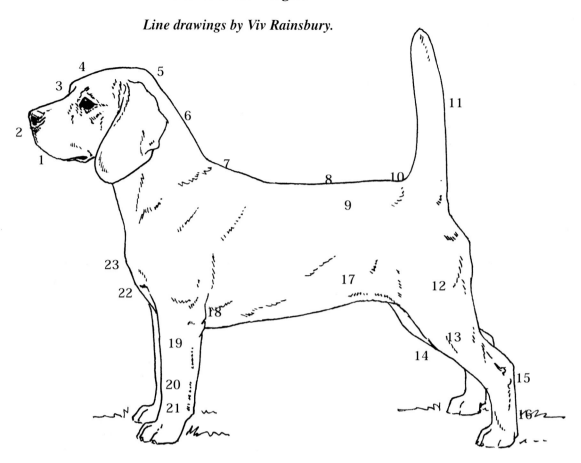

1. Lips/flews	9. Loin	17. Flank
2. Muzzle	10. Croup	18. Elbow
3. Stop	11. Stern	19. Forearm
4. Forehead	12. Upper thigh	20. Wrist
5. Occiput	13. Second thigh	21. Front pastern
6. Neckline	14. Stifle joint	22. Forechest
7. Withers	15. Point of hock	23. Point of shoulder
8. Topline	16. Rear pastern	

a well-laid shoulder, that is one where the shoulder blade (scapula) and upper arm (humerus) make an angle of approximately 90 degrees and the shoulder blades are of sufficient length so that there is little distance between the shoulder blades at the withers. The shoulders should lie close to the dog and be clean and athletic, without any suggestion of undue bulk or overloading. Without the correct layback of shoulder it is impossible to get good forehand extension and the desirable free action. Upright shoulders are a common fault, but sadly often create an upstanding appearance in the static hound which, to the uneducated eye, can be mistaken for "smartness". The forelegs should be perfectly straight and rounded, with quality bone running right down to the feet. In some breeds, notably the sighthounds, a flexibility and length of pastern may be called for, but this would be considered a weakness in the forelimbs of the Beagle. Straight round bone is terribly important to the overall picture of the breed, as often you will find Beagles which appear to have rather "fluted" bone and this detracts from the overall look of quality. There should be no play at the elbows, with them fitting firmly to the chest. When looking at the Beagle in profile, the elbow should be mid-way between the height at the withers and the floor. Also the forelegs should be well under the chest, and not "tacked on" towards the front of the dog, as will invariably be the case in a dog with a straight shoulder and short upper arm. The feet of the Beagle should be tight, like those of a cat, with full, deep and hard pads as these are essential in a working hound. The shortcomings in Beagles' fronts have long perplexed me. It is important that the front should have a certain width, as a narrow "terrier front" is quite untypical, but I have often seen Beagles which, standing, appear to have excellent fronts, yet when they move they do the most peculiar things with their front legs. Sometimes this can be due to poor musculature, but this is not always the case. It is my belief that many Beagles have relatively straight shoulders, and short backs but overangulated rears. Consequently, when such dogs move, the front and rear cannot co-ordinate correctly, and so front legs are forced every which way. Internationally, unduly wide front action in the breed now seems commonplace, and breeders are aware of the need to improve this.

UK Body: topline straight and level. Chest let down to below elbow. Ribs well sprung and extending well back. Short in the couplings but well balanced. Loins powerful and supple, without excessive tuck-up.

USA Chest: deep and broad, but not broad enough to interfere with the free play of the shoulders. Back: short, muscular and strong. Loin: broad and slightly arched, and the ribs well sprung, giving abundance of lung room. Defects: chest disproportionately wide or with lack of depth. Very long or swayed or roached back. Flat, narrow loin. Flat ribs.

In the mind of some fanciers, the ideal Beagle's overall balance is such that it should appear virtually square, with the height to the withers being more or less equal to the length from sternum to rump. In reality, many Beagles are more likely to be slightly "off square", in other words fractionally longer than their withers height, if they are going to move soundly and with scope. The length of body in a Beagle should always stem from its ribcage rather than its coupling, and all too often Beagles are found which are not unduly long in their overall shape, yet their ribcage is far too short, the coupling far too long. While compactness is desired in the Beagle, it is a fact of life that the Beagle which becomes ultra-short tends to be rather "boxy" and lacking scope, this being particularly evident on the move. In my experience the shortest-backed Beagles I have ever seen seldom move with the requisite reach and drive, desired in a working scenthound.

Both Breed Standards draw attention to the need for well-sprung ribs and a chest which is deep, these being vital for providing sufficient heart and lung room. Interestingly, the British Standard calls for a straight and level topline, while the American version makes no reference to a level topline, but includes the provision for a slightly arched loin. In reality, American Beagles in the show ring today invariably possess spirit-level toplines, where the British Beagles are less demanding in this respect. Most breeds of working dog will have a slight arch over the loin, and that arch stems more from musculature than from any spinal formation. The British reference to the correct Beagle underline, i.e. without excessive tuck-up, is important, I feel, as there is an increasing tendency for Beagles to win which have an untypical underline, with almost Whippet-like upward sweep. This quite changes the outline of the correct Beagle and gives a cut-up, unbalanced silhouette. It could perhaps have been pointed out in both Standards that the Beagle should carry enough condition for it to appear fit, taut and well-covered, but should never appear overweight or lacking in shape. When looking down over a Beagle, there should be a noticeable "waist", where the ribs flow into the loin – this is very slight, but should it be visible.

HINDQUARTERS
UK **Muscular thighs. Stifles well bent. Hocks firm, well let down and parallel to each other.**
USA **Hips and Thighs: strong and well muscled, giving abundance of propelling power. Hind Legs and Feet: stifles strong and well let down. Hocks firm, symmetrical and moderately bent. Feet close and firm. Defects: Cow hocks or straight hocks. Lack of muscle and propelling power. Open feet.**

In a hound which is required to cover many miles during a day's work, strongly developed and correctly constructed hindquarters are essential. While few show Beagles are required to endure similar sustained exercise, the physical attributes

should still be there. Some years ago a major fault in the breed was straight hindquarters lacking in turn of stifle, but today we see much better angulation, with the occasional example of what is, actually, over-angulation. Moderation remains the keynote of the Beagle and a dog which has excessive turn of stifle will never have the propelling power of a correctly angulated dog, balanced fore and aft. Another fault I have found in certain lines is hocks which appear to be double-jointed. In other words, when the dog is standing, a little pressure on the hock will force it to push forward with little resistance. This indicates a weakness which will usually manifest itself in the dog's gait.

The Beagle should have well-muscled thighs and second thighs, with rear quarters which appear "hammy" and well-rounded, yet not so much so that they look heavy and over-built. Cowhocks tend not to be too prevalent – this condition refers to a dog where the hind legs bow inwardly to the hocks, the hock joints being relatively close together and the hind feet, as a consequence, turn outwards. Barrel hocks are also sometimes seen, where the whole rear assembly, when viewed from behind, bows, giving the impression of a barrel.

TAIL
UK **Sturdy, moderately long. Set on high, carried gaily but not curled over back or inclined forward from root. Well covered with hair, especially on underside.**
USA **Set moderately high; carried gaily, but not turned forward over the back; with slight curve; short as compared with size of hound; with brush. Defects: A long tail. Teapot curve or inclined forward from the root. Rat tail with absence of brush.**

Many observers may consider that the tail

of a dog is a relatively minor feature, but it is my contention that a poor tail can ruin an otherwise excellent Beagle. Interestingly the requirements of the British and American Standards as regards the tail (or "stern" in hound parlance) vary quite considerably. While the British calls for a "moderately long" tail, the Americans ask that it should be "short as compared with size of the hound". This is very much a matter of interpretation, but, in reality, the American Beagles do, generally, tend to have shorter tails than their British counterparts.

Perhaps where tails differ significantly is in their carriage and set. To the British eye, the ideal Beagle tail is one which is high-set but comes off the topline at a "five-past-the hour" angle. Carriage which is actually perpendicular, or inclined even slightly over the back, would be considered an anathema. In the United States, however, despite the requirements of that country's Breed Standard, many winning Beagles have tail carriage which would be considered unacceptably "gay" for British tastes. Indeed, I believe that some American judges actually prefer more of a "terrier tail", as this tends to give the impression of shortening the dog's back and making it appear "smarter". Many British judges would disregard a Beagle with a forward-inclined tail, even though the dog may excel in other points. The Beagle's tail should show coarse hair on its underside, creating a characteristic "brush" and this completes the balanced picture of the overall dog. Some American exhibitors (despite the AKC Standard listing "absence of brush" as a defect) trim this hair, which, personally, I find creates a rather hard and ugly look, making a "poker tail".

COAT
UK **Short, dense and weatherproof.**

USA **A close, hard hound coat of medium length. Defects: a short, thin coat, or of a soft quality.**

There is little to add about the Beagle's coat, as the Standards say all that is necessary. A quality Beagle coat will feel hard and fit the hound well, yet it should shine with health and vitality. After a run in the rain, a good shake should be all it takes for a Beagle to be relatively dry. A soft, open coat will not permit this and is therefore untypical of the breed.

COLOUR
UK **Any recognised hound colour other than liver. Tip of stern white.**
USA **Any true hound color.**

While blanketed tricolour may be the popularly perceived "proper" Beagle colour, especially in the show ring, all recognised hound colours are equally correct. These include tricolour-mottle, black-and-white, blue-tan-and-white, blue-mottle, white, lemon-and-white, tan-and-white (or red-and-white), lemon-pied, hare-pied, badger-pied, and liver-tan-and-white. These various colours are composed of differently coloured hairs which merge to differing degrees. Some breeders have striven hard to maintain the less popular colours which will always have their loyal devotees. The white-tipped stern is part of the breed's working heritage and is a characteristic which should be maintained.

I feel I should say something about the density of colour in black-blanketed tricolours, though I am sure I will be treading on dangerous ground in so doing. It is my contention that a blanketed tricolour should be just that, and its colours should be rich and definite. Oftentimes Beagle puppies are born as blanketed tricolours and maintain that coat pattern well past their first birthday. However, with maturity the black fades and – in extreme

Unusual colours in the Beagle

Hare Pied.

Blue fawn and white

Blue Mottle.

Orange Mottle.

Black and White.

Badger Pied.

Self Red *White or Cream*

cases – what was originally (and registered as) a black-blanketed tricolour ends up being simply a tan and white. Now, some will argue that this is still a perfectly acceptable hound colour, but I find myself facing something of a riddle: "When is a tricolour not a tricolour?" Puppies which have very solid black blankets, which still appear black when one runs the hand against the lie of the coat, will seldom fade, and whether one is happy with the faded tricolour is, I suppose, a matter of personal taste.

GAIT/MOVEMENT
UK **Back level, firm with no indication of roll. Stride free, long reaching in front and straight without high action; hind legs showing drive. Should not move close behind or paddle or plait in front.**
USA Strangely the American Standard does not mention movement at all.

A well-constructed Beagle in action is a joy to behold. Optimum movement will only be seen in a hound which is correctly built, well-conditioned and muscled without any excess weight. The profile action should be roomy and effortless,

without any suggestion of hackney or high-stepping action, though oftentimes hounds will high-step momentarily until they get into their stride in the show ring, or if they are moved too slowly. The hind action, seen from behind, should show hocks driving away parallel to each other. The front action, seen from in front, should show forelegs moving marginally closer than parallel, and they will converge as speed increases. As I have said earlier, oftentimes Beagle front action is inexplicably wide and loose in front, but the ideal should always be aimed for.

SIZE
UK **Desirable minimum height at withers 13 inches (33 cm); desirable maximum height at withers 16 inches (40 cm).**
USA **There shall be two varieties: thirteen inch – which shall be for hounds not exceeding 13 inches in height; fifteen inch – which shall be for hounds over 13 but not exceeding 15 inches in height. Any hound measuring more than 15 inches shall be disqualified.**

In the United States, while Beagles are

shown as two distinct varieties determined only by size and, consequently, at dog shows, two "Best of Breed" winners will appear in the Hound Group – the Thirteen Inch and the Fifteen Inch – inter-breeding between the two takes place routinely. When I first became interested in the breed in America, I must confess that I believed that Thirteens were only bred to Thirteens, and Fifteens to Fifteens. I soon discovered that this was not true, and the persistent inter-breeding can perhaps account for a lack of consistency in some lines.

. The fact that a Beagle who "measures out" can be disqualified in the United States has resulted in several significant hounds crossing the Atlantic when they went past fifteen inches at the withers. Only an idiot would argue that this has not been beneficial to the Beagle breed in Britain. In the breed's homeland where we recognise just one size, with a minimum height of 13 inches and a maximum of 16 inches (these only being "desirable", I should stress) – the problem we have is that far too many Beagles, notably males, are quite taller than the desired maximum. While I do not believe that a maximum height should be rigidly adhered to, with dogs exceeding it being disqualified, as this would have lost to the show ring some otherwise outstanding sixteen-and-a-half inch hounds, being too forgiving with larger hounds can lead to complacency and a spiralling effect. If we condone 17 inch hounds, it is only a matter of time before we get accustomed to their size and 18 inch hounds start winning. British breeders need to be mindful of the size problem, and to this end the more serious fanciers are always on the lookout for new blood from overseas which may be able to bring size down, while at the same time not losing the excellent qualities which exist.

When assessing a Beagle against the Breed Standard, it should always be remembered that markings can create an optical illusion. Close scrutiny of the dog is therefore essential, as markings should not be taken into consideration.

Studying these two identical dogs they appear quite different. At first glance, it seems that the dog (pictured left) is deeper and better-finished in muzzle. It seems to have a longer neck and better laid shoulder, more height of foreleg and to be shorter in both back and hock, than the dog (pictured right). Close analysis will reveal that this is entirely due to markings. Judges beware!

It amuses me that many of the owners of larger hounds seem to be of the opinion that excessive size and working ability seem to go hand in hand, but I wonder how well versed they are in the history of the breed as a pack hound. In *Beagling,* which was published in 1938, the author, C.B. Shepherd, Master of the South Herts. Beagles, writes: "The limit of 16 inches at the shoulder is imposed at the Hound Show, held annually at Peterborough, but there are several packs in England whose hounds are more than 16 inches in height. Fourteen-and-a-half inches is generally considered the most serviceable size for average country where plough and grass alternate, and certainly this size can show excellent sport under any conditions." I suspect that if an exceedingly good Beagle of fourteen-and-a-half inches was put into the dog classes at a British Championship show today, that dog would be frowned upon by the so-called "working" fraternity – yet, if possessing correct construction, breed type and movement, the dog should be considered nothing but an asset to the breed.

The impression of size can also vary with colour. Lemon or tan and white hounds may appear smaller than their tricolour identical twins, so sometimes the eye can deceive. My own attitude towards size is that one should always try to judge to the Standard in force where one is judging. When working to the British Standard, I would always hope to find Beagles which were between 13 and 16 inches in height, but would be a little forgiving of an otherwise exceptional hound who fell up to an inch either way. I often wonder whether some judges, who happily award top honours to 17 inch Beagles, would be as magnanimous if confronted by a superb hound who stood 12 inches at the withers!

7 SHOWING YOUR BEAGLE

iven that your promising Beagle puppy has been well reared and is maturing into a quality hound, you may be tempted to start showing him – or her; obviously as many bitches as dogs are shown! Assuming that he came from a reputable breeder who has been successful in the show ring, it is advisable to take the puppy back at around five months of age so that the breeder may assess his potential. You should be prepared for the breeder to be honest with you, and if for some reason he feels that the puppy has not blossomed into a potential winner, you should accept that fact and enjoy your Beagle as a companion. If, however, he feels that the puppy could have some level of success in the ring, then you will need to do some hard work to prepare for the rigours of exhibiting.

BASIC SHOW TRAINING

If you have any intentions of showing, your basic training should not include the "Sit" command, which most pet owners assume is obligatory. No show dog is ever required to sit, and indeed I can assure you that it is exceedingly difficult to get a seasoned show dog to sit on command. It just doesn't come naturally! I remember spending hours

with a photographer trying to get Ada and her daughter Birdie to sit together for a photograph – it took forever!

Show training should begin at an early age by standing your Beagle on a firm table in a traditional show stance. The forelegs should be well under the puppy, totally perpendicular, and parallel with each other. The hindquarters should be extended until the hock is also at right-angles to the table. This should create a balanced picture, and the dog's head should be raised by holding it under the chin, stroking gently, with the other hand lifting the tail so that it is carried in a graceful curve.

Table training should always involve food. Beagles are gluttons and anything associated with food will be looked forward to. Once the puppy has co-operated and held the show pose for a moment or two, reward him with a tidbit. After several days of "stacking" the puppy, you can try baiting the puppy with the tidbit, and the chances are that he will hold his tail up unaided. This can be built on, if successful, until the puppy gets into the habit of posing, holding his head and tail correctly while just nibbling at the tidbit. Gradually the tidbit can be moved further and further away from the puppy so that, eventually, he will stand steadily without manual assistance.

EMPHASISING THE DOG'S GOOD POINTS

In the United States, dog judges tend to like all their dogs lined up facing the same way. In Britain judges are generally happy to judge dogs shown however the handler chooses. As most people tend to be right-handed, traditionally dogs are shown with the head to the handler's right, tail to the left. However, before you decide how you intend to handle your Beagle, it is well worth setting him up in front a large mirror to see which, if either, side is the more pleasing. As most Beagles have uneven markings, a dog can look quite different on one side from the other. If, for example, a dog has a deep white collar on one side, he will appear longer-necked if that side is shown to the judge. Similarly, body markings can create amazing optical illusions. I once had an open-marked dog who, when shown left-handed, appeared several inches shorter in back than he did when shown right-handed. It never ceases to amaze me how few exhibitors ever bother to get someone else to set up their dogs so that they can get a "judge's eye" view. It can be very beneficial to see your dog from the other side of the fence, as it were, and you can pick up some very useful handling hints in this way.

Similarly, you should always get someone else to move your dog at some stage early on in his showing, in an attempt to gauge his optimum pace. Some dogs appear to move truer at a slower pace, while others go better at a brisk trot. With the help of a friend, you will be able to ascertain which pace best suits your dog. As we are in the age of the video camera, this can also be enlisted to study your dog, both standing and moving, so that you can work out

when he looks his absolute best. There is a lot more to showing a dog than just standing in a ring holding his lead. The exhibitor who has put in a lot of work beforehand, and is confident in which stance and at what speed his dog looks best, will always have an advantage over a less meticulous handler.

HOW TO SHOW YOUR DOG

Beagle exhibitors tend to show their dogs in one of two ways. There are those who prefer to "stack" their dogs, i.e. stand them in a show pose, while holding the head and tail up; and then there are those who prefer to free-show, with the dog standing unaided, hopefully with the head and tail held high. While I think most people would agree that a Beagle looks at his absolute best if he does free-show, the desire to do so depends very much on the individual dog. Some are "naturals" and take so readily to free-showing; others are less obliging. Despite the fact that she won 42 Challenge Certificates, Ch. Too Darn Hot for Tragband (Ada) would not always free-show in the breed ring. She got bored quickly, and at those times would soon lower her tail, so I frequently had to stack her. However, when she got into the Hound Group, there were different breeds to look at and many more things of interest, and invariably she pulled out the stops and really showed her heart out unaided. One of her old adversaries in the breed was Mal Phillips' Ch. Fertrac Brandy, and I really used to envy Mal, as Brandy would always show relentlessly, head and tail up, totally unaided. Indeed I feel it was his superb showmanship that won the dog so many admirers.

Far too many Beagle exhibitors tend to stack their dogs automatically, and never give them the chance, as puppies, to free-show. My advice is to try to train them to show free, and if they won't, then resort to stacking; but if there is a chance that they have the "attitude" to free-show, then try to build on it, as nothing looks more impressive. The response to free-showing depends very much on the mental attitude of the dog concerned, and I think males tend to free show more readily than bitches, especially once they have been used at stud. If a dog has an eager, inquisitive nature, he will tend to show free, his tail responding to new sights and experiences. Food is again a great help. When Ch. Dialynne Tolliver of Tragband (Mikey) came to live with me, I felt that he had this kind of attitude, and decided to try to free-show him, rather than automatically stack-train. I was never without a tidbit when we were in the garden, and if he struck up a natural pose, head and tail held high, having spotted something of interest, I let him hold the pose for a moment or two and then rewarded him with a tidbit. On a daily basis I spent several minutes baiting him at home, and slowly he caught on. I used to get a little frustrated when well-meaning ringside experts advised me to "string him" when I showed him as a puppy because "he looked a mess standing free"; but letting him mess about as a baby has paid big dividends as his subsequent show record bears out!

TRAINING FOR THE SHOW RING
Training for the show ring should always be fun for the puppy, and in the early stages you will have to get him used to being placed in a traditional show pose. On the ground, you should lift the dog up under the chest, letting his front legs drop perpendicular and parallel. If they don't, you have a constructional fault which you will have to do your best to hide by discreetly realigning the forelegs. Having got the front right, gently run your hand

down along the backline, lift the dog's rear, your hand gently under the rather sensitive bits – so be careful – and drop the hindquarters down so that the hocks are perpendicular to the ground, and parallel to each other. Raise the head so that the line of the muzzle is parallel with the ground, or with the nose pointing down – this angle will always guarantee showing the neck off to its best advantage – raising the tail in a gentle curve with the other. Holding the stern too far out from the back will give an impression of body length, while bringing it too far over the back will create the impression of a dog which is too boxy and stuffy. If your Beagle has a little too much "throat", i.e. loose skin on the neck, this can be discreetly gathered in, pulling it around away from the judge's viewing side.

When it comes to leads, I prefer a fine slip chain on a thin nylon lead. I find that this is unobtrusive, it gives total control, and it can be lifted up behind the ears so that the outline is free from interruption or break. Beagles should never be "strung up" when moving, but I find that if the lead is brought high up behind the ears, and just held so that it is taut, without pressure, the dog will move out freely. Your Beagle should be taught to move in a straight line, in a triangle, and in a circle around the ring. The dog should always be on your left, and the slip chain put on in such a way that when the chain is pulled, the ring attached to the lead pulls upwards. Many people fail to realise there is a right and a wrong way to put on a slip chain.

PREPARING YOUR DOG
As regards presentation for the show ring, the Beagle is a very easy breed to prepare. Most exhibitors settle for just bathing their dogs, and do little else. Some don't even bother with a bath! While I do not advocate "trimming" the breed, I am a

There are two basic styles of handling in the Beagle show ring. Jill Peak (Bayard) is a great advocate of the 'stacking' type of handling. She is seen here showing her own Ch. Bayard Zachariah (above left) and the normally free-shown Ch. Bondlea Poet (below left). Marion Hunt (Bondlea) is a fine example of a free-showing handler and prefers to let her Beagles stand naturally. She is seen here showing her own Ch. Bondlea Poet (below right), and also Ch. Bayard Zachariah (above right) who seems to have taken to the new style like a duck to water.   *Photos: Andrew H. Brace.*

The Beagle requires little grooming for the show ring, but I believe in 'tidying up' my show dogs. The only equipment needed is (left to right): Thinning scissors with one solid and one serrated blade, standard grooming scissors, a fine-toothed flea-comb, and a rubber grooming pad.

Photo: Andrew H. Brace.

great believer in "tidying up" and making every effort to make my dogs look as smart as possible. I am well aware that some more conventional exhibitors will be horrified at my admission, and that is their privilege. I believe in putting dogs in the ring looking as good as it is humanly possible to get them looking, and I am well pleased with the results.

Conditioning for the show ring is not just about giving a dog a bath. It also involves sufficient high-quality food and ample exercise. I believe that up until twelve months of age, Beagle puppies should just be allowed free exercise running around at home or in the local park. Once they get beyond their first birthday, if you have a show dog and are serious about campaigning him, you have to introduce a regime of controlled exercise. To achieve optimum muscular condition, an adult Beagle should get around four miles a day of steady trotting, ideally alongside a bicycle. If that is not possible, exercise machines are now readily available in most countries and these are marvellous for conditioning dogs, as they can be regulated and a formal exercise programme can be developed, adjusting speed and distance accordingly. These machines consist of a continuous rubber belt which runs over two large cylinders at either end of the machine. They are not cruel, as some people suggest, and dogs soon take to them. After a week or so they are eager to

get on the machine and trot away happily, with no restraining lead or collar. Such machines are still very expensive, so are unlikely to appeal to anyone other than the most determined exhibitor. I have also read that they are responsible for bad fronts! Bad fronts come from poor construction and in reality regular exercise will actually tighten up a slightly suspect front rather than the reverse.

Adequate exercise on hard surfaces should ensure that your Beagle's nails are kept short, but if they are not they should be trimmed four days before a show. I find the guillotine-type of dog nail clippers the best, but have to admit that this is the one job I hate. You should be careful not to cut the quick, and if you do cause them to bleed, the dog's feet will be rather sensitive for a few days, so never risk leaving nail-cutting until the day before a show. Preferable to clipping is filing on a weekly basis.

Two days before a show I get the dog on a grooming table and appraise what needs to be tidied up. The only equipment I use (other than nail clippers or file if necessary) is: standard grooming scissors, thinning scissors (with one solid blade and one serrated blade), a fine-toothed flea-comb, and a rubber grooming pad. Unlike many Beagle exhibitors, I trim off all whiskers from the foreface and cheeks, using the standard scissors, as this cleans up the head and enhances softness of expression, but leave the "eyebrows". Using the serrated blade of the thinning scissors, with the whole scissor opened out as wide as possible, I pull the blade through the whole body coat, in the direction of the lie of the coat, starting at the neck and working down the back, over the sides and hindquarters and also up the underside of the tail, being sure not to take too much out of the characteristic "brush" at the white-tipped end. This brings out all the dead undercoat and you will be amazed at how much hair comes out in this way. The tail-end should be discreetly tidied up but not so much so that a hard "poker tail" results. A standard stripping knife can be used equally effectively, as can a hacksaw blade.

Massage the entire body coat with the rubber grooming pad, running with the lie of the coat, and this will bring out any residual undercoat which the serrated blade may have left behind. Beagles will grow slight "frills" of hair down the side of the neck, and on the rear side of both fore and hind legs, and occasionally on their undersides. These can detract from an otherwise clean outline, so I comb them up away from the body using the fine-toothed flea comb, and then scissor them off using the thinning scissors. This should not be attempted by beginners, as, unless you know what you're doing, you can end up with a "knife and fork" effect. So watch someone who knows what they're doing, or practise on a non-show dog first. Any other "straggling" hair can be removed in the same way.

Then bath the dog. I use a safe insecticidal shampoo, well-diluted and applied with a bath sponge, with the dog standing in a human bath on a non-slip rubber mat. Firstly soak the dog through with a shower attachment, then sponge in the shampoo. Every time I bath a dog I

check the anal glands, as they can become impacted. These two glands, situated on either side of the anus, will feel full to the educated touch if you know where to feel, and gentle pressure will release the foul-smelling brown fluid if they are full. Again, I don't recommend this for beginners. Newcomers would be best to consult their vet if obnoxious smells are detectable from the anal area. There is a condition known within the breed as "Beagle tail" (and experienced in other breeds where it is known as "wet tail" and various other names), which is a temporary condition causing the tail to appear limp and dead, usually just the top half. There are various theories as to the cause of this, some people suggesting that it often happens after a bath, and no conclusive proof exists as to what causes it. If your dog suffers "Beagle tail" the chances are that it will fully recover after twenty-four hours – another good reason not to leave bathing till the day before a show. Having shampooed thoroughly, rinse the dog completely. Personally I always use a conditioner on my dogs, and prefer an organic wheatgerm product. This is rubbed into the dog's entire coat and should be left in for about fifteen minutes. Afterwards, rinse thoroughly and towel the dog as dry as possible. Do not be tempted to put a wet Beagle in a crate full of towels. When wet, dogs shake incessantly and it could be that shaking in a crate could be one of the causes of the dreaded "Beagle tail" – who knows?

When the dog is as dry as is possible after towelling, put him back on the table, groom right through with the fine-toothed flea comb and see if there are any straggling hairs around the "frills". If so, tidy them up with the thinning scissors. When fully dry, your Beagle should look bandbox-smart and ready to take on the world.

YOUR FIRST SHOWS

It is never a good idea to take a dog to a major show for his first outing, especially if you too are a novice, so start with something at the lower end of the scale – a match, an exemption show or a fun day, where you can see other more experienced exhibitors and learn the ropes slowly. Your dog will be required to stand on the table for the judge's examination, will be expected to stand in line in the company of other dogs in a traditional show stance, and to move as required by the judge. It is a good idea to go to a few of these small events without your dog, and then come home and have a practice "show" in the garden, perhaps involving family and friends who can act as judge and other exhibitors. Licensed shows are advertised in the canine press and you should apply for a schedule and entry form to the show secretary as listed. Enter following the instructions in the schedule and mail your entry, always using registered post. (If your entry should go astray you will need proof of posting before you would be allowed to show on the day.)

You will need to take your dog-crate with a blanket, your show lead, water and water-bowl and also some dry shampoo or chalk, just in case your hound gets dirty walking into the show. A towel is always a good idea, and of course you should have some tempting tidbits. The British Kennel Club now insists that "water only" should be used in preparing dogs at shows – in my opinion a stupid rule impossible to enforce, but you have been warned!

Get to the show in plenty of time before your class is due. Let your dog exercise, empty himself (always cleaning up afterwards) and let him get the "feel" of the place. When your class is called, try not to stand first in line. If you are inexperienced, it will help if you can see

Hound Group

The American show scene: John and Peggy Shaw's Am. Ch. Shaw's Spirit of the Chase is pictured winning one of the many Hound Groups, handled by Peggy. He represents the sixth generation of Shaw's Champions in direct line, and is also line-bred to the legendary Am. Ch. Starbuck's Hang 'em High. Photo: Booth.

how the other exhibitors show their dogs first. Once the class is assembled, be sure that you have your dog standing as correctly as possible for the judge's first look down the line. First impressions are terribly important and, if a dog catches the judge's eye at first glance, it has caught his interest. As the judge looks at the dogs ahead of you closely, on the table and moving, let your dog relax. Don't try to make him stand properly all the time as he will get bored. Use this time to watch what

The British show scene: Peter Newman and Barry Day's Ch. Symphony of Dialynne is seen winning a Hound Group at Bournemouth Championship show under judge Terry Thorn. Group Two at this show was Bill O'Loughlin's legendary Ch. Bassbarr O' Sullivan, the top winning Basset Hound of all time. Photo: Russell Fine Art.

the other handlers are doing, and note where you will be required to move your dog. As the dog in front of you is moving, having been seen on the table, put your dog on the table and get him to stand correctly. You will probably be asked the age of the dog by the judge, and that is all. Do not attempt to get into conversation with the judge. Move your dog as asked by the judge, and when you come back to him after the final move, get the dog to stand as well as possible, as the judge will probably want to take another look at it standing free. Then file back into line, keeping an eye on which is the last dog to be seen, as then you will have just seconds to collect your dog and get him standing smartly.

If you are selected for further consideration, keep your wits about you and stand where you are told to, always taking full advantage of the ring, and not standing downhill or with your dog's feet in a hole. If your dog makes the first "cut" you will probably be asked to move again, either individually or collectively. You will then have to stand your dog for the final awards. Should you be lucky enough to get in the placings, it always looks sporting to congratulate those who have beaten you. And when you have the opportunity, do try to look closely at those dogs and try to see why they have beaten you. Being able to appreciate virtue in other exhibitors' dogs is essential if you are going to enjoy your days in the show ring. If your dog is beaten, do not be tempted to go home. Put your dog on his bench, or in his crate somewhere cool, and watch the rest of the Beagle judging. You should be trying to learn as much as possible about what is now your breed, and about the intricacies of judging, as one day you may find yourself in the middle of that ring!

8 JUDGING THE BEAGLE

One of the most important, and influential, roles in the sphere of dog showing is that of the judge. Through their decisions, judges can influence a breed to a dramatic degree, as consistent winning dogs tend to be the obvious choice when it comes to breeding, and if judges put up a certain "look", that will be the style of dog which exhibitors choose to produce. I am speaking generally, of course, and there will always be dedicated breeders who prefer to produce dogs of a certain type, size, or colour, regardless of whether or not they find favour in the ring. Such breeders will never become slaves to fashion and derive great satisfaction from "doing their own thing".

The majority of exhibitors, however, want to win and they will be ever-mindful of the type of dog which appeals to the majority of judges. For this reason, it is vitally important that all who presume to judge our lovely breed fully understand the Beagle's essential characteristics, and its original purpose, and are totally conversant with the Breed Standard and all its subtleties.

THE CHANGING FACE OF DOG SHOWING

In recent years the whole face of dog showing has changed considerably. Gone are the large kennels owned by wealthy landowner fanciers who could afford numerous kennel staff to look after their many dogs' every need; to a great extent these have been replaced, largely due to economic forces, by the "hobbyist" exhibitor who owns one or a few dogs. Not too long ago the majority of judges tended to be stockmen who judged not only dogs, but also other forms of livestock, fur and feather. Their knowledge of individual breeds may not have been as thorough as one would now hope for, but they had a natural eye for balance, soundness of mind and body, and quality, and judged accordingly. These were the great "all-rounders" of the past, and the only breed specialists who officiated tended to be senior, well-established breeders who could claim to possess not just a kennel, but a bloodline. They were real specialists worthy of the name, unlike many of today's breed judges who are simply that – people who judge the breed. I feel very strongly that the term "breed specialist" has become much debased in recent years. It is a label which needs to be well earned.

In those "good old days", people who showed dogs did not automatically presume to judge them. In England, after serving a lengthy apprenticeship, they tended to be invited by one of the "breed elders" to judge a few classes of the breed at a small show. Their performance was then monitored and those who showed a good basic understanding of the breed were encouraged to go on; those who did not probably found that their careers had ended before they had begun! The late and much-loved Dolly Macro, who owned the Deaconfield Beagles, was a classic example of the "old school" who came up the hard way and was probably the last Beagle judge of that generation. Dolly had to be forced into judging and then only agreed with great reluctance, despite her amazingly deep grounding in all matters canine. To her death she remained a lady of great modesty, and yet she was without a doubt one of the finest Beagle judges we have seen. When she judged at Crufts, she awarded Ada Best of Breed. That win remains the most treasured of all, and I will always remember her critique, which began with the words: "She came into the ring as if she owned the world."

Today everything is different. Exhibitors who have shown their first dog with modest success want to jump on the judging bandwagon, and I often wonder why. I am frequently asked to speak at judging seminars and I always begin by asking the audience *why* anyone should want to judge in the first place. The answers I receive are many and varied. Some say that it is a logical progression from exhibiting and breeding; others that it is their way of "putting something back". Some, who wish to amuse by their frankness, suggest that it can prove a passport to free international travel!

UNDERSTANDING JUDGING

Personally, I regard judging as an enormous challenge. It is an opportunity to assess a collection of dogs and make a decision as to which is best, armed only with your knowledge of the breed and your basic "eye". The real thrill of judging, however, for me is the faint hope of finding something truly great, maybe a totally unknown or unheard of youngster, which comes into the ring and makes the hairs on your back stand on end. The prospect of discovering a real star is my incentive to judge. It doesn't happen very often, and only a fool would "discover" something new just for the sake of it, regardless of its quality, but when you do find a puppy or junior which you have never seen before, which outclasses all of the competition, it is so rewarding an experience that it is hard to describe.

Judging should never be undertaken lightly. Firstly, you have to understand the Beagle fully, and that means detailed study. Read all the books you can find on the breed, read about its history and development and try to appreciate that feeling of tradition which is so very much part of the breed. Then get to grips with the Breed Standard. Read and re-read it, and try to understand it. Knowing the words of the Standard parrot-fashion is a quite different matter from understanding them. If the Beagle's shoulders should be well laid back, discover *why* they should be so. All Breed Standards were originally drawn up around form and function by the founding fathers of the breed. There was a reason for everything – no requirement of any Standard was inserted on a whim or for purely cosmetic reasons.

Studying the Standard in isolation will only tell you so much, as Standards are by nature quite vague and with considerably wide parameters. You will only fully appreciate the Standard by studying it in conjunction with top quality dogs. When you are in your formative years, watch the

Most Beagles do not mature fully until they are at least 18 months old, so judges of the breed need to understand the various stages of development. At six months, most Beagles will have a definite 'rawness' about them, as seen here in Beagriff Blue Jay, a bitch puppy bred by Steven Seymour in Australia and sired by his Aust. Ch. Tragband Summer and Smoke. Despite her immaturity, Jay's quality and potential are clearly visible.

Photo: Steven Seymour.

Beagles are shown as two varieties in the United States – not exceeding 13 inches, and over 13 inches but not exceeding 15 inches. I judged the breed at Monmouth County Kennel Club in May 1993 and awarded Best of variety in 'Fifteens' to Whiskey Creeks Headliner who came up from the lower classes. He was handled by Sue Delia and is owned by Mark Delia and Michelle Sager.

Photo: Dave Ashbey.

best dogs in the breed when they are in the show ring, and try to relate their good points to the relevant part of the Breed Standard. Only in this way will you begin to develop your "eye". It has often been said that good judges are born and not made, and to a certain degree I would go along with that sentiment. While you can learn most that there is to know about a breed, you will only become an outstanding judge if you have a natural instinct for finding quality, and appreciating harmony and balance.

CORRECT MENTAL ATTITUDES

A vital requirement in a great dog judge is also the correct mental attitude, which has to be totally positive. Judging dogs is about putting the good ones up because of their virtues, not the bad ones down because of their faults. Every dog has his shortcomings, but a successful judge will

appreciate a dog for his outstanding virtues, and see minor faults in perspective. Far too many judges (and novice judges tend to be the worst offenders in this respect) will look at an exceptional dog with, say, a light eye, and see only that light eye. They will home in on what is an obvious, and in this instance, wholly cosmetic and thus decidedly minor, fault and as a result fail to see the wood for the trees. Unless you develop a positive attitude towards judging, you will never contribute anything to the breed – and that is what a judge's brief should be: to improve the breed. It is an attitude which can be self-taught from the day you attend your first show. When you look at any dog in the ring, try to find out what is good about him – what points he has that really make him of use to the breed. It depresses me when I hear exhibitors ringside rubbishing excellent dogs because they are not perfect. Unless you can see beyond what is wrong, and appreciate what is right, then you should never consider judging. You will have nothing to offer.

Given that you have studied the breed, have been successful in the show ring with quality dogs, and have bred typical stock yourself, and you wish to judge, please don't ask for an appointment. That will be resented by everyone. If you have been seen showing good dogs, sooner or later you will be asked – societies which run the smaller type of shows are always on the lookout for new judges as they invariably pull in good entries (working on the "unknown quantity" theory). Prior to accepting your first appointment, I would strongly recommend stewarding at several shows for experienced judges. Not only will this get you used to standing in the middle of a ring, exercising a degree of authority, it will also acquaint you with the official judge's book and relevant paperwork, and hopefully help develop your eye and technique as you watch seasoned judges working at close quarters. Furthermore, most judges appreciate genuine enthusiasm and will be only too happy to discuss their placings with you afterwards if there is a decision which you fail to understand.

Going back for a moment to the point I made earlier about new judges getting large entries, I get rather annoyed with show secretaries (at all levels) who openly admit that their main concern when appointing a judge is the size of the resulting entry. It has always been my contention that the best judges never get the best entries. Why? If you judge a breed regularly, have very definite ideas about the correct type, and are consistent in your judging, exhibitors in the breed with any intelligence will soon work out what appeals to you and what does not. In my own case, few people who have seen me judge would waste their time

by entering considerably outsize Beagles, Beagles with ugly heads, or Beagles with suspect temperament under me, as they would know that I consider correct size, typical expression and sound temperament very important breed characteristics. Conversely, judges who appear to have no type in mind at all and judge one year, putting up long-backed, short-legged dogs, then the next year short-backed, up-on-leg dogs, will tend to get large entries, as exhibitors (understandably so) feel it is a "lucky dip". So judges should not be judged by the size of their entries – strange, but true!

THE TEMPERAMENT OF A JUDGE
So, you have decided to start judging. Are you really ready for this? The centre of the ring is the loneliest place in the world. You will have more friends than you ever imagined possible prior to the show, then afterwards you will be hard pushed to find a handful who will talk to you! Far too many exhibitors take judging personally and are less than objective when it comes to evaluating judging. To many, their dogs are an extension of their very persona, and if you don't like their dogs, they take it as a personal insult. This is true of so many exhibitors, but the serious breeders will appreciate honest and knowledgeable judgement, win or lose. So you have to have a thick skin if you wish to judge. Also you need a high degree of integrity. The breed ring is a terribly incestuous place – many of the exhibitors showing under you one day will be judging your own dogs in the near future. It takes great strength of character to ignore this fact. You will probably also know many of the dogs shown under you – how much they have won, how they are bred, and so on. All these extraneous factors have to be pushed to the back of your mind if you are to

succeed as a judge. Judges are human, and it isn't easy.

A very useful piece of advice I was given many years ago was this: When you judge, and you find a dog that you really like, imagine him being handled by your worst enemy – now, do you still like him as much? Similarly, if you discover a dog that you really dislike, imagine your best friend is showing him – is he still really that bad? It is an interesting academic exercise and helps hone the judging thought process. You really have to discipline yourself and develop the knack of looking at a dog totally 'cold', and judging him, oblivious of all the irrelevancies which can so often cloud the issue.

DEVELOPING JUDGING TECHNIQUE

No one should ever start judging at the smallest Kennel Club licensed show unless they have some experience of handling or "going over" dogs. You need to develop your own technique and, when judging, be consistent in that technique, treating each dog the same. In a short-coated breed like the Beagle, there is little need for over-handling by a judge. I maintain that you can judge the breed well by checking teeth, testicles in the male, muscle tone, and then watching the constructional aspects of the dog through adequate gaiting – but you dare not. Sadly in Britain we tend to attach too much importance to the hands-on aspect (resulting in a new generation of "faith healer" judges – especially the multi-breed judges – who seem obliged to manhandle every square inch of a dog's surface area, presumably in a misguided attempt to display thoroughness), while neglecting lengthy study of movement.

I loathe what I refer to as "The Great British Triangle" as a movement pattern, yet this is what the vast majority of judges

settle for. Personally I feel that once up-and-down, followed by at least twice around the ring, is far more revealing. The shortcoming in the "triangle" is that it involves the dog negotiating two sharp corners. Many of the breed rings tend to be rather small, and if a hound has a brain, he can see the ring-rope ahead of him, so he is already braking as he gets half way across the ring, then he has to change direction, and in this rather restrictive movement pattern, the dog never has time to really settle down and get into his stride. Beagles need to move fluidly and they can only be seen to advantage when they are moving around in a smooth circle, with no corners or stride-breakers to consider. Another important point relevant to our breed is that some Beagles will initially high-step and need to settle into their stride before they display their true action. For this reason, the movement demands made by a Beagle judge should be carefully thought out. It is also important that when judging dogs on the move, the judge actually sees and analyses the movement. Far too many look but do not see – but more of that later.

TYPES OF JUDGING

Let us now talk about ring procedure, assuming that you are about to judge your very first Match or Open Show, but before doing so I would like to share with you a piece of advice given to me by that great American handler and now judge, Frank Sabella. When interviewing Frank many years ago for *Dogs Monthly,* the magazine which I both published and edited for ten years, he told me "When a dog comes into the ring, the first thing I ask myself is 'Is this what the breed is all about?' In other words, a Boxer has to come into the ring and shout 'I am a Boxer', just as a Beagle should scream 'Beagle' at you. Any dog must have an intensity of type about it which comes from certain breed essentials which a dog just has to have, otherwise it becomes just another dog." Words of wisdom indeed. "Is this what the breed is all about?" In the Beagle's case, in my estimation, that means that the dog has to come into the ring merry and alert, of correct size and shape, and displaying a balanced head with mild, appealing expression. Those are the fundamentals as far as I am concerned. But back to your first class...

In the advanced dog showing world there are two types of judging. In countries such as Britain, the United States, Canada and Australasia, dogs are merely judged against the competition. In many countries which are members of the Federation Cynologique Internationale (FCI), judging consists of two stages. Firstly, each individual dog is assessed against the appropriate Breed Standard, given a detailed written critique and graded (Excellent, Very Good, Good etc., or First, Second, Third etc.) based entirely upon the dog's merit relative to the Standard. Then, only those dogs which have achieved an Excellent or First (depending on which country one happens to be in) return to compete with others so graded for the placings. It is a more lengthy and complex system but, in my opinion, one which has great advantages for both exhibitor and judge. But, whatever method is used, the fundamental process remains the same – you still have to find the best dog.

TAKING YOUR FIRST CLASS
Your first class assembles, and the chances are that it will be a Puppy class, so you will have inexperienced youngsters competing. You should bear that in mind and be patient, making allowances for youngsters which you might not in the case of a mature adult. As the class lines up, look along the line from your judging table and see if there is anything there that catches your eye. First impressions are desperately important when judging dogs, as invariably the one which does catch the eye, and has the "it" factor, will prove to be the best, all things being equal.

While still at your table, before you are visibly in the centre of the ring, casually look along the line and watch the handlers and how they are setting up their dogs. Exhibitors can be extremely helpful to judges in pointing out their dogs' faults. You can guarantee that if a dog has a suspect topline, the handler will be fussing about, either tapping the dog under his belly or scratching his loin, so that he firms up in backline. A less than perfect front will be getting maximum attention from the handler who is determined to screw those forelegs into position before you actually see the dog! I have stressed that judging dogs is not a fault-finding exercise, but it is helpful to be told what is wrong with a dog without even having to look for it.

Once the steward has told you that your class is ready, look at the line from the centre of the ring and try to get an overall picture of the dogs and gauge the level of quality. All the time you should be looking for that dog which gives you a little "buzz", a slight sense of excitement, because that is the dog that will probably hold your interest more than any other. Having looked at the line-up in a static position, ask the whole class to move around, at least once. As this is probably a Puppy class, and some of the dogs may be at their first-ever show, they will need at least two circuits of the ring to settle and become acclimatised. As the dogs are going around, study the dogs' carriage and scope (reach and drive) of movement. Is there anything that stands out?

The first and last thing for a judge to assess has to be the overall picture. This photograph of Ch. Dufosee Zenith is one of my all-time favourite Beagle photographs, as it so clearly illustrates what I consider to be correct type, balance and quality. It shows a hound who is all of a piece, substantial and yet with an air of quality, who is completely moderate all through and free of exaggeration. The overall "look" has immense appeal and no one aspect of the dog overshadows the others.

Photo: Thomas Fall.

Begin your individual examination of the dogs on the table. Having got the first dog standing on the judging table, stand well away from him (you will never be able to see a dog properly if you are standing on top of it) and look at the overall picture. This is a point which I will stress repeatedly in this chapter – it is the *overall picture* which is paramount, regardless of breed. Forget the details for the moment; is the dog of acceptable size? is he correctly proportioned as regards height to length? is he well angulated at both ends? does he have a look of quality? is his outline clean and flowing, with no humps and bumps? See the dog as an overall picture. Imagine the dog painted black – a silhouette if you like – that will help you appreciate the outline and overall picture very easily.

Having savoured the outline of the dog on the table, approach him from the front. Some puppies may be a little unsure of things and allowances should be made if a youngster is hand-shy, but in an adult Beagle, anything less than perfect temperament should be penalised heavily. I prefer to show the back of my hand (fingers look so like sausages!) to the dog so that he can sniff and make friends. Before handling

the dog, study the forehand. Look at the head and expression, analysing the earset (which should be low), the eye shape (rounded almond) and colour (mid to dark brown), the balance of skull to muzzle (equal in length), the quality of muzzle (full-lipped without being too pendulous and not snipy), and the stop. The Beagle's stop should be well defined without being too deep, but when you are judging puppies, there are certain aspects of the dog which have yet to develop with age. Judging puppies of any breed is extremely difficult, and this is why all-rounders who have never owned the breed face an impossible task. Breeder-judges who have experience of the various growing stages of puppies will be aware that certain points change with age. This is where they have a decided advantage over the "outsider". They will know that a sloppy front may well tighten, that an outline which is "high in the rear" at six months will settle into a perfect topline, and that a head which appears rather plain and down-faced will invariably "break" and finish up with an ideal stop.

The dilemma about judging puppies is whether to judge them "on the day" against the Standard (which is based on a mature and finished adult), or make allowances for the deficiencies of youth which may, or may not, develop with maturity. It is something of a 'Catch 22' situation. The secret is knowing what a Beagle puppy should look like at a certain age, and that different lines can develop differently. In any event it is to be hoped that you are already sufficiently experienced to realise what allowances can be made in the name of immaturity.

You have assessed head and expression – and please don't make the fatal mistake which some all-rounders do of making strange noises to get a Beagle to "use its ears". The Beagle head should be studied with its low-set ears in repose, not perched aloft, encouraging forehead wrinkles! Handle the head, gently lifting the upper lips to check the bite which should (even in a puppy) be a perfect scissor. Draw out the ear leather to check length (it should reach almost to the end of the nose) and as you do so feel for the desirable fine texture.

Moving your hand down the dog's neck, check for excessive loose skin at the throat, remembering that puppies may have a little loose skin here into which they will grow. Feel the forechest, which should be well filled and in no way hollow, and then check the bone of the forelegs for strength and roundness. Lift up the forefoot to feel for strong and serviceable pads, and when the foot is back on the table consider if it is well knuckled up and tight. Far too many Beagles have flat, open feet, a horrid fault which detracts from the overall picture, is quite untypical, and difficult to breed out. Flat feet do not improve with age, and a Beagle who has poor feet as a puppy, will always have poor feet. The forelegs should drop in naturally parallel.

Having dealt with the forehand, run your hand down the neck to confirm that the

This head study of Ch. Dialynne Princess of Webline shows a beautiful quality head which I feel illustrates particularly the desired eye-shape, ideal stop, and the correct slightly domed skull.
Photo: Courtesy David Webster.

neck is clean and showing a definite arch. Some hounds have an ugly "ewe neck" where the neck profile, instead of showing an elegant crest, is positively concave.

Your hand should continue down the neck to the withers where you can check that the shoulders are well laid back and not too far apart. Upright shoulders go with short upper-arms and in this case you will find that your hand meets the shoulders almost before it has come to the end of the neck. With the other hand, examine the contours of the forechest in profile, to confirm that the dog does have a forechest!

With both hands spanning the body, check spring of rib and depth of chest, and do ascertain how far back the ribs extend. Many Beagles look short and compact, but in reality their body is half ribcage and half loin, instead of being mostly rib with short

LEFT: It has often been suggested that lemon or tan Beagles never have quite the same quality in head and expression as their tricolour relations. I include this photograph of Ch. Norcis Foxy Lady to conclusively disprove that theory! This head shows perfect balance with the characteristically low-set ears, bright expressive eyes and the necessary wide nostril. I awarded Foxy Lady the first of her many CCs as a youngster and still consider her one of the most outstanding Beagle bitches I have ever judged.

Photo: Martin Leigh.

RIGHT: The Beagle bitch's head should be finer than the male's, yet the male head should show power without coarseness but still display quality with the essential mild expression. This study of Danish Ch. Tragband In Hot Water shows great quality and tranquillity of expression, but it could never be mistaken for a bitch's head. I also include this photograph to illustrate the point that softness of expression comes with a mid-brown eye. Eyes which are so dark that they become almost black will result in a very hard expression.

Photo: Courtesy Jesper & Annette Pedersen.

couplings. In handling the body, drawing your hands from front to rear, you will also be able to determine musculation of the loin, and also whether or not the body is too tucked-up with an exaggerated underline (reminiscent of a Whippet). This is a major fault in some countries and on the increase, I believe.

Feel the set-on of the stern by laying your hand flat over the loin, your longest finger touching the tail-base. This will soon reveal whether or not the set is too low but being cleverly handled! Also feel the tail's thickness as it should be noticeably thick-rooted.

The hindquarters can be easily examined

I feel this photograph of Baimor Impromptu illustrates a forehand which clearly has the correct width of front, well-filled forechest, straight forelegs and shoulders which are well muscled without being loaded. Beagles should have a degree of width in front, as too-narrow 'terrier fronts' are quite alien and unserviceable.

Photo: Courtesy Maureen Tolver.

with both hands, thus checking muscle tone and angulation. Having completed your "hands on" examination, again stand back and look at *the overall picture*.

POSITIVE JUDGING
You will note that in this chapter I have chosen to use photographs of certain dogs to illustrate particular virtues, but have not included either photographs or line-drawings to illustrate faults, as the authors of breed books so often do. This is quite

deliberate on my part as I feel that the whole philosophy of judging has to centre around the positive. Any idiot can spot straight stifles, gay sterns or cow hocks in a dog, but it takes a connoisseur to appreciate type, balance and quality. There can be nothing gained by dwelling on the negative, just as you can never begin to learn about recognising excellence by studying mediocrity. Good judges need to be constantly exposed to quality, and it is essential when you begin showing Beagles that you make a point of studying the top dogs in the breed and try to understand what makes them such. You will never get anywhere just looking at average animals, spotting what is wrong with them. It amazes me how some novice exhibitors leave a show before the top awards are given out if they themselves have not won, yet these are often the people who want to judge. How can one possibly be in a position to evaluate other people's dogs without ever taking the time to study the best available? Any judge's ideal – no matter how familiar they may be with a Breed Standard – is moulded completely by the best specimen of the breed they have ever seen. Over the years you will see more and more better dogs, and with time comes discernment and a more critical eye. That eye is constantly developing. I always tend to judge judges by the dogs they themselves put in the ring. I have often asked myself how someone who is a Championship show judge could bear to show such an indifferent dog. If you assume that they like what they show, and they accept that it is good enough, why would you want to pay for their opinion when they are obviously satisfied with poor quality themselves?

EVALUATING MOVEMENT
But back to your first show and your first

Rosspark Mr Muffin was just seven-and-a-half months old when he won his first CC and this photograph was taken. It has been chosen to show that a small (he was fourteen-and-a-half inches), compact dog can have exceptional bone and feet. It also depicts a dog which is amazingly short-coupled, with ribs extending well back. It is my belief that this dog was way ahead of his time, being born in 1968.

Photo: C.M. Cooke.

Ch. Am. Ch. Graadtres Hot Pursuit of Rossut excelled in forechest, as this photograph clearly shows. I judged him at his second British show and awarded him Best of Breed, resolving to use him at stud. The result was the breed record holder, Ch. Too Darn Hot for Tragband.

Photo: Diane Pearce.

I have chosen this study of the free-showing Ch. Newlin Prefect to illustrate excellent hindquarters which show muscular thighs and well angulated stifles. Note the great development of second thigh.

Photo: Diane Pearce.

This photograph of Ch. Dialynne Blueboy shows the most beautiful neck and shoulders, the neck being clean, long and elegantly arched and the shoulders obviously well laid. I consider Blueboy to be one of best Dialynnes ever and have always aimed to line-breed to him.

Photo: Frank Garwood.

class. Having examined each dog individually in detail, you now have to evaluate his movement. You may decide to do otherwise, but I recommend that you first ask the exhibitor to move his dog once up and down. This should establish how true the action is front and back. Watching a Beagle go away from you, the dog should move freely, driving from short hocks which should be parallel at a steady trot. You will find that some dogs move very close behind; less frequently you will discover some who go unusually wide. Either action is indicative of a constructional failure and is less than ideal.

When the Beagle comes towards you, the dog should again move freely, with elbows neat against the chest and the forelegs almost parallel, but as speed increases the forefeet move slightly closer together. This is only very slight and an acute closeness is regarded as "pinning". Many Beagles have a major problem with unduly wide front action. Sometimes this involves unnecessary play at the elbow, which can be due to poor musculation or badly angulated shoulders and upper arms; often the elbows seem quite tight and yet there is still a perplexing "sloppiness" of the forelegs where the dog appears to be pushing his forefeet out in opposite directions, "flipping" his feet. This is poor and uneconomic movement. In the Beagle there must be a certain width in the front, and when you think that the breed was developed to move with its head following a scent on the ground, it is perhaps understandable that, traditionally, front action tends to be less "true" than in many other breeds. What can be confusing for judges is encountering a Beagle which is rather narrow all through, and has what is generally described as a "terrier front", where the front is gun-barrel straight and the forechest poorly developed. Such Beagles may come on dead true and

straight, but this narrowness is untypical for the breed. Given the choice between a slightly loose and wide front and a terrier front, I would have to opt for the former as this is more typical.

Few judges spend sufficient time evaluating profile gait in our breed, but it is vitally important in a hound which should be built for stamina. In profile the Beagle should display a degree of forward reach where the foreleg is stretched fully forward without undue lift. The dog should cover the ground effortlessly, and should be fully co-ordinated with a rear which is equally elastic, showing great flexion of the hindquarters and drive from the hocks. As with the front, there should be no unnecessary lift. I am often amused to hear some Beagle judges applaud the movement of hounds which have a rather exaggerated hind action, in that they flick their hocks upward and back. This albeit flashy kind of action is sometimes seen in more extreme examples of breeds like the American Cocker, where it is accepted and even encouraged. In a Beagle, however, it is quite inefficient and untypical. The Beagle's action should be strong, smooth and elastic, with great scope through minimum effort.

Another reason for paying more attention to side gait than to "up and down" movement is the fact that, when studying the profile, you see the whole dog. This gives you the overall picture again and you can see topline, length of back, tailset and length of neck when the dog is moving naturally. The tale which is then told may be quite different from the stacked outline which a clever handler may have thrown out to you. We can all lengthen necks, straighten toplines and increase angulation if we know what we are doing, but when the dog moves out it is impossible to disguise these faults from the discerning eye. So take time to analyse what the dog is doing with his limbs and his body – check the topline, which should be hard and serviceable, and you will be amazed how easy it is to see shoulder placement from the side when a dog is in action.

I have mentioned elsewhere in this book the natural head carriage of the Beagle and pointed out that what is traditionally perceived to be "show" deportment is not necessarily correct. "Show dogs" are believed to move with their heads held high and proud, yet when the Beagle gaits at average speed the head will be lowered somewhat. Beagles which trot with their heads and necks naturally held up, invariably have a short stride and mincing gait, caused by straight shoulders and short upper arms. This may look "smart" but it is not typical.

Having seen the dog move adequately, after he has completed a second circuit of the ring, I like to see him come back to me and just stand naturally for a few seconds. Not all dogs automatically put themselves into a show stance when they come to rest, and you should not expect them to, but taking a moment or two to see the dog standing on his four legs, without being poked and prodded into position, can be very revealing and remarkably constructive from a judge's point of view. Repeat this individual process with all the dogs in the class, trying not to vary your technique from dog to dog. Having seen them all, you may wish to send them around again together just to have a final look at the class in a relative sense.

MAKING YOUR CHOICES
In England, judges are generally expected to place five dogs. Check with your steward how many prize cards are available and try to end up with that number in your final line-up. Placing six dogs, to then discover

that you have only five places, looks messy, and makes the exhibitor standing sixth feel rather uncomfortable. If you have a particularly large class, you may wish to thin them out by producing a first "short list" before you actually arrive at your placegetters. If you wish to see individual dogs move again, you are free to do so. You want to be certain in your own mind that you make the right decision, and you could well have forgotten how a particular dog moved. There is nothing wrong with that – move him again and be sure. Better that than bluffing your way through and getting it wrong.

The whole judging process is entirely subjective, and that is what makes showing such an inexact form of competition with so many apparent anomalies. It is your opinion, how you interpret the Breed Standard, that the exhibitors are paying for, and you will have your own, totally personal, list of priorities. "One man's meat is another man's poison" is so very appropriate in the judging ring. You may have an aversion to flat feet but be tolerant of light eyes. Next week's judge may turn a blind eye to bad feet but refuse to consider yellow eyes. It is the difference in opinion which makes dog shows work. If there were not different opinions, we would only need to go to one show a year!

While there are certain fundamentals which should be constant and beyond dispute, a lot of decisions taken when judging boil down to personal preferences and taste. These preferences invariably become established through one's experience as a breeder. If you have had a particular problem with, say, straight shoulders, and found them extremely difficult to breed out, the chances are that when you come to judge you will be particularly severe on bad shoulders, whereas you may be quite lenient on a fault

which has never been a worry to you.
Come what may, you should never develop
fetishes. I have heard judges making stupid
remarks about faults they will not tolerate.
The most ridiculous involved a Boxer judge
who was heard boasting that she would
never place a dog with an unpigmented
third eye-lid! I watched the lady concerned
judge some weeks later, and she was true to
her word. There was not a pink haw in
sight, but there were bucket-heads, roach-
backs and straight stifles aplenty!

THE IMPORTANCE OF TEMPERAMENT

All faults should be seen in perspective, but
the one thing on which I will not
compromise is temperament. While I
would forgive a puppy for being a little
unsure of himself, I would not consider a
Beagle which was obviously nervous, and if
I found aggression in the ring I would
dismiss the offending dog. There is no
room in this breed for poor temperament.
The Beagle's naturally merry nature is one
of his greatest assets and must never be
sacrificed, regardless of how outstanding a
specimen's other virtues may be. This is the
one instance where I throw my "overall
picture" theory out of the window!

It staggers me to hear exhibitors making
excuses for dogs who will not show because
they have been frightened by the flapping
tent, an onlooker's umbrella, a waste bin,
an overhead aeroplane or whatever. A well-
adjusted Beagle should be bold and
fearless, happy and totally steady, without
any suggestion of aggression. I am horrified
when I walk past some benches at the
shows and see Beagles lunging out,
snapping at passing dogs. This breed is the
most benevolent-natured dog of all, and his
reputation for being so must be preserved
at all cost.

WRITING CRITIQUES

In judging your class you will have to
weigh up one dog against another and
make a decision. Uppermost in your mind
should be finding which dog has the most
virtues and then taking his faults into
consideration. Ask yourself what each dog
is likely to do for the breed. While decisions
should not be rushed, there is nothing
worse than watching a judge who is
embarrassingly undecided and who dithers
about, obviously unable to make up his
mind. Such judges quickly lose credibility
with the ringside. You have to make a
decision and place your dogs; so, after
careful consideration, place them positively
and decisively, lining them up in the centre
of the ring with the First Prize winner on
your left.

Mark up your judging book and, if a
critique is required (or as the custom of the
country dictates), jot down the notes that
will form the basis of your critique which
will be published in the dog press, as is
customary in Britain, whereas judges who
officiate in FCI countries may have to
dictate a detailed critique on every entered
dog on the spot. Different judges have
different ideas on writing critiques. Having
judged so often in Scandinavia, I find
myself writing – even when judging at
home in the UK – the type of critique they
encourage, i.e. pointing out the dog's
major virtues but also pointing out any
shortcomings which you feel could
improve. This is not damning a dog, it
merely illustrates that you considered the
dog to be a worthy winner by virtue of his
merit which overshadowed those failings.
Some British judges never mention faults,
feeling that is bad form, as other judges
may read the critique and it would then
affect their judging. If judges allow other
judges' critiques to influence their own
judging, they shouldn't be judging! Most

dogs elicit a fairly straightforward critique, and it also helps, I feel, if the critique explains why the First dog beat the Second. Sometimes I read critiques where the First has several faults, while the Second reads like the Breed Standard! That tempts you to draw all manner of unsavoury conclusions. Sometimes you are lucky enough to get a dog which really excites you. If that is the case your critique should reflect your enthusiasm.

In the course of researching for this book I have leafed through tons of old papers, and I happened to come across a copy of the critique I wrote following judging Beagles at Horley Open Show in July 1976. I had given Best of Breed to an unusually promising dog puppy. My critique read as follows: "From time to time when judging one comes across a puppy which stands out so much that it leaves a real impression. This 8 months tricolour dog did just that, and when he came into the ring I knew that he was going to give anything a run for its money for Best of Breed. Royally bred from two great Champions, this young man has all the style and self-possession in the world, his head is well balanced with ample foreface and a soft expression. His neck, shoulder, topline and quarters give him a perfectly balanced, flowing outline and he is well bodied and boned with good feet. I wouldn't want to change him anywhere, he satisfied me totally and I would dare to predict that he could well go down as a "great" in Beagle

history. One I would dearly love to own." Who was this puppy which excited me so? None other than Ch. Beacott Buckthorn, who for many years held the breed record as the winner of the most CCs ever. Bucky did indeed go down as a "great", and it was an honour for me when Ada took his record from him. He was a class act to follow.

Having written your notes and signed your judging book, you will then be ready for the rest of your classes until such time as you have completed the entry and now need to judge Best of Breed. Please remember that wording – "Best of Breed" – and try to judge accordingly. In closing this chapter, I will share with you a piece of advice given to me by one of my mentors when I was starting out as a judge. He said this: "When you judge, judge as if you will never judge again. Judge as if this is your last appointment and the appointment you wish to be remembered for." All too often judges find themselves in a situation where they are tempted to judge "politically". Sometimes they cannot resist the temptation, but they always convince themselves that when they next judge they will do it perfectly straight down the line. Of course they never do, because they have sampled the forbidden fruit of convenience judging.

Think about these words of wisdom and try to understand them. If you remember them when you step into the ring, you will not go far wrong.

9 WORKING BEAGLES TODAY

There are currently some seventy packs of Beagles in England and Wales. These range from the Royle Rock Beagles which were formed way back in 1845, to the West Welsh Foot Pack which was started as recently as 1993. Most of these packs are owned by the committee or trustees of the hunt. Eight packs are run by schools or colleges while seven packs are part of the Army Beagling Association. The majority of the packs are financed by the masters and subscribers, with varied additional funding. All packs are registered with the Masters of Harriers and Beagles Association which was formed in 1891, one year after the birth of the Beagle Club. The Association registers the boundaries of the districts served by the packs, and also maintains the registration of Beagles in its stud book. Much more detailed information on the sport of Beagling can be obtained by reading *Beagling* by J.C. Jeremy Hobson, published by David & Charles in 1987.

Few Beagle breeders and exhibitors in the UK actually hunt with their dogs today, but there is still widespread enthusiasm for keeping the breed's working ability alive, and to this end many enthusiasts attend drag meetings organised by the Beagle Club. The Beagle Club's objects remain unaltered from the original, first published in 1890, which state: "It keeps wide open its doors and welcomes alike to the fold the Master of Beagles who wishes to maintain or form his Pack on ancient lines; the shooting man who keeps a few couples for driving out the rabbits, or putting up the pheasant; the drag hunter who gets an afternoon's healthy exercise with the pleasure of seeing hounds work and hearing hound music; the exhibitor who finds pleasure in breeding for perfection, so far as looks go, and performs most useful work by making the beauty of the breed more generally known; the lady who finds the Beagle the most intelligent and interesting of pets; last, but certainly not the least, the old sportsman whose sporting days are over, but who has a keen remembrance of what has been and joins in, while his recollections and experiences are of inestimable value to a younger generation. All these are now united in the same effort."

DRAG MEETINGS

Much forethought and planning goes into the staging of a drag hunt, which is a favourite sport involving Beagles in several countries. The sponsoring club appoints an

87

The foxhunting Beagle: An unusual study of Am. Ch. Bayou Oaks Cappuccino, the winner of Best of Variety (15 inch) at the National Beagle Club of America Specialty show in 1993, and 17 times Best in Show all breeds. A son of Am. Ch. Barmere's Andretti and Am. Ch. Bayou Oaks Violetta, he is owned and bred by Alyce and Richard Gilmore.

Photo: Glazbrook.

officer to the position of Field Master and it is then his responsibility to appoint the following: Drag Hunt Secretary – who should take minutes of any meeting of drag hunt members, keep records of members attending drag hunts, record the names and ages of their hounds, note any awards made at field trials, confirm drag hunting dates with landowners and also notify members of dates and locations of meets. It is also his job to collect the "cap" (the cash levy made on members and visitors attending a drag hunt to finance drag hunting costs).

While these and any other relevant tasks can be performed by the Field Master himself, it is advisable to delegate at least some of the jobs so that he can devote himself to organising a successful meeting. Whippers-In, numbering three or four, will be required to help the Field Master control the field. They should be keen, regular attenders at drag hunts and be familiar with the local terrain, so that they can assist the Field Master in ensuring that the hounds do not riot. Line or Drag Men or Women fulfil a less glamorous but still

The Stowe Beagles, pictured at the Beagle Club's centenary Show. These hounds are considerably more rangy and lighter-framed than the modern show Beagle.

Photo: Basil Waterton.

Drag hunting is a favourite sport in many countries.

Photo couresy: The Beagle Club.

vital role in that, under the supervision of the Field Master, it is their duty to prepare and lay the line. Consequently they need to have a good eye for the country and appreciate what is a fair obstacle for a drag hunting Beagle, also what is a fair check in the line of scent. A number of volunteers are required to perform this task.

For a drag hunt to take place, a suitable piece of land must be found and the landowner's permission obtained. Ideally a drag hunt requires approximately 125 hectares so that during a morning or afternoon a number of drag lines can be laid within this area, each line being about two or three kilometres (1 1/4 -2 miles) in length. The land should ideally be undulating, with streams and hedges so that the hounds can either be followed on foot or easily seen following the drag line. Co-operation with farmers and landowners is important, and usually personal visits by the Field Master will explain the nature of dragging and undertake to provide compensation for, or make good, any damage to fences etc. The Beaglers'

Perrystar Vivid, owned by Jerry Meek, on her way to winning one of an incredible ten Working Certificates. Jerry Meek is one of the long-standing breeder/exhibitors who has always maintained her interest in the working side.

Photo: Harry Nicholson.

gratitude to the landowner can be shown in several ways, but in Britain the use of land can often be obtained in return for a good bottle of whisky!

It is advisable to have access to a number of different areas of 125 hectares in different regional locations, firstly so that the hounds can enjoy the variety of differing landscapes, and secondly to enable as many members and hounds as possible to participate. The number of locations sought will of course depend on the number of drag hunts to be held during the season, which tends to run in Britain from late September to early April. As far as the hounds are concerned, it is desirable to ensure that hounds are as uniform in size as possible, as it is then more likely that they will run at the same pace. Between ten and twenty-two hounds is a good number to hunt any drag line at any one time, and all involved hounds should be at least twelve months old.

There will usually be between four and eight separate drags of two to three kilometres which have been laid under the direction of the Field Master. He will obviously choose a location which is fairly isolated, and a good distance from any main roads so that interference with traffic

is avoided, and danger to hounds minimised. Laying the actual drag involves pulling a long rope, on the end of which is a length of towel or absorbent cloth, across the ground. This will have been dampened and then soaked in the mixture which will provide the scent.

Any scent used should:
a) Be pleasing enough to the hounds for them to want to follow.
b) Be strong enough so that they are able to do so.
c) Lie on the ground and not rise, ideally, any higher than the hound's elbow so that they can hunt at a steady pace.
d) Last and not evaporate before the hounds have been set on to it.
e) Encourage the hounds to "speak" and not, under any circumstances, to run mute.

There are several favoured recipes for drag scents, notably:
1) Animal excreta (such as hare) to which should be added pure aniseed oil and paraffin. The paraffin acts as a fixative and prevents both evaporation and the scent from rising.
2) Chemical solutions specifically devised by drag hunting packs.
3) Pure vegetable oil mixed with a very small amount of aniseed oil, with a little

paraffin added again to prevent the scent from rising.

However, the first is rather foul-smelling to transport, and the second quite difficult to obtain. A drag scent consisting of 60 per cent pure vegetable oil, 30 per cent pure aniseed oil and 10 per cent paraffin will provide an excellent scent, can be mixed in any quantity required and is easily transported. The mixture should always be well shaken and then sufficient poured on to the damp towel to ensure the drag is impregnated. It is always better to use too much rather than too little, and weather and land condition will also influence the amount needed. This kind of scent will probably be strong enough to hold for about 45 minutes, therefore the drag layers need to cover a considerable distance quite quickly. This can be made easier by dividing the length of the drag into, for example, three sections, with a different person laying each section. Such drag layers can then act as whippers-in from their vantage points to prevent the hounds from rioting.

It is always best to commence laying the drag line out of sight of the hounds so that they do not get too excited, and then to plan the course of the drag line so that it finishes about 30 metres away from the starting point. In this way, owners of hounds who may not wish to follow the entire drag can remain near the starting point, knowing that their hounds will return to them (hopefully!). It is important to use natural obstacles such as hedgerows, streams and "checks" (lifting the drag scent line off the ground for a very short distance) so that the hounds are made to work and speak. In this way the drag line of scent makes for a more natural hunt and is also more interesting for the "field" who can watch the hounds working and casting around for the scent, rather than merely screaming along in a straight line.

The fun for the hounds and the field depends to a large extent on the Field Master and the drag layers. A skilled drag layer must be aware of factors affecting scenting conditions so that he can make allowances for them. For example, adding more fixative (paraffin) to the drag would be advisable in windy conditions. A heavy shower of rain can sometimes obliterate a scent; high wind can cause rapid evaporation, as can a sudden rise in temperature; a frost can check the scent; strong sunlight can deodorise it. Favourable scenting conditions are considered to be when the earth is moist and warmer than the air, and when there is a sudden fall in the air temperature. The best scenting surfaces are grass, sand and earth, and not hard roads, pebbles or stones.

In Britain, at the end of the drag hunting season, Field Trials are held in order that Working Certificates may be awarded to selected hounds, and in order that a Best Working Dog Hound, a Best Working Bitch Hound and a Best Working Hound may be selected. In Britain, these Working Certificates are approved of by, and awarded under the authority of, the Kennel Club.

The Field Trials take into account the following:

a) The Field Master invites two judges with scent hunting or drag hunting knowledge and experience to judge the Field Trials.

b) Acceptance of hounds for the Field Trials is at the discretion of the Field Master.

c) The Field Master divides the entered hounds into groups of five or six, and each group is notated A, B, C, D etc. Each hound in a group is given a light-weight coloured coat – red, black, white, yellow etc. – on which appears a number. This enables the judges to easily identify hounds

Hounds in full cry at a meet of the Beagle Club, held in Leicestershire. Photo courtesy: The Beagle Club.

on the drag line in each group.

d) Five to seven specially prepared and separate drag lines of standard length should be laid. The drag line is marked by flag poles so that judges can determine whether the hounds are following and working the line.

e) On the first drag, each group is run in order over the first drag line, namely A, B, C, D etc. On the second drag line, they run B, C, D, A and so on.

f) Each hound in each group, A, B, C, D etc. is allocated a numbered coloured coat. This colour and number is retained by the hound throughout the Trials, so that Group A consists of five or six hounds each with a colour and number, as do the other Groups; hounds will be identified by the judges as "Group A, Red Coat, Number One" etc.

g) The judges, in this way, do not know the identity of the hounds or their owners. The Field Master gives each judge a list of the groups with five or six colours and numbers for each drag. The judge will then award marks out of ten to each colour and number in each group.

h) The judges will position themselves in the best vantage point – they should carry binoculars to enable them to follow the hounds round the drag line, and so make their judgement on each hound's working ability.

i) At the end of the Field Trials, the judges will decide, with the help of the Field Master or Hunt Secretary, who will hold the Master Record with all details on the hounds in each group, and which hounds – in their opinion – worked well enough to be awarded a Working Certificate. Each Working Certificate must state the name of the hound, the name of the owner, the date and venue of the Trial, and be signed by the judge.

j) From the hounds awarded a Working Certificate, the judges must then select Best Working Bitch, Best Working Dog and Best Working Hound. If necessary, a final drag line may be laid to enable the judges to make their final decision. The only persons who hold the records to enable each hound to be identified in each group are the Field Master and Hunt Secretary.

Drag hunting gives Beagles and their owners a grand opportunity to enjoy the breed's heritage, and owners who may wish to pursue this aspect of Beagle ownership can begin training at home, using a typical scent as detailed above. It has to be said, however, that not all owners will wish their Beagle to "give tongue" at the first suggestion of an exciting scent, and if you happen to live in a built-up area, perhaps drag hunting is not such a good idea.

It is popularly believed that the American situation where the breed is judged as two separate varieties, determined by size, is the result of the show fancy's wishes, but nothing could be further from the truth. In reality, it is the field lobby which virtually runs the Beagle breed in the United States, and the control of the National Beagle Club of America – and thus the Breed Standard – lies firmly in the hands of working enthusiasts, rather than those whose main interest lies in the area of conformation judging. It is the working fancy which first developed the idea of two sizes in Beagles.

Hunting remains extremely popular in the United States and most of the regional Beagle clubs have active working sections which regularly organise field trials. Conformation Specialty shows can only be arranged with their blessing, and invariably are run by a specially set up show committee which may have no major involvement with the club under whose banner a breed Specialty show will be held.

There are four different types of Field Trials held under American Kennel Club Rules: Brace (on Rabbit or Hare); Small Pack (on Rabbit or Hare); Small Pack Option (on Rabbit or Hare); and Large Pack (on Hare). An explanatory leaflet on rules and procedures is published by the American Kennel Club. There are usually in excess of four hundred AKC licensed Beagle field trials held each year, and the majority will be Large Pack on Hare.

The disparity between the American field and show Beagles is even more acute than that seen in Britain, and consequently there is little interbreeding undertaken on either side, each presumably believing that their interpretation of the breed is correct.

WORKING DOGS IN SCANDINAVIA
To become a Swedish Show Champion, a Beagle has to win 3 CCs at shows, but this is not all; the dog has to become a Field Trial Champion first! In Finland the field trial requirement for a Beagle to become a Show Champion is a First prize on hare, and, in Norway also, a First prize on hare or a First prize on roe-deer or fox, plus a Second prize on hare. To become a Field Trial Champion, on the other hand, the Beagle has to have at least a Second prize grading at a "beauty" show, and in addition to have won three First prizes in open classes at field trials, at least one (Norway), two (Sweden) or three (Finland) of which are on hare, which is considered the most difficult game to hunt. These regulations have led to a situation where many of the show Beagles have proved that they are capable of hunting, while most of the field Beagles are, at least, of an average conformation. As not all Beagle owners are hunters, or have access to hunting grounds, you can find many good-looking, untitled Beagles in Scandinavia.

I have to say, in my experience, judging

Beagles at shows in these countries can sometimes be very frustrating, particularly when you are confronted with dogs which are allegedly wonderful in the field, and which are only at the show to gain the minimum quality grading so that they can be bred from. Some of these dogs can be exceedingly ugly and make little concession to the Breed Standard. Also, the movement is often well below the standard we would expect in a merely average show dog. And yet it is claimed they function well in the forests – it makes you wonder!

SCANDINAVIAN FIELD TRIALS

At the field trial the Beagle is hunted for one day in the Open class, or two days in the Elite class. One day means that the dog must be off the leash for a minimum of five hours. At dawn the Beagle and its owner, accompanied by the judge, go to the allotted hunting ground, which should be at least some 600-800 acres, and the dog is let loose. As Beagles in Scandinavia are hunted singly, and not in packs, they should search out well, casting some 200-500 metres, in search of the hare, roe-deer or fox. This behaviour is especially important when hunting the roe-deer, as should the roe-deer become aware of the hunting team, this may cause it to leave the area. If the dog is then persistent, it may be gone for the rest of the day. A good roe-deer Beagle will manage to get the hunted animal to move around in circles, thereby giving the hunters ample opportunity to shoot their quarry. To achieve this, the Beagle has to work the line well, not making short cuts which would make him too fast, and has to give tongue well, so that the roe-deer knows exactly where the dog is. Ideally, the roe-deer will stop and wait for the dog, then make a short rush, and stop again to listen for the dog. When chasing a hare, on the other hand, if the

dog is too slow, this will give the hare time to do more tricks, like doubling back on its own line, or jumping to the side. Then again, to be good at fox-hunting, the Beagle must be willing to take on a cold line, i.e. the night trail of the fox which, in the morning, has usually found itself a resting place in a burrow or maybe on the top of some big rock. Should the fox be aware of the hunter, it will run straight to the next county, and the hunt will be lost for the day! The unaware fox, however, can run in smaller circles, often more curious than scared of the dog. So, every Beagle may not be suited for every game, and also they often develop their own preferences. The majority of Beagles that enter field trials in Sweden will get a prize on hare (70-85 per cent). As a breed they seem to prefer to hunt the hare; indeed in Finland this is the only game they are allowed to hunt.

To get a First prize at a field trial, the Beagle has to chase the quarry effectively for at least 90 minutes, within hearing distance. This often means that they have to hunt for twice that time, as any check that is more than five minutes long will be subtracted from the final time. This also goes for the part of the chase that is too far away for the judging team to hear it. For a Second prize, the dog must hunt for at least 60 minutes, and for a Third prize at least 45 minutes. When it comes to roe-deer hunting, two Second prizes (i.e. 2 x 60 minutes) the same day adds up to a First prize, because it is considered better not to chase the same roe-deer for too long. Two shorter hunts, during a real hunt, also may give the owner a better chance to shoot the roe-deer. During the field trial, however, guns are usually not used. To be awarded a prize, the Swedish rules also stipulate that the dog has to be back not later than three hours after the trial is ended (usually at 3

94

p.m.). Any dog that will not let go of the chase, particularly when roe-deer hunting, will be disqualified. During the trial, the dogs are also graded for the way they search out, the way they give tongue, manage the checks, how obedient they are, etc. Very high points are given to the dog that can be called off at full cry. Needless to say, not every Beagle will be that well trained! Thus, in addition to the time requirements for each prize, a certain number of points also have to be obtained.

QUARANTINE DETECTOR DOGS

While the Beagle's scenting prowess was originally developed as an aid to the huntsman, times have changed and the breed has recently found a new niche where it can help humans – working as Quarantine Detector Dogs. Programmes which employed Beagles at airports were originally developed in the United States and Canada, and, more recently, Australia has set up its "Quarantine Beagle Brigade". Beagles have a remarkable sense of smell, even by canine standards. Their olfactory senses are said to be at least 100 times greater than those of humans. Since they have such steady temperament, they remain calm, even when surrounded by the commotion of baggage inspection areas, and it is these factors which make the Beagle ideally suited to working amongst passengers at international airports.

The Australian Quarantine and Inspection Service (AQIS) monitored the Beagle programmes in the USA and Canada for several years and later contracted a trainer from the US Department of Agriculture to help develop a pilot programme in Australia in 1991. Twenty-eight dogs were initially evaluated in the first recruitment drive and, after careful selection for temperament and veterinary clearance, five dogs began scent recognition training in Brisbane in November 1991. They were trained for various scents including meats (both raw and processed), fresh fruits and vegetables, foliage and eggs. Other scents were added later, including reptiles, bees and – in what is believed to be a world first for a detector

A new role for the 'working' Beagle – Melody and Winston, two valued members of the highly successful Quarantine Beagle Brigade in Australia.

Photo courtesy: Sylvia Tutchener.

dog programme – they were also trained to detect live birds. The Beagles' method of operation is that when they detect a target odour, they simply sit next to the source and await their reward (food) from the handler. This is known as a "passive" response and is the only method acceptable around passengers.

Canine handlers Rachel Holdforth and Harold Smithard were selected from Quarantine Officers in Sydney and Brisbane to undergo training in 1992 and were trained in a pilot programme for five months, being deemed successful after evaluation. They now work full-time with their Beagles in the Sydney and Brisbane International Terminals. The programme has expanded steadily since that time, with four teams now covering Sydney and one each in Melbourne, Adelaide and Perth. A team for Cairns and two teams for State Quarantine work in Western Australia and Tasmania have also been trained, and now Detector Dog teams are working in all International Airports throughout Australia.

The current seizure rates are between ten and twenty per team per day, with approximately four hours actual work time, allowing for breaks between targeted flights. Seizures per 1,000 passengers is averaging around 10.5, with in excess of 80 per cent of seizures being undeclared. The majority of seizures have been of fruit (around 60 per cent) with meat and meat products comprising around 18 per cent. Other seizures include eggs, honey (when combined with target odours), live plants and plant cuttings. AQIS has recently expanded its Detector Dog Programme by introducing "active" response dogs into two international mail centres. The active response involves the Beagle pawing or nuzzling the item producing the target odour, and its reward is the ensuing "tug of war" game. This type of response is ideal in the mail exchange environment, but would not be acceptable around the travelling public.

The success of the Beagle in this sphere of work has brought the breed very much to the attention of the public, and has won him many new admirers. This is a further example of the versatility of this ancient little hound, who will always be guaranteed a place at the side of his human master, whether working, playing or doing what he does like no other – giving endless loyalty and affection.

10 THE GAMBLE INFLUENCE

THE ULTIMATE COMBINATION OF AMERICAN AND BRITISH BLOODLINES

In contemporary British Beagle history, the appearance of one hound can be considered something of a turning point, not simply because he was physically an exceptional dog who heralded the "modern" look, but more importantly because his ability to produce excellence remains unrivalled. This dog was, of course, Ch. Dialynne Gamble. The story of Gamble's ancestry is detailed in the profile of the Dialynne kennel, but it would perhaps be pertinent to speculate as to why this extraordinary dog contributed so much to the breed, not just as a sire of

Champions, but as a sire of dogs and bitches who themselves produced, and a dog who could be intensely line-bred to with great results.

Essentially Gamble was from an outcross breeding between an American imported male and an English bitch. However, both his parents were themselves line-bred to a degree, his dam coming from a half-brother to half-sister mating. His sire, Appeline Validay Happy Feller, was an American import of ideal size and intense quality. Importantly, all his immediate ancestors were high-quality animals, each with something positive to contribute, and his sire, Am. Ch. Herold's Prince Charles had a definite smartness about him with ultra-

The legendary Ch. Dialynne Gamble who revolutionised the breed, siring 26 British Champions. Photo: Diane Pearce.

clean lines. While Gamble's dam is often regarded as being totally British, it should not be forgotten that Ch. Dialynne Nettle was a double grand-daughter of Ch. Dialynne Huntsman. Huntsman was sired by the North American import, Barvae Benroe Wrinkles, a son of Am. Ch. Thornridge Wrinkles out of a bitch who, herself, carried two lines back to Wrinkles. So, in Gamble we virtually had a predominantly American-bred dog with some pretty intense line-breeding behind him. It is interesting to hear, to this day, some American breeders acclaiming Thornridge Wrinkles as "the greatest ever".

I have discussed various "magical formulas" with a variety of breeders in different breeds, and invariably I hear that an outcross breeding from two independently line-bred parents will usually produce excellent breeding stock which breed on consistently.

In this chapter I have included the British kennels who owe the major part of their success to using Gamble stock in their formative years. To this day many breeders aim to line-breed back to Gamble, and it is few successful kennels which carry no Gamble blood at all.

BARRVALE
Peter and Val Davies' small kennel is one of several founded on primarily Dufosee lines. Having shown their first Beagle, bought as a pet, they decided to look for a bitch of show quality and acquired Dufosee Gingham of Barrvale, a daughter of Ch. Dufosee Radleigh of Tragband and Ch. Rossut Fantom. She came from one of the most significant litters ever bred, from a producing point of view. Gingham was mated to Ch. Dufosee Zenith (a full brother to her paternal grandsire, Harris Tweed), and this gave the Davies their first Champion, Ch. Barrvale Opera, a

Peter and Val Davies' first Champion, Barrvale Opera, a daughter of Ch. Dufosee Zenith and Dufosee Gingham of Barrvale. I remember awarding this lovely bitch her first CC at Bournemouth in 1984.
Photo courtesy: Peter and Val Davies.

beautifully made open-marked bitch to whom I recall awarding a first CC at Bournemouth in 1984. Having won her title, Opera took the CC and Reserve Best in Show at the Beagle Association's 25th Anniversary show in an entry of 203.

Gingham was later mated to Ch. Dufosee Mystro of Morsefield – interestingly bred in that he was by Ch. Dialynne Gamble out of Gamble's own great grand-daughter, Ch. Dufosee Quaker Girl of Tragband. This produced Ch. Barrvale Rambler at Morsefield who was campaigned to his title by Mike and Helen Caple. The Davies aim to breed quite closely, just bringing in the occasional outcross when needed. They recently acquired Nivek Madelaine of Barrvale who boasts several lines back to Dufosee Geisha, Gingham's litter sister, while also carrying a line to Ch. Soloman of Dialynne. She became a Champion in 1996.

BAYARD
Jill Peak is well known in the breed for her

great handling skills and also her ability to breed a definite type of Beagle, having forcefully developed a Bayard "look" since the advent of Ch. Bayard Zachariah. One of Jill's earliest significant Champions was Ch. Bayard Olga, a strong and unusually sound bitch of excellent type. Her breeding was a cocktail of Dialynne, Gaytail, Barvae and Rossut, and she turned out to be a good producer. Mated to Ch. Dufosee Zenith she produced Ch. Bayard Zither and her sister, Zena, who was the dam of Ch. Bouldin Zoe of Dialynne. The mating was repeated to produce Bayard Jennifer who was then mated to her half-brother, Ch. Dufosee Influence, to produce Bayard Rachel, the dam of Ch. Bayard Rumba whose sire was Ch. Dialynne Gamble, Rachel's own great-grandsire. Jill also campaigned Ch. Dialynne Vendor of Jayanna and Ch. Dialynne Guardsman of Bayard to their titles. Vendor was used on Jennifer to produce Bayard Gemma, the dam of Ch. Bayard Adam.

The turning point for Bayard came when

Ch. Bayard Rustle is a fine example of the typical Bayard 'look'. Bred by Jill Peak, she was by Ch. Bayard Zachariah out of Bayard Rival, sister to Ch. Bayard Rumba. Having won her British title, Rustle joined Truda Mawby's Clarion kennel in Australia.

Ch. Bayard Zither was bred to Ch. Am. Ch. Pin Oaks Dynasty of Appeline, and this resulted in Ch. Bayard Zachariah. Despite having a First prize withheld from him as a puppy at a still talked-about Championship show, Zac won his title, has competed successfully in many Veteran Stakes like his sire before him, and gone on to be a remarkable and dominant stud dog. Zachariah heralded the modern Bayard look, without doubt. A sister to Rumba, Bayard Rival (from Rachel and her great-grandsire, Gamble), was one of Zac's successful brides, producing Ch. Bayard Rustle who later joined the Clarion kennel in Australia. Honor Eades used Zac on one of my favourite bitches, Ch. Jesson Thrifty, to breed several Champions, notably the multi-ticketed Ch. Jesson Quaintly. Ch. Bayard Adam was also by Zac, and a repeat mating produced Ch. Bayard Larry.

Consolidating her associations with Dufosee and Dialynne, Jill then bought from me Tragband Cat On a Hot Tin Roof at Bayard, a daughter of Ch. Dialynne

Colin Lomax pictured winning Best of Breed at Crufts with his Ch. Bayard Syndicat of Lowyck. 'Sindy' was one of many winners bred from Tragband Cat On a Hot Tin Roof at Bayard by Ch. Bayard Zachariah.

Nimrod of Ramlacim and Ch. Too Darn Hot for Tragband. She proved wildly successful as a producer when mated to Zac, giving rise to the generation of amusingly named 'Cats', the best known of which is the Crufts Group-winning Ch. Bayard Syndicat of Lowyck, winner of many CCs and also Best in Show at Windsor. Mating the CC winning Bayard Sophisticat at Webart to Ch. Bayard Larry, both by Zac, produced Ch. Bayard Harvest Moon. Meanwhile, jointly with Veronica Bradley, Jill had made up Ch. Dufosee Lovebird. Lovebird and Zac gave Jill her latest Champion, Perseverance of Bayard.

BUTTERMERE

Denise and Colin Ashmore's kennel's fortunes took an upward turn when they acquired Dialynne Fairytale of Buttermere, a daughter of Ch. Dialynne Pedlar (by Ch. Am. Ch. Graadtres Hot Pursuit of Rossut) out of Raimex Vita (a daughter of Ch. Barterhound Hammerlyn). Mated to Ch.

A daughter of Ch. Dialynne Pedlar mated to Ch. Soloman of Dialynne produced Denise and Colin Ashmore's first Champion, Buttermere Barleycorn. When mated to her half-brother, she bred the successful sire, Ch. Buttermere Clansman of Dialynne.
Photo: John Hartley.

Soloman of Dialynne, Fairytale produced the Ashmores' first Champion, Buttermere Barleycorn, and her sister Bracelet, who did very well in Australia. Barleycorn was then mated to her half-brother, Ch. Sentinel of Dialynne, the result being Ch. Buttermere Clansman of Dialynne who proved to be an excellent sire before he left for Europe. Dialynne Charity of Buttermere was by Ch. Bayard Adam out of a daughter of Ch. Dialynne Solison. She was put back to her great grandsire, Ch. Soloman of Dialynne to give the Ashmores their latest star, Ch. Buttermere Treasure.

DEANERY

When she was Jean Parker, the owner of the Deanery affix really wanted a Foxhound, but she was advised that Foxhounds do not make good pets, so she settled for a Beagle. From a kennel which kept several breeds, Jean bought a lemon and white bitch who she registered as Newton Everest. The bitch turned out to have some good breeding behind her as she was by Pinewood Custard (Ch. Rossut Triumphant ex Ch. Pinewood Wyrebrig Crocus) out of Danvis (an affix associated primarily with the superb Rough Collies of Tom Purvis) Brocade (by a Rozavel Zloty son out of a Zloty grand-daughter).

When it came to breeding from Everest, Jean had been highly impressed with a dog puppy called Dialynne Gamble. She used the young Gamble and produced her – and Gamble's – first Champion, Ch. Deanery Dream Girl. Her litter sister was subsequently sent to New Zealand in whelp to Ch. Southcourt Wembury Merryboy and the resulting litter helped the breed there no end. Dream Girl was a beautiful quality bitch and her wins included a Reserve Group win and also Best of Breed at Crufts. Mated to Ch. Korwin Monitor, Ch. Deanery Dream Girl produced Ch.

The first Champion for the Deanery kennel, and the first Champion sired by Ch. Dialynne Gamble, was Ch. Deanery Dream Girl.
Photo courtesy: Jean and Wal Westren.

As she had been so successful with the foundation dogs from the Norcis kennel, Jean Westren brought in Norcis The Hooker at Deanery. She was mated to Deanery Draper, a son of Ch. Dufosee Influence and Deanery Destiny (Norcis Uri ex Ch. Deanery Dandylion). A bitch, Deanery Beaulah, was kept from that litter and mated to Ch. Bayard Zachariah. From this came Ch. Deanery Bellboy, a Crufts CC winner and the kennel's first tricolour male Champion. The latest Deanery Champion is also a tricolour male, Ch. Deanery Donald, again by a Norcis stud, Murphy's Law, out of Ch. Deanery Dallas.

Deanery Dandylion, another lemon bitch. Dream Girl also had a litter to Ch. Dufosee Clyde in which was Deanery Day Dream, the dam of Ch. Deanery The Dickler when mated to Ch. Korwin Monitor again. Dickler was tragically killed at a very young age.

In 1979 Jean Parker married Wal Westren, who had bred and shown Beagles and both varieties of Welsh Corgi in his native Australia. Wal duly became a partner in the Deanery affix. Ch. Dandylion had a litter to Norcis Uri, a son of Ch. Korwin Monitor. From this came the Reserve CC winning Deanery Dulcimer. She was in turn mated to Norcis Lars, an interestingly bred dog in that his great grandsires were the excellent producers, Ch. Dufosee Harris Tweed, Ch. Korwin Monitor, Ch. Dialynne Gamble and Ch. Saravere Hardy of Dialynne. This represented a high concentration of Gamble blood. From that mating came Deanery Dulcet. Rossgay Remedy was the chosen stud dog for Dulcet, presumably as he was intensely line-bred to Monitor. That produced Ch. Deanery Dallas, yet another lemon and white bitch Champion for the kennel.

DIALYNNE

To list the show ring successes of the Dialynne kennel, and the influence its dogs have had on other breeders, would take a book in itself. The affix, originally registered by Marion Spavin, later owned jointly with the late Bryan Moorhouse, and now shared with Stuart Milner and Marion's daughter and grand-daughter, Dianna and Melanie, is associated with top-quality Beagles and countless Champions. To date there have been some sixty British Champions carrying the Dialynne name, and the vast majority of these can be traced back in direct line to Marion's original bitch, Derawuda Vanity. Back in the 1950s Marion was breeding Shetland Sheepdogs but she found they were not good doers, having poor appetites. Someone told her that Beagles were natural gluttons, so Marion bought a Beagle to encourage the Shelties to eat!

Vanity, although looking little like the Dialynnes of today, won a Best Puppy award at her first show, and the rest, as they say, is history. Mated to the Canadian import, Barvae Benroe Wrinkles, she produced Ch. Dialynne Huntsman who

Ch. Dialynne Ponder, a dog whose qualities suggest he was ahead of his time. Used on his half-sister, Ch. Dialynne Shadow, he produced Ch. Dialynne Nettle, dam of the immortal Ch. Dialynne Gamble. Ponder's younger brother, Southcourt Tarquin, went on to be an equally important stud dog.

Photo: C.M. Cooke.

was to be the first in a line of exceptionally prolific stud dogs for the kennel. For the Dialynnes Huntsman sired Ch. Dialynne Ponder, his sister, the Harrons' Ch. Dialynne Posy, Ch. Dialynne Opal and Ch. Dialynne Shadow and he was also the sire of Ch. Deaconfield Renown. In those days breeders used to co-operate with each other considerably more than they perhaps do today, and when Marion Spavin and Glenda Young had litters at the same time, they agreed to exchange a puppy to enable each of them to bring in new blood. Glenda's puppy was Ch. Dialynne Ponder's younger brother who, as Southcourt Tarquin, became a very significant sire. Marion's Southcourt-bred puppy became the foundation of the Maldorlynn kennel of the Scratcherd family. Ponder, Posy and Tarquin were out of a daughter of Barvae Benroe Wrinkles, so they came from a half-brother to half-sister mating. Ponder was, in my opinion, a dog born way ahead of his time and I firmly believe that he could win

top honours in the show ring today.

In the meantime Marion had bought Barvae Tamar from the Claytons and she had become Marion's first Champion. By Ch. Barvae Paigan, she was out of a daughter of Radley Triumph of Appeline, and was the dam of Ch. Dialynne Opal. Ponder was used on his half-sister Shadow, and that produced the exquisite Ch. Dialynne Nettle, a superb quality lemon and white bitch. Being closely-bred she was outcrossed to the Appletons' new American import, Appeline Validay Happy Feller. Marion felt that the mating might be something of a gamble, and thus christened a dog puppy in the litter Dialynne Gamble.

It was, as history relates, a Gamble which paid off. Not only was Gamble a magnificent show dog, with style, compactness and substance in a small frame, he proved to be the most remarkable sire. In all he sired 26 British Champions and no matter how a bitch was bred, Gamble would deliver the goods. You could mate him to a cow and produce a Champion Beagle! He is, without question, the dog who changed the breed (very much for the better) in Britain. Many breeders owe their success to using Gamble in their early days, and subsequently line-breeding back to him. The following kennels bred Champions by him: Bayard, Chalmain, Copewell, Deanery, Dufosee, Forrardon, Harque, Kittoch, Mardabevian, Oudenarde, Pinewood, Raimex, and of course Dialynne itself.

In the late sixties, Dialynne Promise, Ch. Opal's son by Tavernmews Rossut Ranter, was mated to Ponder to produce Ch. Dialynne Storm, a handsome masculine dog who won well. Ponder was proving an excellent sire. He was used on Ch. Strathdene Faithful and Dialynne took back a dog puppy who became Ch. Dialynne Strathdene Fettle, later owned by Jack

Peden. Fettle himself sired some interesting stock, including Ch. Dialynne Mystic (out of his half-sister, a Ponder daughter) who was made up by Margaret Foster, wife of the well known all-rounder judge, W. E. Foster.

Gamble Champions came thick and fast, not only for other breeders but for the home kennel too. Among the first was Ch. Dialynne Eldon who went to live with the Ystrad Davies in Wales, and Ch. Dialynne Astra. As is often the case with a kennel which keeps a strong stud team, there were frequent opportunities to buy in puppies by the Dialynne dogs. Sometimes these were from bitches sired by earlier Dialynne studs, but occasionally they were from complete outcrosses. This strengthened the Dialynne kennel's position in the breed enormously, as it presented the opportunity to both line-breed and bring in new blood without actually breeding vast numbers of litters on its own. With her natural eye for picking a promising puppy, many Champions were spotted in the nest by Marion Spavin and brought home to Dialynne. Ch. Solomist of Dialynne was such a puppy, again by Gamble and out of a Fettle daughter. He won well, was used successfully at stud, and then went on to New Zealand where he is found behind many of their top dogs, surprisingly close up in the present-day pedigrees. A Gamble daughter, Ch. Dialynne Tamar of Charterwood, was Jill Philpott's first Champion, while Ch. Saravere Hardy of Dialynne was campaigned by the Dialynnes' most successful protégé, John Emerson. Hardy was by Eldon.

Although she had no immediate Dialynne ancestry, a puppy born in 1975 had been bought in, called Honey of Dialynne. She was the first Stud Book Number winner for a young enthusiast called Stuart Milner. Little did Stuart realise at the time how his family's life would become entwined with that of the Dialynne operation. Using the Copewell affix, Stuart bred from Honey, by Gamble, his first Champion, in Copewell Charity. John Emerson made up another Gamble daughter, in Ch. Symbol of Dialynne, while Bill Hayes began to win well with Dialynne Kelly of Cranwood, the result of mating Gamble back to his grand-dam, Shadow. Kelly later returned to Dialynne where she proved a great producer, as did her brother, Dialynne Kennedy, who sired the Champion sisters, Stuart Milner's Ch. Sonya of Dialynne and Honor Eades' Ch. Sonnet of Dialynne, when used on a Gamble daughter.

Ch. Trewint Speculation of Dialynne was a beautiful bitch for whom I had a very soft spot. Bred by "Stevie" Stevenson in the far southwest, she was by Gamble out of a daughter of the American import, Annasline Page Mill Playboy. She later became a Champion in South America.

Ch. Senator of Dialynne was campaigned by Bill McInnes and Noel Jobson, a son of Hardy out of a bitch who traced back to Elmhurst and Towpath lines. He in turn sired the Jobsons' Ch. Glenivy Intrepid out of Crestamere Trinket of Rossut. Ch. Dialynne Essence was a smart dog who sired well – no surprise as he was by Gamble out of a Gamble grand-daughter, his dam being a daughter of Champions Fettle and Harque to Bella.

One of my favourite Dialynnes of all time was Ch. Dialynne Blueboy, and it is my contention that had Blueboy stayed in Britain he would have had an even more profound influence on the breed. As it was, he contributed greatly to the quality of Beagles in New Zealand. Ultra-smart, with the most lovely neck and shoulder, Blueboy was by the Gamble son, Ch. Oudenarde Gaffer of Rossut, out of Dialynne Bluebell, a Gamble grand-daughter. The few litters

Blueboy did sire before he left the country all contained great producers. That was his strength, the ability to produce dogs which bred on. Despite being up against the mighty winning Ch. Jondor Crocus, Bill and Molly McInnes' Ch. Dialynne Music made her title with some to spare. She was out of Dialynne Kelly of Cranwood and by the interestingly-bred Cranwood Statesman, a son of Ch. Dufosee Harris Tweed (by Gamble) out of Ch. Beston Harmony, a daughter of Southcourt Hatchet, a double grandson of Southcourt Tarquin, Ponder's younger brother. Mating Kelly to Ch. Dialynne Blueboy provided Margaret and Alec Watson with their first Champion, Dialynne Nimrod of Ramlacim, who was a Group winner and a successful sire. Indeed he was the sire selected for Ch. Too Darn Hot for Tragband's second litter, of which more will be found elsewhere. Essence used on the Gamble grand-daughter, Bayard Zena, produced Ch. Bouldin Zoe of Dialynne, while to the excellent brood, Dialynne Lemonade (a daughter of Champions Astra and Hardy), he sired Ch. Dialynne Alice who later did the breed a lot of good in Denmark.

In 1983 the friendship between the Spavin and Milner families had intensified and it was agreed that they should join forces, pool resources and Stuart Milner would become a partner in the Dialynne kennel. They moved to a large property in Lincolnshire and then in 1990 invested in a large boarding kennel and cattery in the Midlands. Today Dialynne is a vast operation where a large Beagle kennel runs in tandem alongside a thriving business. It is very much a family affair with Marion consulting with Stuart, Dianna and Melanie on the breeding programme, Stuart's father George playing a vital part in the Beagles' husbandry, while Stuart's mother, Annice,

cooks – magnificently! – for the family and the endless stream of visitors who enjoy the famed Dialynne hospitality. It is a shame that George Milner has not been persuaded to judge Beagles, as he has an incredible eye for a puppy and never misses a good one.

Stuart had used Gamble on Honey of Dialynne to breed Copewell Candy. She was mated to the American import, Ch. Am. Ch. Graadtres Hot Pursuit of Rossut to produce Ch. Dialynne Pedlar who was my Best of Breed winner at Bournemouth in 1984, that being his second CC. Dialynne also used Hot Pursuit to breed another Champion male, Dialynne Vendor of Jayanna (out of Lemonade), who was campaigned by Jill Peak and then sold to Europe. Vendor's sister, Venetta, was mated to Nimrod to produce Ch. Dialynne Riot, a very smart bitch who was one of many Dialynnes to qualify for the prestigious Pup of the Year competition. As an outcross, the Norwegian bred Amaritas Bim Uno was imported from Denmark where he was a Champion. Used on Ch. Alice's sister, he sired Ch. Dialynne Quentin, the sire of Ch. Bennae Kilroy. Pedlar himself sired the goods. Mated to a bitch who traced back to Gamble several times, he produced Ch. Dialynne Spice of Crestamere, made up by Wyn Mahoney. A repeat mating produced Jill Peak's Ch. Dialynne Guardsman of Bayard, a very classy tri dog to whom I gave a first CC and BOB. and who later went to New Zealand. Pedlar, to a double Gamble grand-daughter, Dialynne Snowflake, produced Ch. Dialynne Beau.

In the early 1980s two arrivals at the Dialynne kennel were to have an enormous impact on the breed. Aileen Kirkland had used Gamble on Kittoch Garland, a daughter of Ch. Beacott Buckthorn out of a Gamble grand-daughter. He was registered as Soloman of Dialynne.

Meanwhile, Di and Carl Johnson, of Dicarl Great Dane fame, had bought Dufosee Geisha from Veronica Bradley, a Gamble great grand-daughter. They had mated her to Ch. Dialynne Blueboy, by a Gamble son out of a Gamble grand-daughter, and there were two very promising bitches in the litter. The Johnsons had kindly agreed to let me have my pick, and I took Dicarl Gay's The Word whom I gave to Ken Sinclair and Adrian Edwards on breeding terms, while the Johnsons kept Dicarl Get Going, later offering her to Marion Spavin as they had decided that they were not going to get that involved in Beagles. Gay's the Word acquired the Araki affix and became the dam of Ch. Too Darn Hot for Tragband, whereas Get Going had Dialynne added to her name and became a Champion. She had several litters to Ch. Soloman of Dialynne, by now a multi CC winning Champion, and produced five British Champions, which remains a record for any Beagle bitch. They were Ch. Dialynne Peppermint (who was made up and later sold to New Zealand), Ch. Dialynne Nymph of Riversong (made up by Basil Waterton), Ch. Dialynne Caesar, Ch. Dialynne Nester of Rosspark (made up by Jack Holland) and Ch. Dialynne Princess at Webline (made up by David Webster).

The Dialynnes acquired Deanery Darkness, bred by Jean Westren, the offspring of Champions Hardy and Dandylion. Soloman was used on her and sired Ch. Dialynne Solison who later went to Christine Lewis and was a key foundation dog for her Fallowfield kennel. A Darkness daughter by Pedlar, Dialynne Actress, was also mated to Soloman to produce Ch. Dialynne Passion. Another Deanery bitch, Dilly, produced Ch. Dialynne Satin to Soloman. When Satin was mated to Lyndex Tango of Dialynne, a Sentinel son out of the good bitch,

Ch. Dialynne Solison became a key stud dog for Christine Lewis' Fallowfield kennel.
Photo: Diane Pearce.

Dialynne Black Lace (by Ch. Dialynne Nimrod of Ramlacim out of Dialynne Actress), she produced Ch. Dialynne Valentine who started winning CCs as a puppy. Soloman, to a sister of Spice and Guardsman, produced Ch. Marcus of Dialynne, made up by Joan Buchan.

When Honor Eades used Soloman on her lovely Ch. Jesson Thrifty, she bred Ch. Jesson Mercy. Mercy was subsequently mated to the American import, Ch. Am. Ch. Pin Oaks Dynasty of Appeline, and a bitch from that litter became Ch. Jesson Chancy of Dialynne. When she was put back to Soloman, she produced Ch. Dialynne Chances Are, made up by Peter Newman and Barry Day. Peter and Barry had earlier made up Ch. Symphony of Dialynne, a lovely bitch bred by the Knights from Soloman and their Adendale Kenine Inca, a daughter of Ch. Dialynne Beau. The Dialynnes had previously made up Symphony's older brother, Ch. Sentinel of Dialynne, who won well in Europe. The Ashmores used Sentinel on their Ch. Buttermere Barleycorn, a Soloman son on a Soloman daughter, to breed Ch.

Buttermere Clansman of Dialynne. When he was mated to Ch. Symphony, the result was the kennel's latest Champion, Dialynne Augustus. Clansman also sired Ch. Dialynne Bryony at Kybo.

I had let my CC-winning Ada daughter, Tragband Sweet Bird of Youth, go to Dialynne on the understanding that I could have a bitch puppy back from her, a grand-daughter to keep Ada company at home. Birdie obliged by producing five males to Soloman! Insisting that I did not want a male, I went along to look at the puppies and some months later Dialynne Tolliver of Tragband took up residence! Before his second birthday he had won 9 CCs and four Hound Groups, and at the time of writing, I am currently enjoying campaigning this personality-plus showman. The postscript to this story is that when Birdie whelped her next litter for the Dialynnes, she produced eight bitches! On a global basis, wherever Beagles are talked, Dialynne and success are synonymous and there are very few prominent kennels which do not owe some kind of debt to Marion Spavin and her breeding.

DUFOSEE
Like so many successful breeders, Veronica Bradley's first Beagle was bought as a family pet. Soon Beagles became very much a family project, the enthusiasm for the breed being shared by Veronica's then husband David (later to become a partner in Liz Calikes' Newlin kennel), her older daughter Sue (with whom I showed several Champions under the Tragband affix) and her younger daughter Jane (who established her own Janfrey kennel having married Jeff May). The Dufosee Beagles are now jointly owned by Veronica and Ken Burgess, who was formerly an exceedingly successful exhibitor and breeder of Welsh

Springer Spaniels under the Plattburn affix.

The original bitch at Dufosee was Belinda of Gwanas, by a son of Ch. Barvae Pilot out of a daughter of the all-American bred Swansford Letton Yale. Belinda was mated to the nearby Ch. Baimor I'm A Rebel, by the American import, Am. Ch. Colegren's Little Rebel of Clovergates, out of a daughter of Ch. Barvae Pilot. In that first litter was Ch. Dufosee Bonnie Girl, the cornerstone of Dufosee and an exceptionally sound bitch whose free and driving movement is still talked about to this day. Bonnie may have been a touch strong for some who prefer a more feminine bitch, but her excellence as a matriarch was irrefutable. In the show ring she won a clutch of CCs and also a Hound Group. Bonnie was mated to Ch. Dialynne Gamble with enormous success. Several litters to him resulted in Ch. Dufosee Clyde, Ch. Dufosee Harris Tweed (whose litter brother, Dufosee Gatsby, was the first Beagle to carry the Tragband affix), and the siblings Ch. Dufosee Zenith and Ch. Dufosee Ziggy.

The kennel then acquired a lovely quality lemon bitch from the Suttons who became Ch. Rossut Fantom. In subsequent generations the combination of Fantom and Bonnie progeny proved highly successful. Indeed, apart from later acquiring a bitch by one of their own studs bred by me, Dufosee have not "bought in" since Fantom. Bonnie Girl's other "husband" was Ch. Wembury Archie, and they produced Danish Ch. Dufosee Kismet, Australian Ch. Dufosee Kinsman and Dufosee Katrina. Kinsman proved an important producer down under, while Kismet, prior to export, was mated to her half-brother, Ch. Dufosee Harris Tweed. That gave me my first Champion in Ch. Dufosee Radleigh of Tragband. Katrina, who stayed at Dufosee, was mated to her

An important family group showing the matriarch of the Dufosee kennel, Ch. Dufosee Bonnie Girl (top centre), and some of her offspring. Top left: Ch. Dufosee Harris Tweed, (a son by Gamble); Top right: Ch. Dufosee Clyde (a son by Gamble); Botttom Left: Ch. Dufosee Radleigh of Tragband (by her son Tweed out of her daughter Danish Ch. Dufosee Kismet); Bottom right: Ch. Dufosee Quaker Girl of Tragband (by Bonnie Girl's sire, Ch. Baimor I'm a Rebel, out of Dufosee Fandangles, who was by Clyde, a Bonnie son, out of Bonnie's dam).

Photo: Thomas Fall.

half-brother, Ch. Dufosee Zenith, resulting in Ch. Dufosee Influence, still one of the smartest-outlined Beagles I have ever seen, and a dog to whom I was happy to give his crowning CC.

A remarkable piece of line-breeding took place when Veronica mated Ch. Dufosee Clyde back to his grand-dam, Belinda, keeping a bitch called Dufosee Fandangles. She in turn was put back to her great grandsire, Rebel, and produced Ch. Dufosee Quaker Girl of Tragband, a bitch of exquisite type whose expression melted many hearts. Ch. Rossut Fantom was mated to Rossut Gaffer, then Ch. Dufosee Harris Tweed, but it was a litter to Ch. Dufosee Radleigh of Tragband that held her first Champion, Dufosee Aria of Tragband, and her litter sister Dufosee Almond of Ivelsyde who was Geoff Place's first big winner. A repeat of this litter, however, produced a litter which has to be

the most significant litter in modern Beagle history, from a producing point of view.

The male, Dufosee Going to Penavon, went to New Zealand where he helped the breed no end. A brother, Dufosee Galleon of Thorndon sired the first Champion for his owner Georgina Kemp, now of the Timamso affix. Three bitches produced remarkably – the home-based Ch. Dufosee Garbo, Dufosee Geisha (dam of Ch. Dicarl Get Going of Dialynne and Dicarl Gay's The Word of Araki – both record producers in their own right) and Dufosee Gingham of Barrvale (who virtually founded the Barrvale kennel). The already intensely in-bred Ch. Quaker Girl had been mated back to her great-grandsire, Ch. Dufosee Gamble to produce the Caples' Ch. Dufosee Mystro of Morsefield. Ch. Dufosee Kirsty was by Ch. Clyde out of Dufosee Topaz, a daughter of Clyde's younger brother, Ch. Harris Tweed, and

Ch. Rossut Fantom.

Meanwhile Ch. Garbo (ex Ch. Rossut Fantom) was first bred back into the Rossut line by using Ch. Rossut Peanut, who was a grandson of Ch. Fantom's brother, Foremost. This resulted in Ch. Dufosee Nobility, who was owned by Jane May, née Bradley. Jane also campaigned Ch. Dufosee Modesty and her dual CC winning sister Madonna. They were by Ch. Influence out of Topaz, a double Bonnie Girl grandson mated to a Bonnie Girl grand-daughter. Ch. Influence also mated a Tweed/Fantom daughter, Dufosee Encore of Tragband, to produce Ch. Dufosee Yen. Used on Encore's older sister, Topaz, he produced Ch. Dufosee Quaver. Influence was also the dog I chose to use on Ch. Too Darn Hot for Tragband for her first litter. From that came Ch. Tragband In Town Tonight at Newlin (campaigned by David Bradley and Liz Calikes), several overseas Champions, and a bitch, Tragband In Favour at Dufosee, who became a great producer for her sire's kennel. Mated to her grandsire, Ch. Zenith, she produced Ch. Dufosee Vindicator. Ch. Garbo had also been taken back to Rossut, but to be mated to their imported Ch. Am. Ch. Graadtres Hot Pursuit of Rossut. Their son, the CC-winning Dufosee Falcon, won a Hound Group before he was sold to Switzerland where he continued his winning career.

Eleanor Bothwell had used Ch. Harris Tweed on her big winning Ch. Norcis Hannah and got Norcis Taurus as a result. When Taurus was used on Ch. Garbo, Ch. Dufosee Wild Flower was produced. Champions Kirsty and Vindicator were mated together for Ch. Dufosee Lovebird and it was Vindicator who sired the latest Dufosee Champion, Capability, whose dam is Ch. Wild Flower. When the Appletons imported from the USA Ch. Pin Oaks Dynasty of Appeline, he was shown by Ken

Burgess from Dufosee to take his title. For Dynasty's first show, however, Douglas Appleton himself handled the dog about whom much had been heard on the Beagle grapevine. "Nugget" (Dynasty) arrived when "Corkie" (Hot Pursuit) was in his heyday. Rumour had it that a "new" American was to make its debut at the Welsh Beagle Club show of 1983. Douglas and Nugget were there, and handler Geoff Corish and Corkie, both entered in Open Dog. This was a nail-biting piece of judging from the ringside's point of view, as never before had we seen such a "Clash of the Titans". Judge Jack Holland gave the nod to Nugget, making what could not have been a more dramatic debut. I believe I am right in saying that the two dogs never met in competition again, though both went on to many more top wins. Corkie had to be content with the Reserve CC that day, but he had the pleasure of watching his baby daughter, Too Darn Hot, take her fourth CC from the Puppy class. Nugget was declared Best in Show. He later passed into the ownership of Ken and Veronica and became a popular stud dog. Ironically, as he was a successful sire, he did not produce a Champion for Dufosee.

I found it amusing that, with both Corkie and Nugget on the scene, it was assumed that one had to like one dog and hate the other. Personally, I admired them both but in different ways, for they were quite unalike. Both had much to offer and, as time proved, both left the breed with various benefits. The Dufosee kennel has provided many younger kennels with foundation stock from which they have bred on. They have kept to a rigid programme of line-breeding and are one of the kennels which have never had a problem with size, all the Dufosee dogs being well within the Standard.

Ada Anderson's first Champion, Ch. Rossmaith Ally, a daughter of Ch. Dufosee Yen and Rossmaith Clarissa, a daughter of Ch. Dialynne Gamble. Photo: Diane Pearce.

ROSSMAITH

Like so many successful breeders, Ada and Tommy Anderson bought their first Beagle as a family pet. A dog puppy called Toby was bought from Jean Westren, who became devoted to the Andersons' late son. In fact he taught the dog to climb the ladder to the loft where they both played trains – sadly his expert ladder-climbing also led to the Andersons losing a window cleaner! Having shown their dog around the smaller shows they decided to buy a Beagle specifically for showing and, in 1978, Deanery Dazzler of Rossmaith joined the household. She won well, despite being an uneasy traveller, and so she was retired from the ring and had a litter to Ch. Dialynne Essence. This resulted in a bitch, Rossmaith Restless. Restless had litters to Ch. Dufosee Zenith, Amaritas Bim Uno of Dialynne and Ch. Am. Ch. Graadtres Hot Pursuit of Rossut. Of these, the Hot Pursuit son, Rossmaith Isis, was the most significant dog for the kennel, winning several Reserve CCs and playing a major part in the future breeding programme.

Dazzler was later mated to Ch. Dufosee Zenith which produced Rossmaith Rosalind and also Rossmaith Gala. Rosalind was mated to Ch. Dialynne Gamble, from which litter came Rossmaith Clarissa. When she was put to Ch. Dufosee Yen, the Andersons had their first Champion in Ch. Rossmaith Ally and her brother Rossmaith Thomas. An Ally daughter mated back to Thomas produced the kennel's current hopeful, Rossmaith Zamba. Gala mated to Isis produced the classy Rossmaith Banjo. When she was mated to Ch. Bayard Zachariah, the result was the lovely sisters, Ch. Rossmaith Watchful and Ch. Rossmaith Whisper. Banjo was the breed's top brood bitch for 1995.

ROSSPARK

Jack Holland has been involved with the breed since 1962, his foundation bitch being Dialynne Nymph. Mated to Int. Ch. Appeline Top Ace, Nymph produced the lovely 14 inch bitch, Rosspark Imp, and Jack has always favoured the compact smartness of American-based lines. Imp's first litter was by the Canadian import, Tonawanda Sibiche, and this gave him Rosspark Miss Muffet. At a Blackpool show, when Miss Muffet was still a puppy, Jack saw Maureen Tolver's Baimor Annasline Solitaire, "a gorgeous tri dog", and despite the fact that he too was a puppy, a stud was booked there and then. When that mating took place, it produced a sensational dog puppy, born well ahead of his time, Rosspark Mr. Muffin. At the tender age of 7 months and one week, Muffin won the CC and BOB at Richmond under Carol Appleton. Interestingly, the Bitch CC winner that day was Dialynne Nettle, also winning her first. Not long after, Nettle's son, Dialynne Gamble, won his first CC at just 7 months of age, the judge being Carol Appleton. At the following Crufts Muffin won both his classes and took the Reserve CC behind Ch. Southcourt Wembury Merryboy who won his crowning certificate that day.

Jack Holland has always aimed to line-breed back to Gamble and his next striking winner was the tan and white Rosspark Elder, out of a double Gamble-bred bitch and sired by a Gamble son. He won a Reserve CC under Reg Wright MH, but sadly he developed a dislike for the show ring. An Annasline bitch was bought in from Judith Ireland and she was mated to Ch. Beacott Buckthorn. A dog puppy, Rosspark Ransom, was retained. Jack used him on a daughter of Ch. Rossut Foreman, Rossut Madcap, and bred a bitch called Rosspark Rosebud. She was the foundation of the highly successful Fertrac kennel. Later a bitch puppy from Dialynne became Ch. Dialynne Nester of Rosspark, one of the famous Soloman/Get Going sibling Champions. She was mated to Ch. Am. Ch. Pin Oaks Dynasty of Appeline, to whom Jack had given his first CC and BOB in this country. A bitch from that mating was Rosspark Reach who won a Reserve CC at Crufts. Mated to Ch. Raimex Kracker, Reach produced Diana Brown's Rosspark Rema of Raimex who is already a CC winner.

TRAGBAND

While my first pedigree dog was a Boxer, I became very interested in the Toy breeds and was doing extremely well with my Pekingese when I one day noticed a Beagle bitch at a local show in my native South Wales. I had seen Beagles before, but found them rather dull and ordinary, but this bitch was compact, smart as paint, with a fabulous head and expression, and I resolved to find out more about her. She turned out to be Imdee Aimee, a daughter of the Appletons' American import,

My first bitch Champion was Ch. Dufosee Quaker Girl of Tragband, by Ch. Baimor I'm A Rebel out of his own great grand-daughter. Quaker was the top winning Beagle bitch of 1979 and went on to produce Ch. Dufosee Mystro of Morsefield.
            Photo: Thomas Fall.

Appeline Validay Happy Feller. Having decided that I could like this breed if they had that "look", I began to investigate who was breeding what and discovered that Veronica Bradley had a litter from Ch. Dufosee Bonnie Girl by Ch. Dialynne Gamble, a Happy Feller son. From that litter I brought home Dufosee Gatsby of Tragband, my first Beagle and litter brother to Ch. Harris Tweed.

At that time I was still living with my parents so could not keep any more Beagles, but one day, when visiting Dufosee, I saw daughter Sue's young dog,

Dufosee Radleigh, in the run. Veronica told me that he would be sold overseas shortly as Sue was leaving for university and would not have the time to show him. I suggested that if they kept Radleigh at Dufosee, I would show him in joint ownership with Sue. Radleigh did very well, winning twelve CCs or so and a Reserve Group placing under the late Arthur Westlake. On a subsequent visit to Dufosee I noticed what I thought to be a fantastic bitch in the paddock. I asked all about her and discovered that she was destined to be a brood bitch as Veronica felt she had a silly temperament and might not be too good a showgirl. I put her on a lead, played with her for a while and found her to be gentle, delightful, and everything I had ever dreamt of in a Beagle. After some coaxing, it was agreed that Dufosee Quaker Girl of Tragband could be owned by Sue and myself, and she too became a Champion. She was a very popular bitch in the breed and it was rewarding that so many people still remembered her when the *Kennel Gazette* published their *Judges' Choice* feature, asking leading judges to name their three favourite Beagles of all time.

Quaker was an impossibility to show. Some days she would love every minute and show as if there was no tomorrow. On other days, and for no apparent reason, she would sulk, hump her back and look an absolute mess. To this day I remember that day at Blackpool when Honor Eades judged for the first time. We knew she loved Quaker, but it poured with rain and Beagles were judged in a muddy corner of a miserable tent, canvas flapping. We decided it was pointless to even attempt to show her, so she remained warm and snug on her bench. As Open bitch assembled, Honor caught sight of Sue and myself ringside and asked in one of her stage-whispers "Where's Quaker?" I suggested to Sue that

A favourite head study of Ch. Dufosee Aria of Tragband, daughter of Ch. Dufosee Radleigh of Tragband and Ch. Rossut Fantom. A repeat mating of Aria produced the historic Dufosee 'G' litter which contained Ch. Garbo, Geisha, Gingham, Galleon and Going to Penavon.   Photo: Thomas Fall.

she should bring her in. Plunged into the mud, Quaker showed like she had never shown before and ended up Best of Breed! She won a clutch of CCs and went on to produce Ch. Dufosee Mystro of Morsefield when mated back to her great-grandsire, Gamble.

Veronica had used Radleigh on Ch. Rossut Fantom and from that Sue and I showed Ch. Dufosee Aria of Tragband – photos of whom still surprise newcomers who think I can only see blanket tricolours, as she was a very sparsely marked bitch, almost white. We also had her younger sister, Encore, who later returned to Dufosee where she produced Ch. Dufosee Yen. At the time I was showing Aria I became friendly with the Johnsons who owned the Dicarl Great Danes. They admired Aria and thought they might have a go at breeding Beagles. They bought Dufosee Geisha, Aria's younger sister, and subsequently mated her to Ch. Dialynne Blueboy, producing Dicarl Gay's The Word and Dicarl Get Going. Seeing the puppies, I fell for Gay's The Word, brought her home and, as I couldn't cope with any more dogs where I was living at the time, gave her to Ken Sinclair and Adrian Edwards who had the Araki Tibetan Terriers, on the condition that I could one day have a puppy back from her.

Having judged the Suttons' Hot Pursuit at his second show, I decided that he was the perfect stud for Gay's The Word, and asked Ken to get her mated to him at her next season. She had five puppies and when they were about four weeks old I went down to see them. One bitch just stood away – paintbox marked and so full of quality. She was going to be mine! I left her there and aimed to collect her when she was about nine weeks old. After dinner, Adrian put on some music and the track playing was "Too Darn Hot" – so she had a name, and Ada was after Adrian. A week or so later Ken telephoned. Mrs Sutton had called him and asked him to take the puppies to Rossut for her to see. "Fine," I said, "but just don't forget which is mine!" After the Rossut trip I had an amusing phone call from Ken who had taken all the puppies for Catherine to see. She particularly liked one bitch and said so. She asked if she could buy it, and Ken agreed. "But which one is Andrew having?" she asked Ken, and he pointed to Ada. "Oh dear," scoffed Catherine, "I fear she may be a touch doggy." I never reminded

Catherine of that conversation, least of all when she gave Ada the first of her seven Hound Groups!

Ada won her first CC at 7 months under Terry Thorn and a further three as a puppy, including Best in Show at the West Mercia Beagle Club's Championship show. Her title came with her fifth CC at LKA. The following year she was the youngest Champion at Crufts. I had been advised by "well wishers" not to go, as the judge, the late Dolly Macro, would not like her, preferring something more substantial. It was Crufts, and I was always told that you never win sitting at home. Ada won the CC and BOB. I was in tears, and that win to this day remains my most treasured moment, not so much for the show, but for the judge who made it. Ada enjoyed spectacular success and ended up with 42 CCs under 40 different judges, giving her the Breed Record, which she holds to this day, winning CCs over seven consecutive years. She was shown at Crufts three times and took the Bitch CC on all three occasions. She was also taken out of the ring for two litters – and it had been suggested by her critics that such a neat "little" bitch (Ada was 15 inches, by the way) would never produce.

Repeating the mating which produced Ada resulted in Ch. Tragband Too Hot to Handle by Rossut, Singapore Ch. Tragband Brother It's Hot of Crouchmead (who was subsequently brought back to the UK when Nancy and Douglas Beaton retired and returned home), and Tragband Hot Gossip About Crickhallow, a good producer for the Dempsters and dam of their first Champion. Ada's first litter was to Ch. Dufosee Influence, identically bred to her great-grandsire, Radleigh. That litter contained Ch. Tragband In Town Tonight at Newlin, Danish Ch. Tragband In Hot Water, Danish Ch. Tragband In For a

Ch. Dialynne Tolliver at Tragband photographed at 18 month of age. A son of Ch. Soloman of Dialynne and Tragband Sweet Bird of Youth, 'Mikey' won 6 CCs as well as an unprecedented three Hound Groups and two Reserve Best in Shows all breeds before leaving Junior classes. He was also the Number One Beagle of 1995, ranking in the Top Ten for all breeds.

Photo: Sally Anne Thompson.

Penny, Tragband In With The In Crowd at Derriford (who was sparingly shown but sired some good stock for the Trewint kennel), and Tragband In Favour at Dufosee, who proved a marvellous brood for Veronica Bradley and Ken Burgess.

Her second litter was to Ch. Dialynne Nimrod of Ramlacim, a Blueboy son, Ada being a Blueboy grand-daughter. From that litter came Australian Ch. Tragband Summer and Smoke, who has had an amazing influence on the Beagles down under; Tragband Battle of Angels at Janfrey, who won his Stud Book number for the Mays before he became just a little too proud of his stern!; Tragband American Blues, who sired well in Holland; Tragband The Rose Tatoo, who went to the Gold Lines kennel in Denmark; Tragband Candles in the Sun, who went to South Africa as a mate for Ch. Tragband Too Hot to Handle by Rossut, Ada's younger brother; Tragband Cat on a Hot Tin Roof at Bayard, a wonderful brood for the Bayard kennel; and my own Tragband Sweet Bird of Youth, who won one CC and several Reserves, then went to Dialynne on breeding terms.

Mated to Ch. Soloman of Dialynne, Birdie produced my latest Champion at the time of writing, Dialynne Tolliver of Tragband, known to all as Mikey. Not only was Mikey Number One Beagle for 1995, but in 1996 he equalled his grand-dam's big ring record of one Best in show, three Reserve Bests in show and seven Hound Groups. When he took Best in Show at the Scottish Kennel Club's Championship show in May of that year, he helped create a further piece of history, in that Ada then became the only Beagle to be a Best in Show winner to produce two daughters who, in turn, produced Best in Show winners (namely Tragband Cat On a Hot Tin Roof, dam of Ch. Bayard Syndicat of Lowyck, and Tragband Sweet Bird of Youth, dam of Ch. Dialynne Tolliver of Tragband).

11 BEAGLES IN THE BRITISH SHOW RING

There have been countless people who have, over the years, contributed to the progress of the Beagle as a British show dog. Many of them are no longer with us, some can occasionally be seen keeping a watchful eye on the Beagle ring though they are no longer active, and others have left the dog world completely to pursue other interests. As this book aims to be a contemporary work, and space is limited, it would be impossible to detail the activities and successes of all those instrumental in advancing the breed, so I intend to concentrate on the progress of the past

twenty years or so. Later in the chapter I will look at the kennel affixes which are still actively exhibiting with notable success, but before doing so I feel it would be pertinent to recall some of the kennel names which were, earlier in this period, forces to be reckoned with, but are no longer regularly campaigning.

BARVAE

It is highly appropriate that the first affix to be mentioned here is that of Gladys Clayton and her daughter Patricia, now a multi-breed judge, as their kennel provided the foundation stock for many of the next generation of leading breeders. The affix was first registered in 1936 by Mrs Clayton who was initially highly successful in Great Danes and several other breeds. Patricia's new-found interest in Beagles resulted in Lindsey Makeway arriving in 1952, a bitch who produced two Champions. The

excellent facilities at Barvae meant that large numbers of hounds could be kept – often as many as 30 or 40 at any one time. Foundation stock was obtained from various sources throughout the country in order to develop not just a line of breeding, but a pure strain. Many later litters bred at Barvae had a five-generation pedigree in which every hound named carried the Barvae affix.

Some of the founding hounds were acquired directly from hunting packs. Limbourne Valiant, registered with both the Association of Masters of Harriers and Beagles and the Kennel Club, and his two daughters, Spotlight and Wilful, came from Mrs C.J. Davies. All three were successful both in the show ring and as Champion producers. Wilful, actually owned by Patricia, became the first Champion Beagle at Barvae. She headed a line of five generations of Champions, namely Ch.

The Beagle Club was formed in 1890 and in 1990 celebrated its centenary with a memorable Championship show.

Photo: Harry Nicholson.

Ch. Barvae Wynder, a Champion bitch sired by Barvae Benroe Wrinkles, is a remarkably 'modern' hound for the time – 1960.
Photo: C.M. Cooke.

Wilful, Ch. Barvae Willing, Ch. Barvae Wynder, Ch. Barvae Shuna and Ch. Barvae Stamford. Perhaps the most fortuitous acquisition, however, was that of Barvae Paigan. Mrs Clayton obtained him, unseen, as a small puppy from a private hunting pack. By the late 50s he had not only gained Champion status, but had become the leading sire in the breed. A contemporary of Paigan, Ch. Barvae Statute, was also to make breed history for his owner, Fred Watson of Derawuda fame. Statute not only became the breed record holder with 17 CCs, but he was the first Beagle ever to win Best in Show at an all breeds Championship show, which he did in 1958 at Chester, the judge being the noted all-rounder, Dr Aubrey Ireland.

In 1959 Barvae Benroe Wrinkles was imported from Canada. He was sired by one of the greats in Beagle history, Am. Can. Ch. Thornridge Wrinkles, sire of over 90 North American Champions. A bitch, Can. Ch. Benroe Belle's Babe, had been specially chosen by Mrs Clayton to mate to Thornridge Wrinkles. She herself contained

two lines to him already, thus ensuring a high concentration of his breeding in the resulting litter. Barvae Benroe Wrinkles was to prove an immediate success at stud. Barvae Varner, who was waiting for him on his release from quarantine, produced Ch. Acrobat in his first litter. Four days after the birth of Varner's litter, Varner's dam, Barvae Progress, also gave birth to a litter by him. This contained Ch. Barvae Aider. In all Wrinkles sired 10 Champions, a breed record which stood for many years.

FORRARDON

The late Pamela Harris and Leonard Pagliero began breeding Beagles at the end of the 1950s, and registered the Forrardon affix in 1959. Prior to that, Leonard had entered the world of pedigree dogs through German Shepherd Dogs and Obedience. Their first Beagle was Derawuda Velvet and the kennel's early breeding programme incorporated Appeline and Limbourne bloodlines. The first Forrardon Champion was Chance, born in 1962. She won three Certificates under three breed authorities, Wilf Herrick, Charles Hardwick and Douglas Appleton, before she was a year old, and at that time dogs did not need to win at least one CC after their first birthday to gain their Championship, as is the case today. Other Champions followed – Ch. Forrardon Chantress, Ch. Forrardon Appeline Beeswing, Ch. Forrardon Frolic, Ch. Forrardon Foxtrot, Ch. Forrardon Rumba, Ch. Forrardon Warrior, Ch. Forrardon Kinsman, Ch. Houndsmark Mindful of Forrardon and Australian Ch. Forrardon Gambol.

The Forrardon kennel holds the unique record of five Bests of Breed at Crufts in the space of twelve years: 1965 – Beeswing (who also won the Hound Group and Reserve Best in Show, still the highest

Ch. Forrardon Appeline Beeswing, owned by the late Pamela Harris and Leonard Pagliero, won Reserve Best in Show at Crufts 1965, the highest award to date for a Beagle at this famous show.
Photo courtesy: Leonard Pagliero.

award to date for a Beagle at this famous show); 1967 – Frolic; 1970 – Foxtrot (who went on to win the Hound Group); 1972 – Foxtrot; 1977 – Warrior. In 1975 Warrior and his dam, Rumba, won the double at the prestigious Hound Show under Janet Lee Gordon, another rare achievement. Many Forrardon hounds gained working certificates from the Beagle Club, and Foxtrot was the first to do so, in the early days being the hound who invariably led the pack. Leonard Pagliero considers Foxtrot to be the greatest Forrardon ever and the epitome of all a Beagle should be. He feels the kennel's most spectacular triumph was at the 1977 Hound Show when Foxtrot, then twelve years old, was shown in the Working and Veteran classes, only having been entered after various people in the breed had prevailed on his owner to let newcomers see this marvellous hound. The judge was Charles Hardwick, Master of Hounds with the Chilmark Beagles, and Foxtrot went on to win Best

of Breed from an entry of 150, beating many of the famous Champions of the day. In his critique the judge wrote of Foxtrot: "Outstanding hound of the day, Ch. Forrardon Foxtrot was still, despite his age, in a class by himself. A clear winner and Best of Breed."

KORWIN
Christine Watson is one of several breeders who established veritable Beagle strongholds in Scotland, Christine buying her first Beagle in 1964. The following year, Rossut Ruffle arrived and when she was mated to Tavernmews Butler, she produced Korwin Bramble who went on to produce the first Korwin Champion, Dancer of Korwin. Christine swiftly established a definite type, and several of her hounds, notably Korwin Butler, while never making their titles, were considered by the cognoscenti to be excellent examples of the breed and went on to produce well.

PINEWOOD
When Ch. Barvae Statute created breed history by winning Best in Show at Chester, Leonard and Heather Priestley were enthusiastic new Pointer exhibitors. However, the sight of Statute convinced them that Beagles were the breed for them. Some months later they bought a daughter of Ch. Barvae Paigan. The Priestleys soon realised Hemlington Rita's limitations and after a few years bought Pinewood Crumpet from Peggy Slapp. She won her first CC and BOB under Reg Wright MH at Bournemouth in 1962, handled by Leonard – the first and only time he handled a dog at a Championship show! Crumpet had a litter by Ch. Appeline Top Ace and this founded the Pinewood kennel, but she herself sadly died at the age of three. The Canadian import, Tonawanda Sibiche, then joined the kennel. A smart,

short-coupled tricolour, he helped stamp his good bone and tight feet on his get. Mated to the rangy, long-backed bitches of the time, he did a lot of good, but, as Heather admits: "It was proved that short backs go with short necks and Sibby was not to be line-bred too closely." One of his most famous daughters was Ch. Pinewood Crocus who, bred to Ch. Rossut Triumphant, produced Pinewood Custard, the proud winner of 1 CC and 11 Reserve CCs!

In the late 70s the Priestleys bought Ch. Southcourt Wembury Merryboy from Glenda Young when he had 3 CCs. They took him on to win another 11 CCs and two Hound Groups. He was also Best Dog at the 1971 Three Counties show under the late all-rounder Herbert Essam. It is my opinion that Merryboy was rather ahead of his time, and could still acquit himself well in the ring today. Merryboy was used extensively at stud. Combined with the Pinewood line he provided the foundation for Silke and Jochen Eberhardt's kennel in Germany. Many more Pinewood exports won top honours overseas. It must give the Priestleys much pleasure to recall that Merryboy sired Ch. Beacott Buckthorn, the breed record-holder for several years, and that Ch. Pinewood Castor was the dam of Ch. Jondor Crocus, holder of the bitch record for some time. These days Leonard and Heather are deeply involved with Cavalier King Charles Spaniels, but through other Beagle kennels the Pinewood name lives on to this day.

SOUTHCOURT

Glenda Young may never have been a large-scale breeder, but her affix has been carried by several significant dog hounds such as the good sire, Southcourt Tarquin (younger brother to Ch. Dialynne Ponder), Tarquin's famous sons Ch. Southcourt

Wembury Merryboy and Ch. Southcourt Wembury Fiddler, and Merryboy's sons, the litter brothers Ch. Southcourt Hatchet and Ch. Barterhound Southcourt Hamilton. Starting with a bitch of essentially Barvae, Derawuda and early Dialynne lines, her own Ch. Southcourt Melody proved that the kennel was not just good at producing males.

WEMBURY

Bette Hastie's small West Country kennel was one where quality was what mattered most. From her Wembury Tinkerbell Chantress came some excellent Beagles such as Merryboy and Fiddler as well as Ch. Wembury Archie who was used to good effect by the Dufosee kennel. Wembury Morag proved a good producing bitch for the Rossuts, and earlier on Ch. Wembury Anna had been an important bitch for Ann Pickthall's Clovergates kennel.

These are just some of the names which come to mind as I think back. It says much for the Beagle's many attributes that a large number who come into the breed stay with it for ever, which is not the case with some breeds where the turnover is rapid. This I feel is a reflection on the great character of the dogs themselves, and also the type of people which the breed attracts. On the whole, Beagle folk are as merry and uncomplicated as the dogs they own.

A–Z OF TODAY'S LEADING KENNELS

ALMARDA

Alan and Margaret Davies' kennel is associated with smart, compact blanket tricolours of ideal size, which is little wonder when one considers their ancestry. Fardene Evening Star was a daughter of the American-sired Ch. Baimor I'm a Rebel out of a Baimor bitch, and she was mated to Pippatine Showpiece, who traced back to Ch. Fardene High Hopes, to produce their first Champion, Almarda Mudlark. When Mudlark was put to the American import, Pin Oaks Dynasty of Appeline, she produced Ch. Almarda Trickster who was the first Champion for Mark Price.

BAIMOR

Maureen Tolver is a fine example of the devotee of the "American" type of Beagle, favouring a compact hound well into the Standard as regards size, and her breeding programme has been developed with this in mind. Starting with a son and daughter of the American import, Ch. Rozavel Elsy's Diamond Jerry, Baimor Annasline Solitaire and Baimor Bettwend Harmony, Maureen bred her first Champion in 1969 when Ch. Baimor I'm A Rebel was whelped. He was by the imported Am. Ch. Colegren's Little Rebel of Clovergates out of Baimor Serenade, a daughter of Harmony and Ch. Barvae Pilot. Rebel's show career was interrupted by his owner's working overseas, but he won his title at five years of age. He was a free and powerful mover who sired particularly good bitches, not least of which was the dynasty-founding Ch. Dufosee Bonnie Girl who inherited her sire's fantastic gait. He also produced my first Champion bitch, Dufosee Quaker Girl of Tragband, when used on his own great grand-daughter. His daughter out of Baimor Sibelle (by the Canadian import Tonawanda Sibiche) helped found the Fardene and Almarda kennels. While not a consistent campaigner, Maureen continues to breed to her ideal type and has recently produced a litter which carries no fewer than 20 lines to Rebel.

BARTERHOUND

Barbara Roderick first hit the high spots in

Bred in 1969 by Glenda Young, Ch. Barterhound Southcourt Hamilton was campaigned to his title by Barbara Roderick. He also sired her Ch. Barterhound Hammerlyn. Hamilton was by Ch. Southcourt Wembury Merryboy, a son of Southcourt Tarquin, out of Southcourt Harmony – herself a daughter of Tarquin and Southcourt Mandy. Both Tarquin and Mandy were by Ch. Dialynne Huntsman, so Hamilton was intensely line-bred to him, having him three times out of a possible four in the third generation of his pedigree.
Photo: Diane Pearce.

the Beagle world with a very slow maturing lemon and white male, Barterhound Southcourt Hamilton, who was five years old when he won his first CC but went on to win five, three of which were awarded at consecutive Bournemouth shows! Hamilton also won a Beagle Club Working Certificate. As Hamilton was intensely line-bred to Ch. Dialynne Huntsman, it was no surprise that he would produce. Mated to Barterhound Bramble, a daughter of Ch. Lanesend Tallarook and a Cornevon bitch, he sired Ch. Barterhound Hammerlyn and, at one stage, Barbara was the only person in the breed to have made up two lemon Champion males. Hammerlyn was a lovely-moving hound and went on to win a

Hound Group. For Barbara he sired several CC winners, and I personally found it surprising that he was not used more by other breeders. One who did, with a result, was Mollie Field who won 7 CCs with his son, Ch. Houndsmark Mudlark. Through another son, Nedlaw Nightowl, he is also grandsire of the Best in Show winning Ch. Julemark Hotspur by Nedlaw. A Hamilton daughter, Barterhound Carol, became an Australian Champion for Noreen Harris in the 1970s, while Barterhound Legend of Dialynne became a Champion in Spain.

BEACOTT

Sylvia Tutchener and her late husband, Phil, bought their first Beagle in 1961 as a companion for their cross-bred terrier. Having got their first taste of showing with two males of average quality, they bought Cornevon Minuet, a lemon and white bitch bred by the Gibsons from Ch. Cornevon Pensive and Ch. Raimex Tally, and added their affix which had been derived from the name of their new home, "Beagle Cottage". When Minuet was around eighteen months old, Sylvia was advised that her bitch would probably benefit from a litter which would give her the body and finish that she lacked at the time. She took that advice and a litter to Southcourt Tarquin produced Beacott Benedict and Bountiful (both lemons), Daphne Ayland's Beacott Brevity and John Marsh's Beacott Boniface. Minuet returned to the ring, winning her title, and she produced three further litters. To Ch. Southcourt Hatchet she produced Ch. Beacott Belle, but her most significant offspring was to Ch. Southcourt Wembury Merryboy, as this mating resulted in the legendary Ch. Beacott Buckthorn.

I recall vividly seeing Bucky for the first time. He was just eight months old and I had him in the Puppy class when I judged

Ch. Beacott Buckthorn, owned by Phil Tutchener, is pictured here in a charming head study which is so reminiscent of his sire, Ch. Southcourt Wembury Merryboy. 'Bucky's' dam was Ch. Beacott Cornevon Minuet, and for several years he held the record for the top winning CC Beagle of all time. His great show career included several Groups – one at Crufts – and he remains the top winning male to date with 38 CCs to his credit.
Photo: Michael Wheeler.

Beagles at a Horley Open show. This dog was charismatic and I had no hesitation in making him Best of Breed despite his youth. The resulting critique appears elsewhere in this book. Weeks later, Bucky won his first CC under 'Beefy' Sutton, and thus started a phenomenal show career which spanned five years and resulted in 38 CCs (still the breed record for a male Beagle), taking BOB 27 times, and 7 Hound Groups (including Crufts in 1981) and he was many times Best in Show at breed club events. He also enjoyed great success in Veteran Stakes, often handled by Jill Peak. At Crufts 1988 he took the

Reserve CC from the Veteran class at a mere twelve years young! Bucky died at the age of seventeen and a half leaving a great gap in Sylvia Tutchener's life, who had lost what was truly "the dog of a lifetime". The late Phil Tutchener spent many hours researching Bucky's pedigree and finally produced eight full generations and the majority of ten generations. Phil also published Andrew Smalley's excellent specialist work, *Any True Hound Colour*. In his research, Phil traced Bucky's ancestry right back to the early part of the century when a Beagle male, Wooddale Pirate, was mated to a Harrier bitch, Roundway Pastime. Pastime's great-great-great-grand-dam, the Harrier, Aldenham Restless, was in fact the offspring of Foxhounds, Whaddon Chase Tarquin and Oakley Sarah. Thus we have a fascinating link with the past.

Bucky had a relatively short stud career and became sterile at an early age; however he produced Ch. Fertrac Anika, the dam of several Fertrac Champions, Sylvia's own Beacott Bellman (sire of Ch. Bondlea Poet), and of course Kittoch Garland who was the dam of Ch. Soloman of Dialynne, an outstanding sire. I was very touched when Sylvia, having awarded Mikey – Ch. Dialynne Tolliver of Tragband – (a Soloman son, and so a Bucky great grandson) his second CC and BOB, wrote "As I watched him in the Group, he bore a strong resemblance to Buckthorn in his youth." Sylvia made up Ch. Fertrac Bramble of Beacott, bred by Mal Phillips, a daughter of Ch. Soloman and Ch. Anika, thus having Bucky on both sides of the pedigree.

BONDLEA
Marion Hunt's affix was first registered in 1970 and her first Beagle, Sonnet of Bondlea (a daughter of Ch. Rossut

Marion Hunt and Jo Norris's Ch. Valsacre Tactful of Bondlea, bred by Val Hargrave out of Ch. Valsacre Liberty by Ch. Raimex Kracker. She is pictured with the cup she won for Best of Breed at Crufts 1995 under judge Diana Brown.

Photo courtesy: Marion Hunt.

Foreman) was bought from the Rossut kennel. Mated to Ch. Deaconfield Rampage, Sonnet produced Bondlea Cherish who won 2 CCs. She produced two litters, but after health problems with the resulting puppies, Marion decided that she needed another foundation bitch. The late Nicky Wetton gave her Chasedene Carmen of Bondlea, a daughter of Brackenvale Bellman (Ch. Dufosee Harris Tweed ex a Ch. Raimex Tinder daughter) and Chasedene Cornelia who was predominantly Chasedene bred, combining Forrardon, Clovergates and Korwin lines. Carmen won one CC and a Reserve CC but it was as a brood bitch that she came into her own. Mated to Beacott Bellman, a virtual outcross, Carmen produced Ch. Bondlea Poet, Marion's first Champion, who won 11 CCs and eight working certificates. He has won well in Veteran classes up to his eleventh year and, with limited stud work, has sired several CC and Reserve CC winners. Carmen's second litter was to Ch. Mistylaw Willy Nilly, which picked up the Korwin lines, and this resulted in Ch. Bondlea Pebbles who won 9 CCs and three working certificates. She also won her Irish title in five straight shows, quite an achievement. She has produced winners, but at one time it looked as if she would not have any puppies, so Marion bought in Valsacre Tactful of Bondlea from Val Hargrave, a daughter of Champions Raimex Tinder and Valsacre Liberty. She was campaigned to her title in partnership with Jo Norris and won Best of Breed at Crufts 1995.

Reg and Hazel Harron's Ch. & Ir. Ch. Broharrons Duffy was out of Ch. Broharrons Harlequin and sired by a brother of Ch. Broharrons Carly. I feel sure he would have won many more CCs had he been based in mainland Britain.   Photo: Diane Pearce.

BROHARRONS

Campaigning dogs from their Northern Ireland home, Reg and Hazel Harron obviously had to travel considerable distances, but their small kennel produced some excellent hounds over the years, several of which would doubtless have done much more winning had they been based in mainland Britain. The Harrons started in Beagles in 1962 with a locally bred dog, O'Mally's Rifleman, who was the first Beagle in Ireland to win a Best in Show. They then bought Barvae Rimple from the Claytons who won the CC under Douglas Appleton at Belfast in 1963. She became the first British Champion for Hazel and her late husband. Dialynne Posy then joined the Harrons' kennel and she too became a Champion. Later three Cornevon hounds were bought in, the litter brother and sister Gaylad and Greensleeves, and Finian. From the combination of Finian

and Posy came beautiful heads, good bone and free movement, and Hazel attributes most of their success to these two hounds. Among their offspring, Ch. Broharrons Thistle won her title, while Broharrons Clover was a marvellous producer. When mated to Ch. Dialynne Gamble she produced Ch. Broharrons Harlequin, a truly lovely bitch.

Later Deanery Deloes, a son of Ch. Korwin Monitor and Ch. Deanery Dream Girl, was bought in and he made his Irish title. His winning get include Ch. Broharrons Silk and her litter sister, Sash, who in turn produced Ch. Broharrons Carly when mated to Kieldorn's Karl, a son of Broharrons Thatch and Broharrons Clementine, similarly bred and tracing back to the Harrons' original Cornevon hounds. Ch. Broharrons Thistle had been mated to Ch. Southcourt Wembury Merryboy, resulting in Broharrons Merrygirl. When she was put to Irish Ch. Deanery Deloes, the result was the start of Pat Huey's run of success with her Lismoyle kennel, Ch.

Broharrons Repeat. The Harrons' own first male Champion was the very handsome Ch. Broharrons Duffy. He was by Broharrons Dooley, full brother to Ch. Carly, out of Ch. Harlequin. I feel sure that Duffy would have won many, many CCs had he been campaigned throughout Britain, and in my opinion he was the best Broharrons ever. A Duffy son, Broharrons O'Connor, produced three Champion bitches – Ch. Broharrons Lace, Ch. Tarlog Brevity and Ch. Tarlog Sweet Chloe.

CAURNIEHILL

Kathleen Cooper must be one of the most travelled of exhibitors, as she has consistently campaigned her hounds from Scotland, missing few shows. Her first Beagle, Cairniehill Lass, was primarily a pet, but competed successfully in Obedience. She had some good breeding behind her on the sire's side, being by Kittoch Archer (Ch. Wembury Archie ex Ch. Grattondown Melba) and she gave Kathleen her first taste of Beagle showing. Mated to Korwin Butler, Lass produced the first Caurniehill Champion, Clarinet, and her sister, Courtesy. Courtesy was mated to Dorabells Consort, a son of Korwin Concorde, and that resulted in Ch. Caurniehill Dancer, in my opinion the best of Kathleen's Champions. Clarinet herself was put to Ch. Newlin Prefect to breed Ch. Caurniehill Fortune, while a previous litter to Ch. Mistylaw Chuckle of Millmar had contained a lemon and white dog puppy called Caurniehill Yokel. Yokel's is something of a fairy story. Kathleen never keeps males, so had sold him to a pet home at eight weeks, from which he was returned a year later in very poor condition. He was built up and then placed in a lovely home for another year until that marriage broke up, and again he returned to Kathleen! She then heard of a couple who were desperate

Ch. Caurniehill Yokel is something of fairytale dog. After being returned from two pet homes, his breeder Kathleen Cooper placed him with the MacAulay family, who attended a Championship show with him for the first time at Crufts 1993. There they watched Kathleen handle him to win the Dog CC. It says much for Yokel's temperament that after a neglected youth he continues to show so marvellously. Photo: Diane Pearce.

to replace a tan and white Korwin dog they had just lost. It was agreed that the MacAulays should collect him from a local show where Kathleen had entered him. He won Best of Breed, the Group and Best in Show! The next time the MacAulays came to a dog show was when Kathleen showed Yokel for them at Crufts in 1993, Harry Jordan judging. He ended up winning the CC and later was to take his crown. A very sound dog, it says much for Yokel's temperament that, despite several homes and not a little abuse along the way, he continued to show with such an extrovert disposition.

CRESTAMERE

Few people in the Beagle world are as popular as Wyn Mahoney, who is always ready to help and encourage young and novice exhibitors. Wyn had originally bred

Wyn Mahoney founded her Crestamere kennel with three half-sisters. Her first Champion, Ch. Crestamere Orchid, was bred by mating a son of one back to his dam's half-sister. Orchid was one of those rare bitches who combine bone and substance with absolute quality.   *Photo: Diane Pearce.*

and shown Labradors when she added Beagles to the kennel. Crestamere Alice of Stubblesdown (Ch. Appeline Glider ex a daughter of Ch. Solomon of Stanhurst), Crestamere Charming of Stubblesdown (her half-sister by Ch. Elmhurst Playmate), and Crestamere Echo of Stubblesdown (another half-sister by Barvae Benroe Wrinkles) proved an unusual and amazingly sensible foundation for the Crestameres. Echo was mated to Ch. Appeline Cannon, and Wyn kept a male from the litter, Crestamere Index. He was then used on his dam's half-sister, Charming, to produce the first of many Champions, Crestamere Orchid, a very popular and much admired bitch in the breed. Mated to Ch. Deaconfield Rampage, Orchid produced Ch. Crestamere Kerry Dancer, while a mating to Rossut Gaffer produced Joan Buchan's first Champion, Crestamere Solomon of Owlden. A Gaffer son, Rossut Paragon of Crestamere, was bought in, his dam being the lovely Ch. Rossut Colinbar

Phantom. This reinforced the Stubblesdown connection, as Phantom was out of Treetops Envy of Stubblesdown, sister to Echo. Paragon was used on Crestamere Katie, a daughter of Charming and Ch. Wendover Bounty, and from that litter Ch. Crestamere Twilight of Rossut was made up. Paragon mated to Crestamare Harmony, an Index daughter, produced Ch. Crestamere Snowdrop.

Orchid had a sister, Oona, who was taken to Ch. Redgate Marquis and this produced Ch. Crestamere Promise of Haliloo. The combination of Promise and Solomon gave Wyn Ch. Crestamere Truth, while Promise and Paragon produced the Champion brothers, Crestamere Ruler and Crestamere Monarch of Owlden. Ruler mated to Crestamere Tartan Lass, a daughter of Ch. Korwin Monitor and Ch. Crestamere Kerry Dancer, gave Doug and Wendy Hall Crestamere Flower of Cliffmere, and helped found their kennel. Truth was taken to Deaconfield Rampant, the result being yet another Champion bitch, Crestamere Chimer. Thelma Hosking made up Ch. Ditchmere Crestamere Norma, a daughter of another Orchid sister, Opal, and Ch. Appeline Cannon. In the mid-1970s, Ch. Norcis Helene of Crestamere was made up, litter sister to the famous Hannah, and a further bitch was brought in and made up in the mid-1980s in Ch. Dialynne Spice of Crestamere, a daughter of Ch. Dialynne Pedlar. Crestamere-bred hounds have also made their mark overseas. The British-titled Twilight was also made up in Australia. Crestamere Hotspur became a Champion in South Africa, Secret in Argentina and Sylvester in Zimbabwe.

DEACONFIELD
The late Dolly Macro first became interested in Beagles back in the 1920s when she watched the Eton College pack

The late Dolly Macro's Ch. Deaconfield Rampage, a significant sire for the Deaconfield kennel.

Photo courtesy: Debbie Taylor.

exercising in Buckinghamshire where she was a kennelmaid for the legendary St. Margaret's Sealyham kennel. Her first Beagle, a stray, arrived in the 1930s and then she acquired a Reynalton-bred hound. Her breeding really began, however, with Stanhurst Rachel, a bitch she obtained from Yvonne Oldman of the Barsheen affix, subsequently more famous in Bloodhounds. Rachel was mated to Ch. Barvae Statute which gave Dolly Ch. Deaconfield Rebecca, born in 1958, and the winner of 10 CCs. Rebecca was taken back to Ch. Barvae Paigan and that produced Ch. Deaconfield Ripple. So successful was that mating that Dolly repeated it in 1962, the result being the Suttons' Ch. Rossut Deaconfield Ravish and Deaconfield Regan, the bitch retained by the home kennel. Mated to the Ch. Appeline Cannon son, Ch. Larkholme Andima Classic Major, Regan produced Ch. Deaconfield Rampage, a hare-pied who sired several significant Champions, among them Ch. Deaconfield Random. Ripple to Ch. Dialynne Huntsman, produced Ch. Deaconfied Renown.

Dolly was one of the generation that had to be coerced into judging, but she awarded her first set of CCs in 1970 when that honour was long overdue. The climax of her judging career was judging the breed at Crufts in 1984, when she gave Best of Breed to Ada, Ch. Too Darn Hot for Tragband. That was the highlight of my exhibiting career, not just for the win, but for the judge who made the award. Dolly Macro was held in high esteem by the Beagle world. Happily, her grand-daughter Debbie Taylor has now taken on the affix and continues to keep the Deaconfield Beagles in the ring.

FERTRAC

Mal and Stella Phillips bought their first Beagle, a grand-daughter of Ch. Appeline Cannon, back in 1977. Having taken her to a few dog shows, they soon realised that she lacked the qualities required of a good show specimen, so two years later they bought Rosspark Rosebud from Jack Holland, a very well-bred bitch whose grandsires were Ch. Beacott Buckthorn and Ch. Rossut Foreman, very much the vogue dogs of the time. For their first litter, the Phillips felt that the obvious choice of stud dog was Buckthorn (though I feel not many newcomers would have found such a daring in-breeding quite so obvious!), and their hunch paid off as it yielded their first Champion, Fertrac Anika. Anika won 7 CCs, but she excelled as a brood bitch, having three litters to Ch. Solomon of Dialynne which, of course, doubled up on the Buckthorn blood. The first litter contained Sylvia Tutchener's Ch. Fertrac Bramble at Beacott and Wyn Griffiths' Ch. Fertrac Benita at Barneydore, both bitches, but it was the lad who stayed at home that rather eclipsed his sisters. Ch. Fertrac Brandy won 31 CCs, taking Best of Breed 25 times. He also won 20 Reserve CCs. In addition he won several Hound Groups and was twice Reserve Best in Show at general Championship shows. He won the Contest of Welsh Champions one year and was twice Best of Breed at Crufts. He has gone on to be a successful sire, with several Champions to his credit, passing on his extrovert nature and tremendous showmanship as well as unusually good hindquarters. Two repeats of this mating which worked so well produced Ch. Fertrac Coira (also a Champion in Ireland), Fertrac Cognac who went to Germany, Fertrac Carisma who became a Champion producer in New Zealand, the Reserve CC winning Fertrac Damsel, and Fertrac Debutant who also went to New Zealand.

JANFREY

For some time Jane (née Bradley) and Jeff May showed their Beagles using a joint interest in the Dufosee affix of Jane's mother, but they later registered their own Janfrey kennel name. Up until then they had shown with success a variety of Dufosee hounds including Ch. Dufosee Nobility, Ch. Dufosee Modesty and her dual CC-winning sister, Dufosee Madonna. Madonna's daughter by Ch. Soloman of Dialynne, Janfrey Angelica, became the first Champion for the new affix. Janfrey Fashion was Madonna's daughter by Ch. Dufosee Nobility, and she was mated to Ch. Dialynne Tolliver of Tragband to produce the current Janfrey winners.

JESSON

One of the most consistent kennels for type in recent Beagle history has been the Jesson establishment of Honor and Jesper Eades. The Jessons began with Forrardon Rhapsody, a very sound and free-moving tan and white daughter of the Forrardon Champions, Foxtrot and Chantress. Honor Eades has always been a stickler for

movement in her hounds and when it came to breeding from Rhapsody, Ch. Houndswood Havoc was the chosen stud dog, a son of Ch. Deaconfield Rampage. This mating succeeded and produced the famous tan and white "twins", Ch. Jesson Fencer and Ch. Jesson Fantasy. Rhapsody then had a litter to Ch. Dialynne Gamble from which came the CC winning male, Jesson Ranter. When Ranter was used on his half-sister Fantasy, Jesson Whimsey was the result. Meanwhile Honor had begun to develop a second line by bringing in Ch. Sonnet of Dialynne, a Gamble grand-daughter who, Honor maintains, had the most perfect front and neatest feet she has ever seen. Sonnet was mated to the Gamble son, Ch. Dufosee Harris Tweed, whose free movement had obvious appeal to Honor. This produced one of the most exceptional Jessons ever – Ch. Jesson Saddler. He was a high-quality dog with great style which carried him through to win 16 CCs and a Reserve Hound Group. He rather overshadowed his litter brother, Seeker, yet it was Seeker who won Best in Show at the Hound Show in 1982. A repeat breeding produced Ch. Jesson Lancer and his sister Lacy.

In an attempt to unite the two lines with which she had been working, Honor mated Whimsey to Saddler. The first litter from these two produced Ch. Jesson Barley, while a repeat resulted in Ch. Jesson Thrifty. I particularly remember Thrifty as I judged her at Birmingham City show when she was just 10 months old. Her older sister, Barley, had won the Open Bitch class and was sitting on two CCs. Thrifty had won Puppy Bitch. I imagine that Honor was hoping to win a third CC with Barley, but I just could not resist Thrifty's charms and gave her the CC and also BOB, with Barley taking Reserve. Happily they both went on to complete their titles. Thrifty

The Jesson 'twins', Ch. Jesson Fantasy and Ch. Jesson Fencer, bred by Honor Eades from Jesson Rhapsody and Ch. Houndswood Havoc.

Photo: Diane Pearce.

was mated to Ch. Soloman of Dialynne to produce Ch. Jesson Mercy, and for her second litter was put to Ch. Bayard Zachariah, both of which represented line-breeding but in slightly different directions. To Zachariah, Thrifty produced Ch. Jesson Quaintly who won 33 CCs, a great feat indeed for a lemon bitch, and her tricolour brother, Ch. Jesson Quester. Mercy in turn was mated to the American import, Ch. Am. Ch. Pin Oaks Dynasty of Appeline (Zachariah's sire) and this produced Ch. Jesson Clinker and Ch. Jesson Chancy of Dialynne. The two lines were again brought together by mating Quaintly to Clinker, resulting in Ch. Jesson Firefly. The kennel's latest Champion is Ch. Jesson Swiftly, a daughter of Ch. Mercy by Ch. Dufosee Yen. Chancy has, for Dialynne, produced Ch. Dialynne Chances Are when mated back to her grandsire, Soloman. Jesson remains one of the few kennels which has never appeared to have a problem with either size or body length, the majority of their hounds coming very much out of the same mould.

LISMOYLE

Pat Huey had lost one of her two pet Beagles and so decided to buy a replacement to keep the surviving dog

company. She had been visiting shows in her native Northern Ireland with a friend who was showing an Afghan Hound, and had admired the Beagles she had seen winning in the ring, most of which came from the Harrons' kennel. In March 1977 a telephone call came from Hazel Harron telling Pat that they had a promising male which she could have. For Pat it was love at first sight, and this open-marked tricolour became Ch. Irish Ch. Broharrons Repeat. "Pete" had many admirers in mainland Britain and Eleanor Bothwell was one who used him on her Crestamere Martha (Ch. Crestamere Ruler ex Ch. Norcis Helene of Crestamere) and thus produced Ch. Norcis Ashes.

Pat was now keen to establish her own kennel and bought from Eleanor Norcis Beaula, a daughter of Martha and Norcis Taurus (Ch. Dufosee Harris Tweed ex Ch. Norcis Hannah, litter sister to Martha's dam, Ch. Helene). As was originally planned, Beaula was mated to Pete and this gave Pat two Champions, Ch. Irish Ch. Leaburn Bracken and Ch. Irish Ch. Lismoyle Bonnet. Staying with similar bloodlines, Beaula was later put to Rossgay Remedy, very closely line-bred to Ch. Korwin Monitor, the sire of Hannah and Helene. This combination proved even

Ch. & Irish Ch. Leaburn Bracken was bred by Pat Huey from her first Champion, Ch. & Irish Ch. Broharrons Repeat and Norcis Beaula. Photo: Diane Pearce.

more successful, resulting in Ch. Irish Ch. Lismoyle Chorus, who was a Group winner in Ireland and also won the title of Northern Ireland Hound of the Year in 1992, Irish Ch. Lismoyle Caliban, and Linda Hawley's Ch. Lismoyle Circe of Bennae. Bonnet had a litter to Ch. Bondlea Poet and from this Pat is currently campaigning Irish Ch. Lismoyle Dexter and his sister Debutante. The latest Lismoyle litter was sired by Rossgay Rambler, reinforcing the lines which Pat used in her foundation breeding.

LOWYCK
Although Pat and Colin Lomax's Lowyck affix is often assumed to have first appeared with the arrival of Bayard Syndicat of Lowyck, they had in fact kept Beagles since the late sixties and started off with a daughter of Ch. Appeline Cannon. They mated her to Pinewood Caddy and kept Lowyck Blackberry Girl who, to Ch. Southcourt Wembury Merryboy, produced Lowyck Challenger who won his way into the Stud Book. Bringing up a young family and the demands of starting a business

meant that the Lomaxes took a back seat for some years, but they later bought Bayard Ruth of Lowyck, a Zachariah daughter, from Jill Peak and also Bayard Syndicat of Lowyck, again by Zachariah but out of Tragband Cat on a Hot Tin Roof. Syndicat had a marvellous career, winning a string of CCs, Best of Breed at Crufts under Veronica Bradley, and also Best in Show all breeds at Windsor one year. Ruth was mated back to her grandsire, the imported Ch. and Am. Ch. Pin Oaks Dynasty of Appeline, and this produced the CC winning Lowyck Honeysuckle. Syndicat recently had a litter to Ch. Dialynne Tolliver of Tragband, an interesting combination in that they are out of litter sisters, which produced the 'Pup of the Year' qualifier, Lowyck Kissin Cousin.

MILLMAR
Another of the highly successful small Scottish Beagle kennels is owned by Isobel Miller who has owned the breed since 1963. Using Ch. Easthazel Miniman on the home-bred Millbar Joyful Miss, Isobel bred her first CC and BOB winner, a tan and white male called Millmar Mellow

Isobel Miller's home-bred Ch. Millmar Brevity, daughter of Korwin Butler and Millmar Barley Sugar, and dam of Ch. Millmar Beeswax. Photo: Diane Pearce.

Russet. However, the kennel's breeding programme really took off with the purchase of Mardabevian Bangle, a daughter of Ch. Dialynne Gamble and Pinewood Charlotte. Bangle to Ch. Kernebridge Young Jolyon produced Millmar Barley Sugar, and when she in turn was mated to Korwin Butler, two tricolour Champions emerged – Ch. Millmar Brevity, campaigned by her breeder, and Australian Ch. Millmar Barrister of Korwin who was sent to Australia by Christine Watson. In 1986 Mistylaw Chuckle joined the kennel, a son of two Mistylaw Champions, Willy Nilly and Homespun. Chuckle won 7 CCs and has sired three Champions to date, including Ch. Millmar Beeswax (whose dam is Ch. Brevity). Both Chuckle, in 1989, and his daughter Beeswax, in 1993, had the honour of winning Best in Show at the Beagle Club's Championship show.

MISTYLAW

Betty Lawson-Whyte's kennel has long been associated with Boxers, and more recently with English Setters and Siberian Huskies, but it is for Beagles that it is best known. The Mistylaw affix was first registered in the early 1950s when the kennel was entirely committed to Boxers. Having been attracted to the breed, in conjunction with a fellow Beagle enthusiast, Meg Hunter, Betty took out the Linister affix, and these two ladies founded their Beagle kennels with Barvae Faithful, Rossut Bluetit and Linister Polly Wolly Doodle, who had Wendover and Barvae lines behind her. A busy boarding kennel prevented Betty from the serious campaigning of a show team in those days, but even so the unusually coloured Bluetit, a blue, tan and white, won a CC and Reserve CC. At that time, all the Linister Beagles had experience of hunting hare. Subsequently the Beagles were absorbed

into the Mistylaw kennel. Barvae Faithful was mated to Ch. Deaconfield Rampage to produce Linister Harvester, a hare-pied of some influence who was used to good effect by Christine Watson of the Korwins. Polly Wolly Doodle had been taken to Ch. Easthazel Miniman to produce Linister Mini Mum. She in turn was mated to Harvester to get Linister Damson. Damson was then mated to Int. Ch. Korwin Concorde, a direct descendant of Harvester, and this resulted in Ch. Mistylaw Homespun, Mistylaw Helter Skelter, and Mistylaw Henchman who went to Germany where he obtained a working certificate on hare, duck and roebuck. Homespun was a remarkable bitch of great quality, and such a sound mover. I vividly remember my – and many others' – surprise the day she won the CC and BIS under me at the 1990 Scottish Beagle Club's Championship show when she was more than ten years old, looking less than half her age.

Helter Skelter was mated back to her grandsire, Korwin Butler, which gave Betty Mistylaw Lydia. When it came to breeding from Lydia, Betty did not rush off to use the latest Champion, but decided on the little-known Zedell Luque, a son of Butler out of Korwin Ilyana of Mistylaw (Ch. Dialynne Gamble ex Ch. Dancer of Korwin). That close mating produced Ch. Mistylaw Party Piece and her brother Ch. Mistylaw Willy Nilly. Ch. Homespun had been outcrossed in the meantime to the American import, Ch. Am. Ch. Graadtres Hot Pursuit of Rossut. From this came the CC winning brothers, Mistylaw Atlas and Mistylaw Abbot of Keepersgate.

One of the most memorable shows for the owner of the Mistylaws must surely have been Crufts 1987 when Madge Openshaw judged. The Dog CC and BOB went to Hot Pursuit himself, but the

Mistylaws walked off with all the other major awards. Ch. Homespun won the Bitch CC, her son, Atlas (by Hot Pursuit), won the Reserve Dog CC, while Mistylaw Comfort of Korwin (Homespun's daughter by Ch. Mistylaw Willy Nilly, and sister to Ch. Mistylaw Chuckle of Millmar) won the Reserve Bitch CC! Ch. Willy Nilly has sired five Champions to date and was the top sire in the breed for 1990. So successful was his mating to Ch. Homespun that, not surprisingly, it was repeated. From this came Ch. Mistylaw Gentleman who won Best in Show at the 1990 Beagle Club's Centenary show. In fact, three Mistylaw males have won Best at the parent club's Championship event – Willy Nilly and his two sons, Chuckle and Gentleman.

NEDLAW
Patience and Patrick Walden's foundation bitch was Houndsmark Mulberry and all of their current winners trace back to Mulberry's children by Ch. Barterhound Hammerlyn. Two daughters, Nutcracker and Nutmeg, have produced consistent winners including Karen Hoggarth's Nedlaw Nutshell of Marshcourt who won a memorable first CC in her tenth year (by Pancrest Sirocco out of Nutmeg), and the consistent winning Nedlaw Night Jester (by Ch. Mistylaw Willy Nilly out of Nutcracker). However, the brother to the "Nut" sisters, Nedlaw Nightowl, was to become a sire of some repute when he was used by Maureen Dundas on her Leeshir Sunflower at Julemark back in 1985. A lemon and white male puppy from that litter, Julemark Hotspur by Nedlaw, was nine months old when he went to live with the Waldens, owned jointly by Patience and his breeder. He won his way through to 23 CCs, 16 of them with BOB. He was Best of Breed at Crufts in 1990 and 1991 under two senior lady specialists, Betty Lawson-

Whyte and Patricia Clayton. His most memorable win was Best in Show at Windsor in 1992 under Leonard Pagliero, but his co-owner assures me that, almost as exciting, was the win of Reserve in the Hound Group at Darlington when I was judging! I suppose this would be because Hotspur would not be what was generally presumed to be "my" type, but his balance, construction and movement were something impossible to ignore. Hotspur won two working certificates and has sired several Champions, including the multi-CC winning Ch. Raimex Kracker.

NEWLIN
The Newlin kennel was founded by Liz Calikes who was later joined in partnership by David Bradley, previously of Dufosee note. Liz began with two puppies, bought as pets, from George Cook's Eskaidee kennel, Eskaidee Snoopy and Eskaidee Peanut. These two were duly mated together to produce Newlin Nutmeg. She won well at Open shows and was then mated to Ch. Korwin Monitor, her great grandsire on both sides of the pedigree, to produce the seemingly ageless Ch. Newlin Prefect. Norcis Roxanne at Newlin, a daughter of Ch. Dufosee Radleigh of Tragband and Ch. Norcis Hannah, was then bought in as a mate for Prefect to whom she produced Ch. Newlin Opium. A younger sister of Opium, Newlin Kersey, was sold to Hazel Deans who mated her back to her grandsire, Prefect, to produce Ch. Newlin Gempeni Truant. For Kathleen Cooper, Prefect also sired Ch. Caurniehill Fortune.

In the meantime David and Liz had got from me Tragband In Town Tonight at Newlin, a son of Ch. Dufosee Influence and Ch. Too Darn Hot for Tragband. He won Top Beagle Puppy in 1986, the same year that Opium was Top Beagle Bitch.

Liz Calikes and David Bradley's Ch. Newlin Gempeni Truant, a son of Ch. Newlin Prefect out of his own grand-daughter, Newlin Kersey.   *Photo: Diane*

When In Town Tonight, by now a Champion, was used on a Prefect daughter he produced Madika Talkback to Newlin, who won one CC and several Reserves. A lovely quality bitch, she was unlucky not to have made her title. Talkback in turn was mated to Truant, doubling up on Prefect, and that produced the latest star at Newlin, Ch. Upsadaisy, who won her first CC some months after producing an exciting litter to Ch. Dialynne Tolliver of Tragband. One of these puppies, Newlin Abbie from Tragband, is one of the first British-bred puppies for many years to be exported to the USA where she is being shown and bred from by Terri Giannetti and Ted Swedalla of the Beowulf kennel. Her litter sister, Newlin Aniseed, caused a sensation when she won the Bitch CC at the 1996 Scottish Beagle Club's Championship show, aged just 7 months!

NORCIS

The most successful Scottish Beagle kennel today has to be that of Eleanor and Frank Bothwell. They first owned a Beagle in 1967 and from her bred their first litter in 1968. The Bothwells were fortunate in buying a dog puppy, Korwin Monitor, from Christine Watson who became their first Champion. Monitor was by Korwin Tatler out of Rossut Ruffle and carried a lot of Tavernmews breeding. He was a stylish-moving tricolour who proved a popular stud dog. He sired seven Champions, and many breeders still aim to line-breed back to him with excellent results.

They then obtained Ch. Southcourt Hatchet, one of the famous brothers sired by Ch. Southcourt Wembury Merryboy. Next came a Korwin bitch, suitably bred for mating to Ch. Monitor, in the form of Korwin Rachel. She produced the famous Ch. Norcis Hannah, a group winner with 25 CCs to her credit, and her litter sister, Ch. Norcis Helene of Crestamere, made up by Wyn Mahoney. Hannah was, for Eleanor, the dog of a lifetime and I have a sneaking suspicion that it was no coincidence that some years later Ch. Norcis Foxy Lady was retired from the ring when she was just one CC away from Hannah's record. Korwin Eager had also been brought in to strengthen the kennel's bitch team, and she was mated to Ch. Hatchet, resulting in Norcis Glory. Glory was then mated to Ch. Monitor, to bring the lines closer, and Norcis Invader was a son of that mating. The Bothwells had also acquired Eskaidee Malady, a daughter of Monitor who had valuable Tavernmews lines. Malady to Invader produced Ch. Norcis Nelson, a Champion for Tommy and Sandra Smith.

Eleanor had taken back Crestamere Martha, a daughter of Ch. Helene and Ch. Crestamere Ruler. Mated back to Ch. Monitor (her grandsire), she produced Ch. Norcis Uist. Uist mated to Ch. Mistylaw Chuckle of Millmar became the dam of Ch. Norcis Moonweaver. Meanwhile Ch. Hannah had been mated to Ch. Dufosee

Eleanor Bothwell's Group winning Ch. Norcis Hannah won 25 CCs. She was sired by Eleanor's Ch. Korwin Monitor out of Korwin Rachel.   Photo: Diane Pearce.

Harris Tweed and from that came the good producing Norcis Taurus and his brother Teacher who went to the Newlin kennel. Taurus to Ch. Uist produced Norcis Etoile, the sire of Norcis The Hustler. In pursuit of an outcross Dialynne Sherbert, a daughter of Ch. Soloman of Dialynne, was bought in as a mate for Etoile. The result of this was the fabulous Ch. Norcis Foxy Lady who won 24 CCs – and I am proud to say I gave her the first! Taurus had also been used on Crestamere Martha to produce Pat Huey's foundation bitch, Norcis Beaula.

Eleanor had admired the Irish-based Ch. Irish Ch. Broharrons Repeat and used him on Crestamere Martha. That produced Ch. Norcis Ashes and Pat Huey's Norcis Angus. Running two bloodlines in tandem, Ashes was mated to Ch. Soloman of Dialynne and produced Ch. Norcis Ike. Ch. Ike mated to The Hustler gave Eleanor a bitch, Norcis Odile. She was mated to Deanery Brigand (a son of Norcis The Hooker at Deanery, Hustler's sister) and from this came another Champion, Norcis Poosie Nansie. Odile also had a litter to Ch. Sentinel of Dialynne, resulting in Ch. Norcis The

Fisher King. Ch. Moonweaver was used on a Korwin-bred daughter of Ch. Ike to breed Ch. Norcis Thrissle. Ch. Foxy Lady was mated to the imported Ch. and Am. Ch. Pin Oaks Dynasty of Appeline, and from this litter came Norcis Black Gold of Peppermoor, owned by Meg Dixon, to whom I gave a first CC and BOB in 1995. Norcis lines have played a major part in several other kennels' development, notably Deanery, Lismoyle, Newlin and Rossgay.

PERRYSTAR

Jerry Meek's kennel has always been small by design and was founded on Forrardon Linnet, a daughter of Ch. Appeline Forrardon Beeswing who was Reserve Best in Show at Crufts in 1965. Her first litter to Ch. Deaconfield Rampage produced seven puppies, three of which went to Sweden where they excelled in the hunting field. Perrystar Vesper won the prize for the best hunting Beagle in 1974 and also became a Finnish Champion. Linnet mated to Ch. Houndsmark Manful gave the Perrystars their first Champion, Vanity, who went on to win 7 CCs and 12 Reserve CCs. She also won a working certificate, as Jerry has always taken a keen interest in the hunting activities of the breed. Ch. Vanity was mated to Ch. Crestamere Monarch of Owlden and produced a bitch, Perrystar Vogue. Vogue was in turn taken to Ch. Houndsmark Mudlark and Perrystar Vixen was retained from the litter. Mated to Forrardon Digby, a son of Ch. Houndsmark Mulligan, Vixen produced the next Champion, Ch. Perrystar Vinca, who won 5 CCs and also a working certificate. Ch. Bondlea Poet was then used on Ch. Vinca, from which litter both Voyager and Visible won Reserve CCs. Perrystar Vivid won an amazing ten working certificates.

Jerry Meek's Ch. Perrystar Vanity, a daughter of her foundation bitch, Forrardon Linnet and Ch. Houndsmark Manful. This was the kennel's first Champion and won seven CCs as well as a Working Certificate.

Photo: Diane Pearce.

RAIMEX

Diana Brown's first foray into the dog world was with Boxers, her first being Gremlin Inklette, sister to Marian Fairbrother's legendary Ch. Gremlin Inkling. The first Boxer litter to carry the Raimex affix was born in the mid-fifties. Having decided to add a Beagle to the household, Diana bought two bitches from the Barvae kennel, Scribbler and Tokay, and it was the latter who was to serve as the foundation of the Raimex Beagles. A litter from Tokay by Barvae Spotlight produced a very feminine bitch with a gorgeous head and expression, Raimex Tiffin. When mated to Ch. Barvae Pilot, Tiffin produced the first Raimex Champion, Ch. Raimex Tally, who was born in 1965. Like many of the Raimex hounds, Tally proved to be a laster and won over ten years. He won 13 CCs and also topped the Hound Group at Three Counties in 1968. Tally's sister, Raimex Twinkle, produced the kennel's next Champion, Ch. Raimex Wager, by Southcourt Tarquin, the influential if untitled younger brother to Ch. Dialynne Ponder. Australian Ch. Raimex Widgeon was a great help to the breed down under, siring many leading hounds.

Wager's sister, Raimex Walnut, was mated to Ch. Raimex Tally, her dam's litter brother, bringing the Raimex breeding closer, and this produced Ch. Raimex Tinder. Tinder was then used on a daughter of Wager to breed Raimex Victoria, line-breeding still further. Victoria was taken to the major stud force of the time, Ch. Dialynne Gamble, and this gave the kennel what is strangely its only Champion bitch to date, Ch. Raimex Pheasant, who won 11 CCs and was a very beautiful type of bitch. This litter also contained South African Ch. Raimex Phoenix of Tanqueray and, at home, Raimex Psousi, who joined the Subarrah kennel. The next Champion, Ch. Raimex Magician, was also by Gamble but out of Raimex Merinda, a daughter of Tinder. Bringing her lines closer again, Diana then used Magician on Pheasant and produced another Champion male, Ch. Raimex Peacock. Previously Pheasant had been mated unsuccessfully to some of the great stud dogs of the time, so this litter brought great joy. Peacock's litter sister, Raimex Pipit, had been mated to Ch. Houndsmark Mudlark and this produced Ch. Raimex Muffler who later went to Australia where he did much good.

Back-tracking somewhat, Raimex Victoria (dam of Ch. Pheasant) had been mated to Ch. Barterhound Hammerlyn and had a daughter, Raimex Vita. She was then mated to Ch. Dialynne Gamble from which came a bitch, Raimex Clement. She in turn was outcrossed to the imported Ch. Am. Ch. Pin Oaks Dynasty of Appeline and bred a bitch, Raimex Cressida, who went to live with Val Hargrave for whom she founded the Valsacre kennel. Diana had a puppy

133

A delightful study of Diana Brown's Ch. Raimex Kracker, Best in Show at the 1992 Hound Show. He was by Ch. Julemark Hotspur of Nedlaw out of a bitch sired by Ch. Soloman of Dialynne out of the sister to Ch. Raimex Pheasant.   Photo: Diane Pearce.

back from Cressida by Ch. Raimex Peacock, Raimex Rosefinch. She was then taken to Ch. Mistylaw Willy Nilly and produced Ch. Raimex Ramsey. The most winning Raimex to date has been Ch. Raimex Kracker, winner of Best in Show at the 1992 Hound Show and a Group winner at general Championship shows. He was sired by Ch. Julemark Hotspur of Nedlaw out of Subarrah's Kismet of Raimex, a daughter of Ch. Soloman of Dialynne and Raimex Psousi, Pheasant's sister. Despite the use of various outcross

stud dogs, the Raimex hounds always seem to be of the same type, presumably due to some very close line-breeding in the early days which fixed a definite look of very sound, well balanced hounds.

RIVERSONG

Basil Waterton's original bitch was called Draul's Trifle, a combination of American and pack stock. In 1966 she was mated to Ch. Beston Bugler and thus began the Riversong kennel. From the start Basil decided he wanted to develop his own line and the Riversongs have succeeded in establishing a type. Sticking to the lines he admired, he has bred four Champions and made up another. Ch. Riversong Rhapsody won 7 CCs. Her first four were won at breed club shows at each of which she was also Best in Show, and they were in England, Wales, Scotland and Ireland, so she can claim to be a truly British Champion! She was by Ch. Kernebridge Trooper out of Riversong Pastime who traced back to Basil's original stock. Mated to Lanesend Raimex Talmer, Rhapsody produced the second Champion, Riversong Wishful. In 1984 she won Best Puppy in Show at the Border Counties Hound Club Championship show.

Riversong Serendipity, sister to Ch. Rhapsody, was mated to the essentially Dufosee-bred Ivelsyde Fugue and this produced Ch. Riversong Prelude, sire of Ch. Cadellin Phantom. Prelude was an excellent type dog, compact and solid, but at fifteen and a half inches he was often referred to as "Basil's little dog"! At the time he was up against some big winners, in more ways than one. Riversong Thimble was yet another bitch from the Trooper/Pastime mating and when she was mated to Ch. Soloman of Dialynne, Basil got Ch. Riversong Rehoboam. The other Riversong Champion was Ch. Dialynne

Basil Waterton's first Champion, Ch. Riversong Rhapsody, was a truly 'British Champion, winning the first four of her seven CCs at shows in England, Wales, Scotland and Ireland!   Photo: Diane Pearce.

Nymph of Riversong, one of the famous Soloman/Get Going children.

ROSSGAY

Brenda Haslam started her kennel in 1969 with a pet bitch from June Middleton's Gaytails. Brenda decided her puppy needed company so bought a ten months old bitch of Tavernmews breeding. Neither of these were deemed a suitable foundation for breeding, so Brenda then bought Grattondown Lady from Don Lester, a daughter of Ch. Southcourt Wembury Merryboy. Lady was first mated to Pinewood Caddy and from this came South African Ch. Rossgay Random of Beagay. Her next litter to Ch. Dialynne Eldon produced Rossgay Rival, a sound tan and white bitch who, Brenda admits, was "big enough". For her third litter Lady was put to Ch. Korwin Monitor. In this litter was Rossgay Rachel who became a good producer for the Dalzells' Torrabarn kennel while Brenda kept the male, Rossgay Rannoc. A fourth litter from Lady was by Pancrest Sirocco, resulting in the lovely-size tricolour, Rossgay Rythem.

Rival mated to Ch. Dufosee Harris Tweed produced the Reserve CC winning Rossgay Roulade. Roulade mated to Rannoc bred Rossgay Ragtrade who was mated to Norcis Lars to get Rossgay Ryderman, the winner of several Reserve CCs. Rythem was put to a son of Rossgay Rachel which resulted in Rossgay Rumba, a lovely bitch who died tragically early, but she did have one litter to Pancrest Sirocco

Jim and Julie Woodcock's Ch. Rossgay Roddie was bred by Brenda Haslam from two home-bred Rossgays. Not only did this dog win Best in Show at the Beagle Club Championship Show, he also won the Viscount Chelmsford Memorial Champion Stakes for Dog Hounds at the 1992 Hound Show. Photo: Edward T. Jones.

which contained the CC winning Rossgay Remedy. Rythem also had a litter by Ch. Deanery The Dickler which produced Rossgay Rymer, winner of several Reserve CCs. Rythem to Ch. Barterhound Hammerlyn produced Rossgay Rustler. Roulade to Rustler produced Brenda's first Champion, Ch. Rossgay Roddie, though he was actually campaigned by Julie and Jim Woodcock for whom he won several CCs and was Best in Show at the Beagle Club Championship show. He also won the Viscount Chelmsford Memorial Stakes for dog hounds at the 1992 Hound Show. Roddie's brother, Rossgay Rummage was bred to Deanery Dawn Run of Rossgay to produce Rossgay Ranak. Ranak sired Ch. Sabinhay Outlaw for David Nicholson and when Outlaw was used on Rossgay Ragtrade, the CC winning Rossgay Rallywood was the result. Deanery Dawn Run of Rossgay also had a litter to Rossgay Remedy to produce Rossgay Riff Raff. She won Reserve CCs like so many of Brenda's hounds, but when mated to Ch. Rossgay Roddie, she produced the kennel's latest star, Ch. Rossgay Rambler. Brenda claims to use Ch. Korwin Monitor as the keystone of her breeding, and the Rossgay hounds are well known for their construction and soundness.

ROSSUT

The Rossut story spans more than thirty years and the Sutton family's involvement with the breed, and indeed the world of pedigree dogs at large, is vast. The late Group Captain "Beefy" Sutton and his wife Catherine founded the kennel back in the late fifties and today the kennel is continued by their daughter Patricia. Catherine Sutton had previously been involved with Boxers (like several other notable Beagle breeders) and ran a large boarding kennel when she decided to go in

A key stud dog in the early days of the Rossut kennel was Rossut Joker who sired the first three Champion males made up by the Suttons.   Photo: Sally Anne Thompson.

for Beagles. She quickly established a broad base of breeding bitches from a variety of backgrounds, some pack-bred, some carrying strong Appeline lines and some being the progeny of early American imports such as Showman and the Rozavel dogs.

The kennel's first Champion, Rossut Treetops Hasty Footsteps, came from the eminent all-rounder judge Judy de Casembroot whose Treetops kennel was one of the leading lights in the Cocker world. Some of the early Rossut dogs were bred from dogs listed as "unregistered" in the Kennel Club's Stud Book. Such a male was the sire of a bitch called Veronese who was mated to her half-brother Holbein (sired by United Pack Bellman) to produce Rossut Wistful. She was mated to Rozavel Texas Star and from this outcross came Rossut Joker, one of the key males in the early days of Rossut. Joker sired the first three Champion males for the kennel, Ch. Rossut Vagabond, Ch. Rossut Triumphant and Ch. Rossut Juggler. Meanwhile Ch. Rossut Deaconfield Ravish was made up, bred by Dolly Macro.

Treetops Envy of Stubblesdown, sister to Wyn Mahoney's founding Echo, and owned by Lady Moynihan, had been mated to Rossut Plunder, a son of Ch. Barvae Paigan and Joker's sister, Joyful. From this mating came Ch. Rossut Colinbar Phantom, a significant bitch in the kennel's development. Ch. Vagabond had been used on a Stormerbanks/Letton-bred bitch and sired Ch. Rossut Nutmeg, a very classy bitch of the time. A repeat mating of Ch. Rossut Vagabond resulted in Ch. Rossut Gaiety, another prolific winner, and also her brother Gaffer who was to prove a remarkable stud dog. The kennel won well with Ch. Rossut Redgate Trueman, bred by the young James Gordon Hall, enjoying a great run in the early seventies.

Three Champions followed – all by Gaffer. Ch. Rossut Daffodil was out of Dialynne Debbie, a daughter of Rossut Joker, while Ch. Rossut Bobbin and Ch. Rossut Foreman were both out of Ch. Rossut Colinbar Phantom. An early breeding of Phantom and Gaffer had produced Paragon and Pegasus, Paragon being owned by Wyn Mahoney. Ch. Rossut Fantom (a double grand-daughter of Ch. Rossut Colinbar Phantom) went to the Dufosee kennel where she proved a marvellous producer. Rossut Chestnut was by Ch. Fantom's brother, Rossut Foremost, out of Ch. Daffodil, thus a Gaffer grandson to a Gaffer grand-daughter. He proved a good sire and produced Ch. Rossut Peanut when mated to Wembury Morag of Rossut, a Foreman daughter. Peanut enjoyed a great run in the early eighties.

By this time, the Suttons senior were doing a great amount of judging, both being established all-rounders, and the kennel had now passed into the sole ownership of their daughter. However, Patricia's equine commitments made it difficult for her to attend many shows, so

Patricia Sutton handling Ch. Rossut Foreman who, for some time, held the breed record for CCs. Foreman later became a sire of note. *Photo: Diane Pearce.*

the Rossut hounds were frequently handled in the show ring by Geoff Corish, a professional handler. Ch. Oudenarde Gaffer of Rossut was made up by the kennel, being a Gamble son, while it was Gaffer who sired Ch. Dialynne Blueboy. There was great excitement in the breed when Geoff Corish appeared at Border Union show in 1982 with the Rossuts' latest acquisition, the American dog, Am. Ch. Graadtres Hot Pursuit of Rossut. At his first show in England he went through to Best in Show All breeds under Percy Whitaker. A few years later, the same judge made his daughter, Ch. Too Darn Hot for Tragband, Best in Show at Blackpool. When Percy later judged the breed at Midland Counties, he ended up with Corkie and

Ada as his CC winners, giving Ada Best of Breed, and I recall him wondering whether, ever before, a breed judge had awarded the CCs to a dog and a bitch, both of whom they had previously made Best in Show all breeds.

There was no denying that "Corkie" was "different" but he had that stallion look in a compact frame, with great substance, yet very clean lines, and a wonderful rear. He also had tremendous ring presence and natural "style", coupled with a delightful temperament which can still be seen in his descendants today. I judged him at his next show and was delighted to give him the breed, resolving to use him as soon as possible. Corkie was a love-or-hate dog. That year he went to eight shows and won 7 Bests of Breed, and soon became a major threat in the Hound Group. The following year was Corkie's year. He attended twenty shows, winning 18 CCs and 15 BOBs. At one show he stood Third in Open Dog and at one took his only Reserve CC of the year, to "the other" American dog, the

Appletons' Am. Ch. Pin Oaks Dynasty of Appeline, who made his debut at the Welsh Beagle Club where Jack Holland made him Best in Show. Interestingly, at Corkie's last show of the year, he was beaten for Best of Breed by his daughter, still a puppy, Too Darn Hot. Corkie was an interestingly bred dog as he was by a son of Am. Ch. The Whims Buckeye out of a Buckeye grand-daughter. Those of us who did use him at stud had great results, but I feel he was very underrated as a sire and not taken advantage of by some breeders who could have benefited from what he had to offer. Still, through his progeny his line lives on.

I had given the Suttons a dog puppy from a repeat of the mating which had earlier produced Too Darn Hot and he became Ch. Tragband Too Hot to Handle by Rossut who was later sold to the Streatfields in South Africa. Handled by Jack Peden, "Pete" kept the breed in the spotlight there for several years. More recently Patricia Sutton has been able to get to more dog shows than she had in the past

Ch. Webline Katy, owned and bred by David and Mary Webster and Mickie George, was bred from Webline Countess by Ch. Deaconfield Rampage. Countess had earlier produced the first Webline Champion, Ch. Webline Holly.

Photo: Diane Pearce.

and we happily now see her regularly exhibiting. She made up Ch. Rossut Ensign, a son of Ch. Peanut out of Dufosee Jewel of Rossut, a Corkie daughter out of Ch. Dufosee Garbo, and later Ch. Rossut Posy, the last Champion sired by Corkie out of a daughter of Ch. Oudenarde Gaffer of Rossut.

WEBLINE
Although David is the half of the Webster marriage we associate more with the breed, it was in fact his wife Mary who bred their first litter of Beagles in 1959. This was from Letton Glitter. David became a partner in the Webline affix when he retired from the RAF in 1964, and later "Mickie" George, an English Springer breeder with an interest in Beagles, joined them. Glitter to Barvae Benroe Wrinkles produced Webline Actor. Their Barvae Dainty was also mated to Wrinkles to produce Webline Bellmaid. Actor and Bellmaid were then mated together to produce Webline Countess, and when she was taken to Stanhurst Placid, the result was the first CC winner for the kennel, Webline Holly, who subsequently became their first Champion. Countess also produced the next

Champion, Ch. Webline Katy, but this time to Ch. Deaconfield Rampage. From the Priestleys came Ch. Pinewood Crib of Webline, a class-bred son of Ch. Southcourt Wembury Merryboy and Ch. Pinewood Chimer. To Ch. Webline Katy he sired Webline Quilley who was exported to the Eberhardts for whom she became an International Champion. Crib was also used on Ch. Webline Holly, resulting in Webline Rainbow. She was mated to Ch. Beacott Buckthorn to produce Webline Viscount, a very handsome dog who won a CC. The breeding line suffered a dreadful setback when two hounds drowned in a tragic accident, but Dialynne Princess was bought in and became a Champion in 1987. Her daughter, Webline Princess Beauty, subsequently became a CC winner. Currently Dialynne Sadie rules the roost at Webline, winning 6 Reserve CCs but the next step up has eluded her.

There are many other Beagle breeders and exhibitors, whose mention space prevents, but who are steadily making a name for themselves by breeding quality hounds and, constantly, the breed is attracting new devotees.

12 BEAGLES AROUND THE WORLD

AUSTRALIA

There are six Beagle clubs throughout Australia, with most clubs holding two Championship shows each year. Entries range from around 50 in Perth to over 200 at the larger Sydney and Melbourne clubs' events. There is also a National Beagle Council which, among other duties, nominates clubs to host National Shows. Such shows are held at intervals of several years and are, not surprisingly, regarded as the most prestigious of all to win. The Council is also in a position to issue "Awards of Merit" to Beagles which it regards as having made an outstanding contribution to the breed, which can be based on achievements in the show ring, as a producer, or even as an obedience competitor.

INFLUENTIAL IMPORTS

As far as breeding is concerned, British bloodlines have been the main influence on Australian Beagles, but some of the British imports have themselves had a strong American background, and there has also been some stock imported directly from the United States. The 1960s saw the arrival of Aust. Ch. Lees Pennon and, later, Aust.

The winner of the first Australian Beagle national Show, held in 1985 and judged by Sylvia Tutchener, was Truda Mawby's Aust. Ch. Clarion Choice. He went on to become one of the breed's great show dogs and subsequently received the Australian Breed Council's Award of Merit.

Photo courtesy: Steven Seymour.

Ch. Lees Banjo, from Pat Curties' Lees kennel in England, these two Beagles going to the Scotts in Sydney. Pennon, who was sired by Am. Ch. Renoca's Best Showman, won the very first Beagle Club show in Australia and went on to become a prolific sire. Among his progeny was Aust. Ch. Martinique Just Joe who, to this day, holds the breed record for the most all breeds Best in Show awards. Other successful Beagle kennels of this era included Balihai, Belview, Bluebell, Clarion, Nangunyah, Timbillee and Torbay.

Over the next few years British imports arrived from the Dialynne, Rossut, Rozavel, Wendover and Velmere kennels. Early Rozavel stock was particularly influential with Aust. Ch. Rozavel Kiwi, Carol and Happily all winning CCs at breed club shows. It was Australia's gain when the late Thelma Gray decided to make Adelaide her final place of retirement, and she took with her to Australia several Beagles, including Ch. Rozavel Giftbox, Onform Kooky of Rozavel and Am. Ch. J'Dons Salt of the Earth, whom she had imported into England.

The seventies saw the arrival of several influential dogs, notably Aust. NZ Ch. Annasline Fanfare and Aust. NZ Ch. Annasline Highlight. Both were originally imported from Judith Ireland in England to New Zealand by Mollie Grocott of the Moerangi kennel, who later sent them both to the Scotts. These two half-brothers (they were both by the American import, Annasline Page Mill Playboy) were to become exceptional producers, and Fanfare also had a truly outstanding show career. The combination of Fanfare and Pennon daughters was particularly successful. and this formula helped establish several kennels, presumably in part due to the fact that Fanfare was a grandson of Showman, Pennon's sire. Both Aust. Ch. Lees Pennon and Aust. Ch. Annasline Fanfare were awarded the Breed Council's Award of Merit. Most memorable of Fanfare's progeny was his son, Aust. Ch. Manahound Matchpoint who, like his sire before him, was a top class show dog and a prepotent stud. There are few who would dispute that the Fanfare/Matchpoint era was a major

contributing factor in establishing the Beagle as a breed which could win top honours in the all-breed ring. Matchpoint also received the Breed Council's Award of Merit.

Two of the breed's top bitches are a Matchpoint daughter, Aust. Ch. Manabay Milady's Ace, and a Matchpoint grand-daughter, Aust. Ch. Bayhound So Sassy. Both received Awards of Merit. His half-brother, Highlight, was nothing like as popular as Fanfare, yet he still produced several top winners, including Aust. Ch. Flemando Hightime, who won Best in Show at a Sydney Spring Fair Show from an entry of over 4,000 entries and also received an Award of Merit. Highlight also sired Aust. Ch. Kindilan Hi Tristan, a multiple Best in Show winner.

Other dogs of influence at the time were Aust. Ch. Dufosee Kinsman (litter brother to the bitches Kismet and Katrina), Aust. Ch. Barterhound Carol, Am. Ch. Page Mill Oscar, Aust. Ch. Annasline Go Jo and Aust. Ch. Page Mill Lady Luck. Australia was also extremely fortunate to see the arrival of Aust. Ch. Beacott Buckwheat, full brother to the legendary Buckthorn. This dog was greatly overlooked by many judges because of his tan and white colouring, but fortunately his qualities were appreciated by clever breeders, and many kennels made good use of his breeding, including Bonnymead, Braylodge, Filnor, Nangunyah and Semeru. Among Buckwheat's most notable grandchildren would be Aust. Ch. Nangunyah Yeodler who was a consistent winner at Specialty level, and Aust. Ch. Filnor Humphrey, also a Specialty winner.

DEVELOPMENTS SINCE THE EIGHTIES
The eighties saw a big increase in imports from the UK with kennels such as Buttermere, Chalmain, Crestamere,

Dialynne, Newlin, Perrystar, Raimex, Tragband, Webline and Velmere sending stock, while American bloodlines came in from the Chardon, Crisette's, Page Mill and Pin Oaks kennels. Aust. Ch. Raimex Widgeon produced several top winners. His son, Aust. Ch. Kinbrace Maestro, won the Group at a Sydney Royal and had many other major wins, while Aust. Ch. Casalbeau Clairvaux, a Widgeon daughter, won Best in Show under both Marion Spavin and Diana Brown when they judged breed shows "down under". Clairvaux was also an All breeds Best in Show winner who received an Award of Merit.

In the late eighties I sent out to Steven Seymour a young dog called Tragband Summer and Smoke, from Ch. Too Darn Hot for Tragband and Ch. Dialynne Nimrod of Ramlacim. After a successful career in the ring, Summer and Smoke went on to produce more than 20 Champions in Australia and New Zealand. Many of the earlier imports traced back to Ch. Dialynne Gamble, and this kind of breeding seemed to really click with him. Many of the breed's top bitches were bred to him and this resulted in no less than five different CC winners at club shows and several all breeds Best in Show winners. Most notable among his children was Aust. Ch. Belvaux Hot Summer Night, who was a multiple Best in Show winner and won the hound Group at Melbourne Royal from an entry of more than 6,000 dogs.

During the nineties Truda Mawby (owner of the Clarion kennel and as famous for her green hats as her dogs) imported Ch. Bayard Rustle from Jill Peak in England. Rustle did some useful winning and produced several Champions. More recently Clarion imported Aust. Ch. Daragoj Starsong from Eeva Resko's kennel in Finland. She won the National Specialty in 1995. There has also been an influx of

Aust Ch. Tragband Summer and Smoke was a son of Ch. Too Darn Hot for Tragband and Ch. Dialynne Nimrod of Ramlacim, and was sent out to Steven Seymour when he was six months of age. He was a good winner but excelled as a sire, producing more than 20 Champions in Australia and New Zealand.
Photo: Cabal.

American blood with the return of Lesley Hiltz (née Funnel) who married and lived in the USA for several years. Lesley's husband, David Hiltz, bred the influential Am. Ch. Starbucks Hang 'em High, whose son, Aust. Ch. Starbucks Torbay Colours, is already a Group winner in Australia and proving to be a popular stud dog. Colours' dam, Aust. Ch. Torbay Hot 'n' Spicy, has been imported into Australia by Jan Jeffs of the long established Mingus kennel.

THE NATIONAL BEAGLE SHOWS
The first Australian National Beagle Show was held in 1985 and Sydney hosted the event. Britain's own Sylvia Tutchener drew a marvellous entry of 203 individual dogs and the top award went to Truda Mawby's Junior male, Aust. Ch. Clarion Choice. This young hound went on to be one of the breed's great show dogs and in due

Aust. Ch. Belvaux Hot Summer Night, a multiple Best in Show winner who also won the Hound Show at Australia's largest show, the Melbourne Royal. Owned and bred by Troy Johnson.   *Photo: Cabal.*

course received the Breed Council's Award of Merit. The second National Show was held in Melbourne in 1992 with Eleanor Bothwell, another British breeder, judging. This time there was an entry of 224 dogs and Eleanor's Best in Show winner was again a Junior dog, Aust. NZ Ch. Burnsdale Anything Goes, bred by Ruth Mason in New Zealand and owned at the time by Steven Seymour. Also a Specialty Best in Show winner in New Zealand and a Group winner in both countries, he went on to produce several Best in Show winners in Australia. His young son, Aust. Ch. Hilldamar The Way To Go, won Best in Show at the 1995 New South Wales Specialty under Catharina Linde-Forsberg of Sweden. She has since succeeded in buying the dog, who is now already winning well in Sweden. He too was an All breeds Best in Show winner. Anything Goes seems to have clicked particularly well with daughters of Summer and Smoke, and it is my feeling that this combination will produce some of the best stuff in

Australasia over the next few years.

The third National was hosted by the South Australian Club and held in Adelaide in September 1995. Danish breeder Jesper Pedersen judged and found his Best in Show in the aforementioned Aust. Ch. Daragoj Starsong. She was Best in Show at her first outing in Australia and would seem to be destined for great things. Australia very much looks forward to the year 2000 when Sydney will host the fourth National Show.

NEW ZEALAND

When you think that New Zealand is a very small country with a population of a mere three-and-a-half million, it is surprising that the overall quality of their Beagles is so high. While New Zealand may not have the numbers of other countries, I – and many other visiting specialist judges – have been of the opinion that, overall, the New Zealand Beagles can take on the best in the world. To cater for the country's scattered population, over the years three Beagle Clubs have been founded. The New Zealand Beagle Club is based in Wellington (North), the Auckland Beagle Club obviously in Auckland (also North), while the recently formed South Island Beagle Club is based in Christchurch (South). All three clubs hold fun days, walks and shows.

Beagles in New Zealand are quite active participants in Agility and have further attained top gradings in Obedience. Hunting is very much alive and well, with packs attached to the New Zealand Beagle Club and the South Island Beagle Club. There are, additionally, two privately owned packs, the Hawera Pack of the Steele family, and the Walton Pack, owned by John Storey. Early in 1995 the New Zealand Government's Ministry of Agriculture and Fisheries recommenced the Quarantine Detector Scheme, which employed Beagles to sniff out foodstuffs which were being illegally imported at the international airports. This is a follow-on from a very successful scheme in Australia.

The recent history of the breed in New Zealand really begins when Mollie Grocott imported Annasline Fanfare from Judith Ireland. I have mentioned Fanfare earlier, in the Australian section, as he was later owned by the Scotts in Sydney. Fanfare's influence on the breed in New Zealand was as extensive as it was to be later in Australia. In 1965 Bryan Giles and Lloyd Ellis bought their first Beagle from Mollie Grocott, their Leeavon kennel being instrumental in establishing the breed in New Zealand. They imported several dogs, some of whose influence can still clearly be seen today. Firstly NZ Ch. Royalbrae Rossut Spirit was imported from the UK and then, in 1968, Rozavel Battle Cry and Rossut Howboro Hasty arrived, also from the UK and in whelp to Ch. Rossut Triumphant. Bryan and Lloyd campaigned Ch. NZ Ch. Solomist of Dialynne and Aust. NZ Ch. Scottholme Willem Two. Hasty was mated to NZ Ch. Annasline Fanfare and produced NZ Ch. Leeavon Superstar and NZ Ch. Leeavon Starglow. The home-bred NZ Ch. Leeavon Huntsman was an all breeds Best in Show winner.

ONE OF THE GREATEST

In 1974 Elizabeth (Polly) Middleton (now Mrs Phil Kersey) bred her first litter of Beagles. She was lucky enough to obtain NZ Ch. Rossut Howboro Hasty from the Leeavon kennel, who was duly mated to NZ Ch. Annasline Fanfare (for the second time) to produce what is commonly known as the "How" litter. A bitch from this litter, NZ Ch. Merrybrook How Hasty, is widely regarded as one of the greatest Beagles New Zealand has ever produced, not only

NZ Ch. Merrybrook How Hasty was bred by Polly Middleton Kersey from NZ Ch. Rossut Howboro Hasty and NZ Ch. Annasline Fanfare, both imported from the UK. She is still widely regarded as one of the greatest Beagles ever produced in New Zealand.
Photo courtesy: Noelene Hughes.

by local breeders, but also by visiting specialist judges. What is more, she bred on superbly and, when mated to the follow-up Annasline import, NZ Ch. Annasline Highlight, she produced the country's most prolific winner to date, NZ Grand Ch. Merrybrook Jamie Luck. He won Best in Show all breeds four times, in addition to an incredible 110 CCs. Lucky was owned by John and Sandra Green, of whom more later. The Merrybrook kennel of Polly Middleton has bred some 32 Champions and of late has incorporated Clarion lines from Truda Mawby's Australian kennel, as well as incorporating an Australian line which comes down from Aust. Ch. Tragband Summer and Smoke. Merrybrook has also exported stock to many countries around the world, including Aust. NZ Ch. Merrybrook Buddy Hal to Peter Nordstrom in Australia.

John and Sandra Green's NZ Grand Ch. Merrybrook Jamie Luck won an incredible 110 CCs as well as four All Breed Best in Show awards. Bred by Polly Middleton Kersey he was produced entirely from British exports, his dam being Hasty (by an Annasline dog out of a Rossut bitch) and his sire NZ Ch. Annasline Highlight.

Photo courtesy: Noelene Hughes.

KEY STUD DOGS

In 1974 Joyce and Noel Hodgson established their Penavon kennel. Over the past twenty years they have consistently produced winners and, perhaps more importantly, key stud dogs which have bred on for other kennels. The breeding programme was originally based on a blending of lines which incorporated Annasline Fanfare, Annasline Highlight and Solomist of Dialynne. Several Merrybrook bitches were purchased as well as a son of Ch. Southcourt Wembury Merryboy, who was bred by Dawn Graham and Helen Salt from their Deanery Donna, imported in whelp. The resulting Butterscotch of Gra-Sal was the breed's first tan-and-white Champion. The combination of these lines eventually produced NZ Ch. Sandstorm of Penavon, who was recognised by specialists in the show ring, and bred on for several other significant Auckland kennels.

Penavon has also been involved in importing a number of other Beagles, most notably Aust. NZ Ch. Dufosee Going to Penavon, a male from one of the most significant litters ever bred.

Recently Penavon, now based in Auckland and owned by daughter Noelene Hughes and her husband Geoff, have incorporated lines from Sue Bownds' Nangunyah kennel in Australia. A daughter of Aust. NZ Ch. Nangunyah Jazzsinger and NZ Gr. Ch. Merrybrook Jamie Luck, Aust. NZ Ch. Penavon JL's Jazz, won two Specialty CCs in Australia as well as numerous Group and in-show awards, and has progeny currently winning in Australia. The imported NZ Ch. Nangunyah Penavon Seeker is an All breeds Best in Show winner, also with winning progeny.

STICKING MY NECK OUT

Patty Glenie's Buckhound kennel, established in the early 1980s, began with a daughter of NZ Ch. Penavon Bonzo Boy (the sire of Sandstorm) and NZ Ch. Merrybrook High Hopes. She was mated to Penavon Sandbagger (Aust. NZ Ch. Dufosee Going to Penavon ex NZ Ch. Semeru Sunset) to produce the first two Buckhound Champions, NZ Ch. Joyful and NZ Ch. Lord Samson of Buckhound. Later Patty purchased a Sandstorm son, NZ Ch. Littlejohn of Penavon (ex NZ Ch. Gra-Lynne Corrina). When Littlejohn was bred to Joyful, NZ Ch. Kayla of Buckhound was produced. Owned by Jill Southard, she was the first of two all breeds Best in Show winners to be bred at Buckhound. The second was a Littlejohn son out of NZ Ch. Burnsdale Wild Affair, NZ Ch. Sir Poldarc of Buckhound.

In a later partnership with Lyn Dixon as Buckvael kennels, Littlejohn was mated to a Sandstorm daughter, NZ Ch. Paragon of Tamaleigh (bred by Pat and Dave Herd) to

When I judged the Auckland Beagle Club's 1992 Specialty, I made a four-and-a-half month-old puppy Best male. He grew up to become NZ Ch. Buckvael Solomon Grundy, and was a son of Mystro's T Thumb. He is owned by Noelene and Geoff Hughes and is pictured on the day he became my youngest ever winner.

NZ Ch. Burnsdale P for Prudence is pictured winning at 11 months of age. Sired by Aust. Ch. Tragband Summer and Smoke out of NZ Ch. Burnsdale Eclipse, Prudence is typical of the outstanding type and quality produced by Ruth Mason's small but highly successful kennel in New Zealand's North Island.

Photo courtesy: Ruth Mason.

produce NZ Ch. Buckvael Lady Genna, dam of NZ Ch. Buckvael Bossanova (by Aust. NZ Ch. Torbay Final Formula) and NZ Ch. Buckvael Solomon Grundy (by NZ Ch. Penavon Mystro's T Thumb). I particularly recall Solomon Grundy – I have something of a name for frequently sticking my neck out and giving rather young dogs top honours. When judging in Auckland in 1992, I really excelled myself with Solomon Grundy, as I made him Best Dog at the Beagle Specialty when he was just four-and-a-half-months old! Puppies of that age can be shown in New Zealand but they are not eligible for the CC. I was happy to discover later that he had gone on to make quite a reputation for himself.

When Aust. NZ Ch. Burnsdale Anything Goes won the Australian National in 1992, beating an entry of 240 Beagles, it was really a cause for celebration in New Zealand, as many of the long-established New Zealand Beagle affixes were there in

his pedigree. His breeder, Ruth Mason, who is based in Pokeno in the North Island, started off with a bitch from Jackie Cudby's Huntingdale kennel, NZ Ch. Huntingdale Primrose (Ch. Dialynne Blueboy ex NZ Ch. Huntingdale Honey's Hit), who was mated to NZ Ch. Sandstorm of Penavon to produce NZ Ch. Burnsdale Eclipse, the winner of several Specialty CCs under overseas judges. She was subsequently mated to Aust. Ch. Torbay Too Hot to Handle to produce NZ Ch. Burnsdale Hot Shot and NZ Ch. Burnsdale Wild Affair. Hot Shot was mated to a second Blueboy daughter, Semeru Silhouette, to produce Aust. NZ Ch. Burnsdale Anything Goes.

A GREAT LOSS TO THE BREED IN BRITAIN

Down in Wellington at the base of the North Island will be found one of the country's longest established kennels still

currently breeding. Jackie and Michael Cudby's contribution to Beagles has spanned almost a quarter of a century. Stalwarts of the New Zealand Beagle Club for the entire period, the Huntingdale kennel has bred many winners. Initially Jackie exhibited a Leeavon bitch and incorporated the Fanfare line through a daughter imported from Australia, NZ Ch. Stuartview Black Velvet. In latter years Huntingdale has become very involved in English bloodlines and imported several hounds, including Pancrest Southern Cross, Rossut Hot Mango, and two dogs to which I awarded CCs in the UK – Ch. NZ Ch. Dialynne Peppermint (who was exported in whelp to Ch. Dialynne Beau) and Ch. Aust. NZ Ch. Dialynne Guardsman of Bayard. They also have a close association with Ch. Dialynne Blueboy, imported to New Zealand by Ann and Arnold Caithness. I have said earlier in the book that I felt Blueboy was a great loss to the breed in Britain. Interestingly, much of the quality Australian stock now being bred through combining Summer and Smoke stock with Anything Goes represents quite intense line-breeding to Blueboy.

Dawn Graham is no longer breeding; however, for many years the Gra-lynne kennel produced some of the top winners in New Zealand. Early residents at Dawn's kennel included Beagles of Leeavon and Houndswood breeding. When Dawn combined with Helen Salt (Houndswood) to import Deanery Donna from the UK in whelp to Ch. Southcourt Wembury Merryboy, the Gra-Sal name was born, which dominated the New Zealand show scene countrywide for many years. NZ Ch. Grand Image of Gra-Sal, a dog retained from that breeding, produced NZ Ch. Gourmet of Gra-Lynne, who subsequently produced NZ Ch. Gideon of Gra-Lynne,

an all breeds Best in Show winner. Gideon sired NZ Ch. Harlequin of Gra-Lynne, who was Marion Spavin's Best in Show winner when she judged the Auckland Beagle Club's Championship show in 1985. Quin's dam, NZ Ch. Gra-Lynne Halloween (Aust. NZ Ch. Dufosee Going to Penavon ex NZ Ch. Torbay Tarella), was also a top winning bitch of her time.

Lynn and Andrew Ward's Sarangrave Kennels have been established for a number of years, but, following a move to Wellington from the Auckland area, they were lucky enough to obtain NZ Ch. Saucy-Kate of Gra-Lynne from Dawn Graham. Katie was mated to NZ Ch. Swimbridge Snowman, an all breeds Best in Show winner resident at Sarangrave, bred by Hilary Bott in Auckland. The litter produced NZ Grand Ch. Sarangrave Show Gunn, one of the country's top winning Beagles. He is the first home-bred Grand Champion in the breed, and to obtain the title he had to win 50 CCs and three Bests in Show at all breeds shows.

MULTIPLE ALL BREEDS BEST IN SHOW WINNER

John and Lorraine Perfect's Jedburgh kennel, based at the top of the South Island in Nelson, first became interested in Beagles in 1968. On a visit to the UK Lorraine bought the half-brother and sister, Rozavel Battle Cry and Rozavel Fanny. Both became Champions in New Zealand and Fanny was a multiple Best in Show winner. Together they produced NZ Ch. Jedburgh Fieldmaster, also an all breeds Best in Show winner. A second litter from Fanny, but this time by the imported NZ Ch. Rozavel Hugset Ragnor, produced NZ Ch. Jedburgh Harkaway. When mated to NZ Ch. Merrybrook How Handsome, Harkaway produced Aust. NZ Ch. Jedburgh Good Tracker, a multiple all breeds Best in Show winner with Specialty Bests also under his belt. Holding Thelma Gray's Rozavel lines in high regard, Jedburgh later imported a daughter of Aust. Ch. Rozavel Pluto from the Sligrachan kennel in Australia, NZ Ch. Sligrachan Stardust being one of only three Grand Champion Beagles in New Zealand, and to date the only bitch.

Gretaglen kennels, owned by Ken and Pat Cliffin, and based in Christchurch, have played a very important role in the development of the Christchurch Hunting Pack as well as winning in the show ring. NZ Ch. Gretaglen Urchin is a Specialty Best winner, gaining the award under the Barvae expert, Pat Clayton. Ken and Pat were also the driving force behind the recently formed South Island Beagle Club.

I have already mentioned Helen Salt's connection with friend Dawn Graham under the Gra-Sal kennel name. Helen's own kennel, Houndswood, was, however, successful in its own right, initially involving lines from Leeavon and Colin Dehn's Kotoku kennel (basically Fanfare lines). Helen owned Merrybrook How's That, but the most notable Houndswood winner was NZ Ch. Houndswood Highlight, sired by NZ Ch. Leeavon Superstar out of NZ Ch. Arlette of Kotoku. Also NZ Ch. Houndswood Dime a Dozen was a top winner for Pat and Lawrie Stephens in Auckland in the late 80s.

At the very bottom of the South Island a relatively new kennel is enjoying a very high degree of success, and has already had a great impact on the show scenes on both sides of the Tasman. John and Sandra Green were the owners of the previously mentioned NZ Grand Ch. Merrybrook Jamie Luck. They also have the distinction of having bred a litter containing two All breeds Best in Show winning brothers – NZ Ch. Jest Hit and Run being based in

New Zealand, and the other, Aust. Ch. Jest Smash and Grab, being campaigned by Truda Mawby from Clarion in Australia. They are sired by Merrybrook Mayday and are out of NZ Ch. Rallydon Greengables, the bitch who was my CC and Best in Show winner when I judged the 1992 Specialty for the Auckland Beagle Club. The Greens also campaigned NZ Ch. Merrybrook Final Forte to two All breeds Bests and several Specialty CCs. While New Zealand may not have the numbers, what it lacks in quantity it certainly makes up for with quality dogs and enthusiastic breeders. The overall type of Beagle being produced in New Zealand is, without a doubt, world-class, and long may that remain so.

SOUTH AFRICA

In 1895 the first Beagle was registered in South Africa, a bitch named Venus, by Ajax out of Flora, Registration Number 507 and owned by H.E. Wilmot. Further details are that Venus had a litter, by Ploughman, and a dog from that union, Roderick, was registered in 1896. In 1907 a Mr Hourgebie registered two dogs and a bitch from one litter and these were the first traceable registrations where more than one Beagle from the same litter was recorded. In the 1930s Lady Mary Grosvenor, of the Westminster affix, brought out from England a four-couple draft from the Cheshire pack, and later others from the Newcastle and District and Shropshire and Dee Valley Packs. These hounds were worked, being followed on horseback, and they hunted mainly jackal. Some of Lady Mary's subsequent litters were registered, but unfortunately further information is not available as to their descendants, since they were pack hounds and did not venture into the show ring. It is, of course, possible that some of these dogs were used at stud and the offspring may have been shown

The first Open Show for Beagles in South Africa, held in 1981. Three of the four major winners (Best in Show, Best Opposite Sex, and Best Opposite Sex Puppy) came from Oonagh Gore's Duxfordham kennel which has sent quality stock to several countries.

Photo courtesy: Ros Glaysher.

later, but verification is impossible. Records show that the first Beagles to have become Champions in South Africa were Mr Jorrocks' Juggins of Leisureleigh and Jupiter, both males, who were gazetted as such in November 1960.

In the 1950s there were several imports from the Barvae and Cannybuff kennels in England, and these did much for the breed, introducing established breeding lines which resulted in a noticeable upturn in quality and substance, the Barvae bitch line proving to be particularly dominant. In 1967 Ros Glaysher and her family arrived in South Africa from England, complete with their Beagle dog, Jason. Although purely a pet, bought to replace a much loved and recently departed Boxer, Jason had quite an impressive pedigree which contained several Rozavel dogs as well as hounds from the East Nene, Eton College and United Pack lines.

In the late sixties and early seventies the Johannesburg show scene was relatively small as far as Beagles were concerned, with John Ellis' Copperhills kennel, Maurice Orton's Chelldales and the van Smaalens' Darlyn kennel, which was also active in Welsh Corgis. John Ellis had imported from the Pinewood kennel dogs such as Pinewood Honeycomb and Pinewood Clippy, both of which had beautiful heads and the desired soft expression. Maurice Orton imported Rozavel Matches, a male who was subsequently taken over by Ros Glaysher, who then discovered that

coincidentally he had very similar breeding to her original Jason. The van Smaalens' stock was greatly influenced by Barvae lines and Ros Glaysher was fortunate in acquiring a bitch, Darlyn's Abigail of Towri. Abigail had been rehomed several times but, when she was outcrossed to a Rozavel dog, she produced several Champions for what was now the Tanqueray kennel. One of the resulting bitches, Tanqueray's Tanya, was the top winning bitch of her time, one of her first Certificates coming from the late L.C. James, of Wendover fame.

In Natal, Norman Roseveare with his Craigham kennel had imported several dogs from the Dialynne kennel, notably Dialynne Viceroy, Dialynne Norseman, Mardabevian Melody of Dialynne and Bartek Cracker of Dialynne. The Craighams did very well in the show ring and some quality litters resulted from their imported stock. Sadly, through domestic problems, the kennel was later disbanded. Mrs Anderson in Cape Town bred Boxers, Corgis and Beagles under the Towri affix, her Beagles being based mainly on Barvae lines which her friend Mrs Hockey had imported. Generally the Towri hounds had lovely heads, good bone and excellent hindquarters, although some of the bitches tended to be rather hefty.

INFLUENTIAL IMPORTS
1976 saw the arrival of Jack Peden in South Africa, a Scotsman complete with tartan

jacket who took his Beagle, Denorsi Dusty Rebel, right to the top when he won the prestigious Goldfields Dog of the Year competition in 1977. Rebel, who was campaigned throughout South Africa, was a real stallion hound and used his driving movement to perfection, fair steaming around the ring. The 1980s saw more Beagle imports from the Duxfordham, Crestamere and Raimex kennels, and later the British Champion, Tragband Too Hot to Handle by Rossut, was sold by the Suttons to John and Wendy Streatfield. In South Africa Pete hit the show scene with a bang, being handled by Jack Peden, who took him through to many Best in Show wins at all breeds level. His daughter, Malton Lady Luck of Belvoir, shared the same handler and she too enjoyed great success, as did the Pete son, Towri Beerburrum.

Raimex Phoenix at Tanqueray, imported by Ros Glaysher, was most successful both in the show ring and at stud. He was awarded 28 CCs and 43 BOBs with many Group placings and Best in Show at the Natal Sporting Hound Association, both as a puppy and as an adult. He was twice Beagle of the Year, and won Best in Show at all the Beagle Club Open shows from 1984 to 1989, except in 1987 when he took Best Opposite Sex to his daughter, Harriet. His grand-daughter, Tiffin, won Best in Show at the Beagle Club of Transvaal's first Championship show under Sylvia Tutchener, whilst Best Opposite that day was Micklegrange Briar, a son of the imported Crestamere Hotspur of Isibindi. In 1989 the Tanqueray kennel was decimated through organophosphate poisoning which resulted in the loss of Harriet (who was in whelp) and the subsequent putting down of Phoenix, who never recovered sufficiently to enjoy any quality of life. This tragedy devastated family and friends and resulted in a dramatically restricted breeding programme which has still not fully recovered.

THE BEAGLE CLUB OF TRANSVAAL

The Beagle Club of Transvaal was formed in 1979 and Ros Glaysher was its chairman until she moved to Cape Town in 1990. The first president was the late L.C. James, the British Wendover expert. The club held its first open show in 1981, produced a newsletter, and later introduced drag hunting for its members. Drag hunts are still one of the most popular outings for local Beagle enthusiasts and some of the hounds work really well.

The Club applied for Championship status in 1990 and at the qualifying show there were 43 Beagles entered. To retain such status, a specialist breed club must have 30 dogs present and exhibited at the show. This began to prove difficult, and in 1993 it was decided to forego the Championship shows and concentrate on Open events for the time being.

The gene pool in South Africa is quite small, although there have been three recently imported males, one from the United States, one from England, and one from Australia. They have yet to prove their worth at stud, however, as they are still quite young. South African breeders have expressed the opinion that the breed is currently rather in the doldrums, and prevalent faults need eradicating through seriously considered breeding programmes. This will entail ruthless evaluation of stock and avoiding any kennel-blindness.

DENMARK

In recent years, Denmark has acquired an enviable reputation for producing top class Beagles. The breed always attracts one of the highest entries at the Danish shows, and the breed club shows can invariably

150

muster 150 dogs. Not only does the breed have numbers – the Danish dogs have for some time been of excellent overall type and size. During the past 15 years the Beagle has proved a very popular breed in Denmark, both as companion and a show dog, with impressive results in the show ring in competition against all breeds. This situation has not happened by accident, but is the result of years of hard work and enthusiastic dedication to the breed by a hard core of breeders.

THE DANISH BEAGLE CLUB
The Danish Beagle Club is only 14 years old, but before that there was a club which catered for both Beagles and Bassets, this being founded in the late sixties. The founding father of the breed in Denmark was I.C. Christensen, a highly innovative, active and ambitious chairman of the club and himself a Beagle breeder of some standing during the early, rather difficult, years of the Danish Beagle. He managed to make the club into much more than a vehicle for showing and breeding; he developed the social side, organising parties, obedience training, and published an excellent magazine, helped greatly by the fact that he was a journalist. The Danish Beagle Club still maintains these traditions and it has an incredible 1,300 members – and this in a country which registers only 3 to 400 puppies a year. Certainly the Danish Beaglers know how to enjoy themselves, as any judge who has officiated at one of their club shows, and joined in the revelling at the post-show party, will confirm!

The obedience aspect of the club is a very important element, and no less than 25 experienced instructors, who are themselves Beagle owners, teach novice Beagle owners how to deal with what is not always the easiest of breeds. Today there are Beagles on the Danish national Obedience team, and also on the national Agility team too. Several Beagles have obtained the difficult title of Danish Obedience Champion, a prospect that would have been laughed at 15 years ago.

Danish Beagles are not required to hunt, and this is arguably one of the reasons for the Danish Beagle Club's success, when compared to other national clubs where there tends to be considerable in-fighting between the hunting and showing factions. As a result there are no hunting-based restrictions imposed on the club where breeding is concerned. To quote Jesper Pedersen: "Restrictions never improved the quality of a breed; quality comes with ambition and competition."

EARLY DANISH BEAGLES
To begin with, the Danish Beagles were very much influenced by some imports from Finland, not necessarily great show dogs themselves, but I.C. Christensen hoped to improve their type and temperament, and to that end imported the American dog, Seven Hill's Black Gold. He was a small and very smart dog and constituted nothing short of a revolution on the Danish Beagle scene. He produced many Champions, but, more importantly, he opened the eyes and minds of all who saw him, who consequently realised the need for a much smarter type of Beagle with softness of expression. His importance in the development of the Danish Beagle can never be underestimated.

In Sweden, Catharina Linde Forsberg bred a litter by Black Gold. One of the puppies, Gold Smuggler (thus christened because his semen was actually smuggled into Sweden!), became the sire of Black Gold II when mated to Pinewood Courtesy, one of several influential Pinewood exports to Scandinavia. A friend

151

Dk Ch. WW77 Black Gold II revolutionised Beagles in Denmark. He was by Gold Smuggler out of Pinewood Courtesy, and for nine years was the leading stud dog in his country. Many breeders still aim to line-breed back to him.   Photo: Birthe Damkjaer.

of I.C. Christensen's, Kristian Hansen, bought Black Gold II in Sweden, and Denmark now had its first Beagle superstar, winning Best in Show at International dog shows and bringing the breed into the limelight. He was also a very dominant stud dog who transmitted his type so easily. Many breeders in Denmark still try to line-breed to Black Gold II, and his importance in pedigrees remains enormous. He was the most important dog in the Pårup kennel of Kristian Hansen, who was the most successful Beagle breeder in Denmark during the seventies. For an amazing nine years Black Gold II was the 'Gold Stud Dog' there.

The Daragoj kennels were well established by that clever Finnish breeder Eeva Resko, when she was approached by an ambitious new Beagle enthusiast in Denmark, Jess Schmidt, whose kennel affix was Dazzlers. Jess imported some dogs from Eeva, the most important of which must be Daragoj Casio. I remember vividly giving the young Casio his first Best of

Breed. Some years later he was shown under me at what turned out to be his retirement show, and he again took the Breed. Casio was a great winner, ultra-smart with wonderful balance and a look of quality. In 1982 Casio was the top winning Hound in Denmark, and he is the sire and grandsire of many of today's top winners, producing more Champions than any other, I believe. It was interesting to see how Casio was behind so many of my winners when I judged the Danish Beagle Club show in January 1995. He has certainly been of great benefit to the breed.

SMALL, SMART AND VERY 'AMERICAN'

In 1979 Annette and Jesper Pedersen bought their first Beagle, a male called Canto, who was to mark the beginning of the Gold Line kennel. During the past twelve years, they have ten times been the top breeders in Denmark, and hold the record of producing nine World Winners since 1985. Canto himself was a Champion, and a marvellous moving hound. He became World Winner in 1985 and for many years was the Beagle with most international titles in Denmark. Now his son, Gold Lines Better Be Bookie, has beaten him with 15 international titles. The Gold Line kennel based their breeding on bitch lines from the Pårup and Minette kennels, coupled with Danish and Brazilian dogs. The Brazilian imports were Bangor Corn Flakes and Bangor Tuborg, each tracing back to Seven Hills; both were small, smart and very 'American'. The most important Danish-bred dog, apart from Canto, is probably Daisy Hills Dynamiske Domino, a son of Casio, owned by Jette and Jan Olsen. He is the sire of many Champions for the Gold Line and other kennels, including Gold Lines Wild X-Ample who won Best in Show at the big international show in Berlin in both 1994 and 1995.

Several British kennels have exported to Denmark, such as Deanery, Dialynne and Norcis. An eager importer was Claus Sorensen who died so tragically young. His Magic Noire Beagles helped elevate the overall quality to a considerable degree. I have exported three dogs to Denmark. Tragband In Hot Water and Tragband The Rose Tattoo went to the Gold Line Kennel, while In Hot Water's sister, In For A Penny, went to the Dazzlers kennel. The Gold Line kennel has also imported two American males, Navans To All the Girls Luv'd and White Acres Murphy's Law. Murphy won Best of Breed at the 1995 World Show under Eleanor Bothwell.

LEADING BREEDERS

An affix which is held in high regard by all Danish breeders is Minette, the kennel name of Tove Pitzner. She started in the late sixties and was one of the pioneers in the breed. Her bitch line had great quality and was based on imports from the Annasline kennel in England. Daisy Hill is another kennel still active, and with more than 25 years experience. It has combined basically American-based stock with Casio to great effect, and the Vinther family which owns the kennel is very much involved with the Obedience side of the club. Indeed, Finn Vinther has for many years been chairman of the Obedience section.

There are several up and coming breeders who are already making their mark on the Danish Beagle scene, and I feel sure they will continue to keep the breed high in quality and popularity. One such breeder is Lotte Jensen who owns the Skansehøj kennel. At the 1995 show of the Danish Beagle Club I was very impressed with the quality of dogs coming from this kennel,

and my Best in Show winner was a nine-months puppy bred by them. Skansehøj's Johanne was a daughter of Daisy Hills Dynamiske Domino out of a bitch who went back to Buglair and Pin Oaks lines from the USA, and Dialynne and Trewint lines from England. I felt that the stock from this kennel had much to offer in construction and movement and I will watch their progress with interest. The Beagle is now firmly established in Denmark and can only go from strength to strength, as long as the breeders continue to work together and do not become blind to some of the faults which may be appearing.

THE REST OF SCANDINAVIA

For the purposes of this book I have excluded Denmark from Scandinavia, under whose umbrella it is often included, as the Danish Beagle scene is much larger and more show-orientated than that of any of the other Scandinavian countries, namely Sweden, Finland and Norway. The Swedish Beagle Club was established in 1953, and the Finnish Beagle Club in 1961 by people with a major interest in hunting. Before this time Beagles were only sporadically found in Scandinavia. In Norway the Beagle people have joined the Norwegian Hare Hound Club which has a main interest in the various breeds of Scandinavian scenthounds, or Stovares. There are currently plans to form a Norwegian Beagle Club. (In Scandinavia, the Kennel Clubs will only recognise one club for each breed.) The main purpose of all the Scandinavian Beagle clubs is still to promote the hunting ability of the breed but, unlike the situation in the UK, the breed has not developed along separate lines – one for the show bench and one for the field. The reason for this is to be found in the Show and Field Trial Regulations laid down by the breed clubs and sanctioned by the Kennel Clubs. The Swedish Beagle Club has sixteen regional clubs organising the shows and field trials and around an incredible 2,000 members, whereas the Finnish Beagle Club has 60 regional clubs and about 2,700 members. Approximately 600 Beagles are registered each year in Sweden, 850 in Finland and 350 in Norway. The number of entries at Field Trials is about 450 per year in Sweden, 250 in Finland and 125 in Norway. A special Stud Book is published in Sweden and Finland containing details of all the dogs that have qualified at the trials. Some of the currently leading Beagle kennels in Sweden are Beagler's, Champhurst, Gunfire, Merryant's, Starmaids, Trewelyn and Ullikas, all owned by fairly small breeders producing, at most, one or two litters per year. In Finland the most famous breeder is Eeva Resko of the Daragoj kennel, and in Norway the Amaritas and Røraskogens kennels of Anne-Marit Olsen and her husband Olav Olsen respectively.

Catharina Linde-Forsberg made Aust. Ch. Hilldamar The Way To Go Best in Show when she judged a Specialty in 1995. She later imported him to Sweden where he won the Nordic Winner title. He is pictured taking Group Three at Stockholm
Photo: Lillemoor Boos.

US AND UK INFLUENCES
So how have British and American show Beagles influenced the breed in Scandinavia? Catharina Linde-Forsberg is a world expert on artificial insemination and holds a senior post in the Department of Obstetrics and Gynaecology at the Faculty of Veterinary Medicine in Uppsala. She is also an enthusiastic breeder, exhibitor and judge of Beagles, owning the Beagler's kennel. During the late 60s she imported a bitch, Rossut Promise, from Catherine Sutton, who had some pack Beagles in her pedigree and it is said that her grandsire, Appeline Dancer of Camerlyn, had 17 Show Champions and 14 Field Trial Champions in his pedigree. Promise

produced some very good field dogs, especially when combined with Carin Lindhe's import, Barvae Rinkles. Both he and Barvae Pelham sired Champions in Sweden. Three Perrystar imports, Valinda, Vesper and Vandal (by Ch. Deaconfield Rampage ex Jerry Meek's foundation bitch, Perrystar Forrardon Linnet), were very successful at field trials, although none of them gained their crown. They did, however, produce some good hunting stock.

Catharina imported Pinewood Courtesy (by Ch. Southcourt Wembury Merryboy ex Ch. Pinewood Chimer) from the Priestleys in 1973. Courtesy took several Groups at major shows and was later inseminated with semen from the American male, Am. Ch. Seven Hills Black Gold, imported into Denmark by I.C. Christensen. Black Gold himself qualified as an International

Champion through a field trial in Germany. The most famous offspring from a son of this combination – Beagler's Gold Smuggler – were Danish Ch. Beagler's Black Gold II, with ten Best in Show awards at all breeds Championship shows, and his younger full brother, Beagler's Black Gold (all very confusing with three 'Black Golds' appearing in pedigrees!), who was the breed record holder for Bests of Breed in Sweden. Black Gold was also one of the foundation dogs used in Eeva Resko's Daragoj kennel, siring, among others, Danish Ch. Daragoj Piece of Gold, the top winning show dog of all breeds in Finland for 1989.

Some years later, Pinewood Courtesy was mated to Black Gold's half-brother, Great Pumpkin of Starcrest, a lemon and white who was imported to Sweden from the USA by the famous Swedish all-rounder judge, Marianne Furst-Danielsson. Pumpkin was the sire of Catharina's Int. Nord. Ch. FT Ch. Wild Honey who, apart from being a beautifully constructed hound was, in her owner's words, "the best field dog I've ever hunted with". Pumpkin threw a very strong interest for hare hunting in his puppies.

During the same time, Marianne Furst-Danielsson imported from England Annasline Diadem and, later, the well-known winner, Ch. Southcourt Wembury Fiddler and Annasline Pompous (full brother to Annasline Gayboy who went to Norway). Diadem was by the American import Rozavel Elsy's Diamond Jerry out of Annasline Rozavel Lovely Ring. Pompous was from the same breeding on the dam's side, while his sire was the American import, Annasline Page Mill Playboy. All three threw some good field dogs. Diadem, in addition, was Dog of the Year in Sweden for 1970. This, together with the introduction in Sweden of the

popular cartoon character, Snoopy, led to an almost threefold increase in the number of registered puppies for the breed. As happens so often in these cases, this led to a deterioration in the quality of the breed.

In 1981 Catharina imported the littermates, Boddiga Royal Occasion and Boddiga Royal Celebration, from Madge Openshaw Miller in England. They were line-bred to Page Mill Oscar, who mated four bitches in England before going on to Lesley Funnell (now Hiltz) in Australia. Behind them are mainly Page Mill and Whiteacres lines, but also some Colegren blood. They turned out to be amazingly good field dogs, the kind you could only find once in a lifetime. Celebration was a Swedish Show and Field Trial Champion when she was barely two years old, and Occasion an International and Nordic Show Champion and Field Trial Champion at three years. They remain the only two British exports to Sweden to have won their titles, and both produced exceedingly well.

Mated to Eeva Resko's American import to Finland, Starbuck's Classic, Celebration produced Int. Nordic Ch. FT Ch. Mälardrotts Yankee Boy, among other good dogs. Occasion, being a male, has naturally had a greater influence, producing fifteen dual or Field Trial Champions to date. Beacott Banker (sired by the American import, Am. Can. Ch. Chardon Yankee Clipper) and Beacott Bellmaid, going back to Ch. Beacott Buckthorn, have also done well at both shows and field trials, and have in turn produced good stock.

Catharina judged the American dog, Briarhill Own Own Brucie, at a show in 1991 when he was just a puppy. He was later sold to Eeva Resko in Finland. By way of imported semen, Brucie has produced many good winners including, in Sweden,

Champhurst Bark At The Moon, a multiple Group winner with a First prize on hare at field trials, and his litter sister, Champhurst Batteries Not 'Ncluded, a consistent Best of Breed winner. Their dam, Merryant's Daisy Strax of Champhurst, herself has many BOBs as well as two Specialty Bests in Show. She is by the Danish import, Gold Line's Sound of Harlem (by Brazilian Ch. Bangor Cornflakes) out of Beagler's Myrten (Beagler's Black Gold ex Int. Nord Ch. FT Ch. Wild Honey). Line-bred to both Beagler's Black Gold and Ch. Boddiga Royal Occasion, Beagler's Baryton is now proving a successful winner for Catharina.

Enhancing still further the marvellously cosmopolitan bloodlines with which the Scandinavians can work, Catharina has recently imported to Sweden the dog she made Best in Show at a Specialty show in Australia, Aust. Ch. Hilldamar The Way To Go. As he is a son of the New Zealand-bred Aust. NZ Ch. Burnsdale Anything Goes, I am quite envious of this latest acquisition.

FINLAND

Most breeders in Finland, as in the other Scandinavian countries, breed Beagles for hunting only. The Beagle is second only to the national scenting breed, the Finnish Stovare, in popularity as a field dog. The only Beagle so far to have qualified for the title of International Field Trial Champion is the Finnish-owned, but Swedish-bred, Bravur's Donny. One Finnish breeder has, however made a great name for herself world-wide as a producer of high-class show dogs, and that is Eeva Resko of the Daragoj kennel.

Prior to falling victim to the Beagle's charms, Eeva had successfully bred Borzois and Basset Hounds, and she has also produced many excellent Lhasa Apsos. However, it will undoubtedly be for her

Danish Ch. Daragoj Piece of Gold was the top winning show dog of all breeds in Finland in 1989. She illustrates the typical Daragoj 'look' which Eeva Resko established, having cleverly blended bloodlines from several different countries.   Photo: Bruce Smith.

Beagles that Eeva will be best remembered. The kennel was based on British Pinewood lines coupled originally with American blood from the Colegren and Johjean kennels. Subsequently, Eeva brought in outcrosses from Starbuck's in the USA and Torbay in Australia. To this day, each litter bred at Daragoj traces back to Clovergates Pleasure (by Ch. Saravere Hardy of Dialynne ex Ch. Clovergates Liberty Belle), the kennel's original British import and the foundation of a very strong bitch line. Her double grand-daughter, the appropriately named Am. Ch. Daragoj Double Pleasure, was the first foreign-bred Beagle to win Best in Show at an all-breeds Championship show in the United States, and she became the dam of nine American Champions. Her daughter, Am. Ch. Daragoj Royal Ascot, went to the USA at six years of age and won a Beagle Specialty twice, the second time as a veteran, and always owner-handled. Another daughter, Brazilian Ch. Daragoj Royal Rendezvous won very well in that country, while

Double Pleasure's grand-daughter, Danish Ch. Daragoj Piece of Gold, was in turn ranked Number One show dog of all breeds in Finland in 1989.

Over the years, Eeva has established mutually beneficial relationships with other breeders in the USA, Brazil and Australia and has cleverly blended different bloodlines to produce an unmistakable Daragoj "look", that of a smart, compact, well-boned Beagle with excellent topline and rear angulation and typical Beagle temperament. All in all, the Daragoj Beagles have Champions in four continents, a remarkable record.

NORWAY

During the early 50s, notable imports included Elmhurst Warden, Barvae Mongoose and Barvae Titlark. Titlark and Warden produced the first Norwegian Champion, Montebellos Bella, while Mongoose sired Norwegian Ch. Pobby who was to become an important stud dog. It has been said that Bella herself was not of show quality, being rather coarse and short on the leg, but she produced several generations of successful field dogs. Barvae Warpaint, an imported tan and white, also produced some good stock although none became Champions. In 1964 Barvae Riby (brother to Rinkles who was sent to Sweden) was imported to Norway, originally being owned by Arne Tjomsland. He did well at shows with a Group win at a Norwegian Kennel Club all-breeds show as a youngster. On Mr. Tjomsland's death, Riby went to the Amaritas kennel of Anne-Marit Olsen, who entered him at field trials organised for the (long-legged) Stovares, where he was awarded a Second prize on both roe-deer and hare. At this time there were no special field trial rules for Beagles. Barvae Riby won 7 CCs, so under the present rules he would have been a

Champion.

In 1967 and 1968 Letton Chicago Gangster and Annasline Lovely Blazette came to the Amaritas kennel. Blazette became the first Beagle in the Nordic countries to win a Best in Show at an International show. She also became a Danish Champion. Chicago Gangster and Blazette's son and daughter (by Ch. Rozavel Elsy's Diamond Jerry), Amaritas Lovely Diamond Jerry and Jerrina, each won 2 CCs in Denmark before the border was closed because of rabies. Other sons of Blazette and Ch. Rozavel Elsy's Diamond Jerry were Jerrico (who won a Group at a Norwegian Kennel Club show when a mere 11 months old) and Jeremy (who was sold to Sweden where he produced 14 offspring with field trial merits and notable show wins). Letton Chicago Gangster produced Beagles who used their tongue more ideally when following the deer or hare than did hounds from the old lines. He also impressed in the way he worked, searching out much more efficiently. He produced one Champion and some more with field trial merits, and he was a particularly good producer of brood bitches.

During the 70s, Annasline Gayboy (by the American import, Annasline Page Mill Playboy) came to Anne-Marit. Himself a wonderful dog, he acquitted himself well in the show ring and produced nine offspring with prizes at field trials. His most famous son was Amaritas Örjan who, at two-and-a-half years of age, was sold to Sweden, where he became the first Beagle ever to win the full title of International Nordic Champion and Field Trial Champion. Like his sire, he was a superb stud dog, as 27 of his get were awarded prizes at field trials, several of them winning their titles, among them Int. Nordic Ch. FT Ch. Beagler's Hello Dolly, a daughter of Pinewood Courtesy. Örjan's dam was Baimor Gleam (from the Rebel-Glitter litter). A Gleam daughter in Sweden was mated to Int. Nord. Ch. FT Ch. Boddiga Royal Occasion to produce the well known Swedish FT Ch. Ödmårdens Bobby McGee.

In 1971 Maureen Tolver of the Baimor kennel in Britain visited the Amaritas kennel, bringing with her three Beagles: Baimor Tinsel who was in whelp to the American import, Appeline Validay Happy Feller (sire of the legendary Ch. Dialynne Gamble), Baimor Glitter who had been mated to Ch. Baimor I'm A Rebel, and Baimor Solitary Star who had won 2 CCs in England. Star won Best of Breed in both Norway and Finland, but sadly died of pyometra after having a litter to Chicago Gangster. They produced Amaritas Rusky Dusky who became a top winner. Tinsel's daughter by Happy Feller, Amaritas Noble Nymph, also enjoyed a successful career in the show ring and was later to prove one of the kennel's best brood bitches. Glitter herself was a super hunter, taking a First prize on roe-deer before sustaining an injury. She won 7 CCs and was a Group winner at a Kennel Club show, later producing two Champions, Amaritas E'viva (by Clovergates Midnight, brother to Ch. Clovergates Liberty Belle), one of the best producing bitches in Norway, and Amaritas

Örba (by Barvae Riby) who, along with her litter brother Öbertus, produced several field trial award winners. Barvae Riby and Baimor Glitter remain the only British imported Beagles to have won prizes at Norwegian field trials.

In 1983 Anne-Marit Olsen brought the American male Colegrens Blue Devil Imp from Ann Pickthall in England, owner of the Clovergates kennel. He won well and also produced good hunting dogs. Interestingly, Imp's blood found its way back to Britain in a very roundabout way when Marion Spavin imported, from Denmark, Danish Ch. Amaritas Bim Uno of Dialynne. He was a grandson of Imp on his sire's side and went on to be a Champion producer in England.

It is fascinating to me how Beagles from so many countries, and with essentially different immediate backgrounds, have been combined by talented breeders to produce the goods. In the Beagle breed we have been fortunate in having a number of open-minded breeders who can look past their own doorstep and see quality in other countries, then acquire new blood to improve certain points. This is very healthy for the breed and long may it continue, for this is the way forward.

13 BEAGLES IN NORTH AMERICA

While the Beagle is native to Britain, the development of the modern British breed owes much to the influence of American imports in the fifties and sixties. Generally speaking, a number of key imports helped to improve compactness, firm up toplines and improve the finish of the heads. In recent years the number of imports has declined dramatically, with only two significant dogs arriving in the early eighties – Graadtres Hot Pursuit of Rossut and Pin Oaks Dynasty of Appeline. Since that time British breeders have worked almost exclusively with local bloodlines.

In recent years I feel that the breed in the USA and the UK has polarised somewhat. While the British Beagles may have something of a size problem – many of our hounds are at the top end of the height recommendation – we have largely managed to maintain good construction, excellent movement which demonstrates both reach and drive as well as being true "up and down", and a lot of very good heads and expressions.

The Americans, on the other hand, seem in many instances to have become preoccupied with the "compactness" of the breed, and the production of an ultra-short back appears to have become all-important. This is often accompanied by excessive rear angulation, and yet the forehand is frequently disproportionately upright. When you shorten the back, you invariably also shorten the ribcage, the neck and the upper arm. This results in a rather upright shoulder. Given that a Beagle has a short back, upright shoulder and yet great angulation of the hindquarters, it follows that when the dog comes to move, the front and rear will not co-ordinate, and a complementary forehand reach is impossible to achieve. The result is that the hindquarters propel the dog forward to a greater extent than the front can cope with, and consequently the forelegs tend to fly every which way! When the drive from the rear is too great for the front assembly to cope with, the dog will employ a delaying tactic so that the concussive force is well spent before the front foot hits the ground. Such tactics also include high-stepping and paddling.

On a visit to the 1995 National Beagle Club of America Specialty I was one of a ten-strong party of British breeders who visited. While I admired the general evenness of type in the 15 inch dogs, and their obvious compactness, I did find the

breed, I found that the dogs which appealed to me were frequently from the Bayou Oaks, Beowulf, Page Mill, Shaws, Tashwould and Whiteacres lines. They seemed to be a more moderate kind of dog which would fit in quite easily with some of the British dogs.

A COMPARISON OF THE US AND UK BEAGLE

In view of the obvious differences which have evolved, I felt it would be pertinent to ask an American breeder to offer an overview of the breed at the present moment, and I am grateful to Richard Gilmore M.D. for the following:

The importation from the USA of Appeline Validay Happy Feller by Douglas and Carol Appleton did British Beagle breeders a great favour. Mated to Ch. Dialynne Nettle, he produced Ch. Dialynne Gamble, the greatest sire the breed has ever known in the UK. In years to come, Gamble was to be the cornerstone of many successful kennels.

Photo: Joan Ludwig.

"Over the past three years, I have had the pleasure of travelling abroad to England and Australia from my native United States, and have observed the Beagle breed at conformation shows on numerous occasions. On my return to America, the most remarkable insight has been on the American rather than the English or Australian Beagle. What I thought I had always known about our breed here was widened by the look abroad, allowing me to be more critical and appreciative of the Beagle in the United States. What follows is an attempt to share my views of the subject with breeders everywhere.

The show scene in America is largely regional, as distances between show sites in the US preclude the owner/handler from extending the exhibition of his or her dog beyond a regional level. Likewise, breeding programs tend to cluster in areas of the country, as there is a tendency to use local stud dogs to avoid the risks, inconvenience and expense of shipping bitches over long distances. As a result, one may see dogs of only a certain type at any given local show and draw some faulty conclusions about the American breed. Exceptions to this do

movement, particularly in front, something of a worry. Having said that, I found some excellent hounds which I felt would help the breed in Britain. More often than not these were dogs which some American fanciers may have considered slightly long-cast, but to our eyes their balance was perfect and quite in keeping with a hound which should move with great scope. Having seen a wide cross-section of the

America's Beagle of the Year 1987/88/89 was Am. Ch. Keith's Wilkeep Nicodemus, the 15-inch son of Am. Ch. Starbuck's Full Count and Am. Ch. Wilkeep Love Notes. Bred by Brenda Ahlhardt and Alene Peek, Nicky was owned by Barbara Cosgrove and handled to many major victories by Denny Mounce. Photo: Missy.

exist, however, and generally one will see a broad entry at the annual National Specialty, no matter in which region it is held, and occasionally at regional Beagle Specialties. Some of the more prestigious all-breed shows, such as the Westminster Kennel Club show in New York, may also provide a national entry, albeit of very limited size. Thus one must either attend the National Specialty or do a fair amount of travelling if one is to get a true and balanced look at the American show

Beagle. Also, because of the distances involved, campaigning a top winning Beagle in a competitive manner has meant employing a professional handler most of the time. Thus winning the points in America can be an expensive proposition.

THE SMALLER SIZE OF THE AMERICAN HOUND
Probably the first identifying feature that the international visitor would discern is the smaller size of the American hound. As

we generally have much smaller hare and cotton-tail rabbits here, Americans developed the Thirteen-inch and Fifteen-inch Beagles for hunting reasons, as the smaller hound would better match his quarry in size and range. Height is a disqualification, so one rarely exhibits an oversize dog for very long in the show ring, as the judge can and should measure suspect hounds at his or the other exhibitors' discretion. As with any other breed, miniaturisation while maintaining type is very difficult. Although the Breed Standards are the same for each, there has been difficulty in maintaining quality in the Thirteen-inch variety. As if "mother nature" has not made it difficult enough for us, there has been a serious loss of Thirteen-inch male bloodstock abroad, as the financial incentive to sell to fanciers in the Far East has been quite compelling. As a result, a quality Thirteen-inch male in the United States remains a rare bird indeed. Nevertheless, an exceptional bitch is often seen. The most notable Thirteen-inch bitch has been the recently retired Ch. Lanbur Miss Fleetwood, bred by Jon Woodring and Wade Burns, and shown meticulously by Eddie Dziuk. Breeders and judges alike have acclaimed this lovely hound, with gorgeous type, smooth flowing gait, and exceptional temperament, as she became the top winning American Beagle of all time.

Another feature distinguishing the American Beagle from its overseas relatives is the apparent shorter back in relation to leg length. The biggest reason for this probably lies in the American Standard which calls for "back short, muscular and strong". While it is my impression that the writers of the Standard meant to imply "short between the couplings", the phrase has been taken quite literally, producing a hound that is short between the head and the stern. This distance is composed of shoulder layback, proper ribbing, coupling and croup. Shortening any one or all of these will produce a shorter head-to-tail interval. Unfortunately there has been a trend in the US to produce and promote dogs that have the striking silhouette of a short back at the expense of steep shoulder angulation and short ribbing. This "fashion" of breeding short-backed animals is commonplace in many breeds in the US, not just the Beagle, as the majority of judges here put heavy emphasis on this one trait. These dogs, while stunning in the stacked photographs, generally have been short-strided and lacking in the aerobic capacity that would be necessary for a full day in the field. Since the American Standard does not include a specific description of the gait, we rely instead on the logic that "form follows function". Unfortunately, since few show exhibitors hunt with their hounds, this connection is not often made, and this trend is likely to persist.

The American Standard calls for a tail that is "short as compared to the size of the hound", while the British Standard calls for a tail "of moderate length", and clearly American tails are shorter. There is generally more curvature of the tail, as the American Standard calls for a slight curve, but excessively curved tails over the back are considered a conspicuous fault. There is nothing that stamps type on the Beagle more than the lovely head and pleading, gentle expression. I wish I could say that we were doing a good job in producing this in the American breed, but feel that we often fall short, largely for two reasons. First of all, while many aspects of the head conformation have to do with scenting and hunting ability, judging the type of a good Beagle head is largely a function of aesthetics. Most judges of Beagles in

America, in contradistinction to the United Kingdom, have never bred Beagles. As a result, there is considerable variation in their ability to judge type and reward the good Beagle head in the ring. Secondly, the price for maintaining the smaller Thirteen-inch size in the US can often be refinement of the headpiece, with shorter, "snipey" muzzles and shorter, high-set ears. Nevertheless, the dedication of several breeders has ensured the survival of many quite beautiful heads in the gene pool.

Another noticeable difference in the American Beagle is the amount of rear angulation, which is generally more than is seen anywhere else, except perhaps in Western Australia. While controversial, I believe this to be in accordance with the Standard which describes "stifles – well let down" and "hocks – moderately bent". In addition to providing the mechanical frame for proper drive, this rear angulation, combined with the shorter back, often leads to a very striking profile as compared with the English silhouette. Unless coupled with a well laid-back shoulder up front, however, there can be considerable lack of balance, resulting in a hound which cannot reach sufficiently for his drive. This can produce a variety of movement disorders and unsoundness.

In terms of markings, the classic American Beagle is a black-saddled tricolor, although the Standard says that all hound colors are acceptable. Tan and white, or red and white, Beagles have become more popular and acceptable lately. The prevalence of the depigmentation gene in the American gene pool does allow for the occasional blue dog to be exhibited, although the corresponding generally lighter eye can make big winning difficult, by detracting from the pleading expression. A notable exception to this has been Ch. Merry Song's High Performance, who was campaigned to numerous Group wins and an all-breed Best in Show award. Livers are allowed in the Standard, but rarely exhibited, because of the fierce countenance that the yellow eye can produce. Mottles and open-marked hounds are, at the current time, just not seen.

Despite the problems mentioned above there are a number of kennels in the United States that have consistently produced quality animals and remain, in the current time frame, important sources of breeding stock. Space constraints prevent me from mentioning all, so I will concentrate on the breeders whose bloodlines have been widely used outside their own kennels.

SHOULDER LAYBACK AND SOUNDNESS

Page Mill, a well-known kennel in the US owned by Carroll Diaz, continues its bloodline, begun in 1959. Certainly the most influential sire produced by this kennel of late has been Ch. Page Mill On The Road Again, who was used extensively across the US and has been noted for the shoulder layback and soundness of his progeny. Notable hounds produced by "Willie" include National Specialty Best of Breed winners, Ch. Page Mill Upset The Applecart, bred by Ella Mae De Capri, and Ch. Rancho Glen's It's A Snap, bred by Mary Lynne and Michael Katusich. Today, many of "Willie's" sons and grandsons continue to influence our Beagles throughout the US.

Washington State's White Acres Kennel, founded by Margaret White and continued now by her grand-daughter, Carol Tyte and husband Ed, continues to figure in breeding programs nationally. While the breeding stock has dramatically changed from Margaret White's original bloodline, the acquisition of Ch. Whisper's Inflation

Fighter has played a prominent role in the kennel for the last decade. He has produced over fifty Champions, including the Specialty and Group winners, Ch. White Acres I'm Heavenly Too and Ch. White Acres Second To None, the latter a National Specialty Variety winner. Daughters of Inflation Fighter have done considerable winning on their own, and have produced well, including Ch. White Acres Libby On the Label. Her son, Ch. White Acres Designer Label, a dog of stunning silhouette with short back and striking rear angulation, was a prodigious sire in the last decade.

Moving from the West coast to Texas, the Yaupon Row kennel of the late S.R. Whittaker Jr. figured prominently in the breeding programs of several important kennels of the area. Rigorously line-breeding on the old White Acres and Colegren bloodlines, his kennel produced a larger, longer-cast hound with a beautiful shoulder, neck and headpiece. Although Mr. Whittaker rarely campaigned a dog past its Championship, he did produce a multiple Group winning bitch, Ch. Yaupon Row Bayou Oaks Cocoa, from one of his last litters. Ch. Yaupon Row Sailor Boy CDX, an all-breeds Best in Show winner, provided the original sire line for Hugh and Alene Peek's Wilkeep kennel.

EXCEPTIONAL SHOW TEMPERAMENT

Blending the Yaupon Row stock with Page Mill and Starcrest lines, the Wilkeep kennel produced several quality Beagles, including National Specialty Best of Opposite Sex winner, Ch. Wilkeep Point of View, and the multiple Best in Show winner, Ch. Keith's Wilkeep Nicodemus, the latter co-bred by Brenda Ahlhardt. Nicodemus was an outstanding show dog with exceptional show temperament, heavy bone and short

The great American stud force Am. Ch. Starbucks Hang 'em High, a son of Am. Ch. The Whim's Buckeye and Am. Ch. Elsy's Shooting Star. He was owned and bred by David Hiltz.   *Photo: Missy.*

back. Although Nicodemus was used on only a limited basis at stud, his sons, Ch. Barmere's Mario Andretti and Ch. Wilkeep's Bayou Classic were sire and grandsire respectively of the Best in Show winning litter mates, our own Ch. Bayou Oaks Cappuccino and Ch. Bayou Oaks Chianti.

On to the Mid West, where no discussion of the American Beagle would be complete without mention of Ch. Starbuck's Hang 'em High. Bred by David and Linda Hiltz, Hang 'em High was the product of an outcross between the great Thirteen-inch sire, Ch. The Whim's Buckeye, and Ch. Elsy's Shooting Star. He has had a tremendous genetic influence on the American breed, after being campaigned to a long and distinguished show record of over twenty Best in Shows and National Specialty wins. He has produced over one hundred and thirty Champions and, although deceased, continues to sire puppies from frozen semen collected years before his death. Hang 'em High has also proven to be a sire of sires as well. Ch.

Hickorynut's Hangman, a son out of a Colegren bitch, was an outstanding sire for many kennels and produced the lovely National Specialty breed winning bitch, Ch. Fairmont's Sound of Music. Another son of Hang 'em High, multiple Best in Show winning Ch. Chardon Kentucky Derby, proved invaluable for the Chardon kennel of Charles and Donna Kitchell. A full sister of Hang 'em High, Ch. Starbuck's Meadow Song, proved to be a "blue hen" for Annette Didier's Meadow Crest kennel, producing multiple Champions and prepotent sons whether line-bred or outcrossed, including Ch. Meadow Crest Grand Slam, National Best of Variety winner Ch. Meadow Crest Winjammer, and Ch. Starbuck's Full Count, sire of Ch. Keith's Wilkeep Nicodemus. The Merry Song kennel of Mara Baun and Nancy Bergstrom has also used intensive line-breeding on Hang 'em High and produced multiple Best in Show winners, including Ch. Merry Song's High Performance, and National Specialty Best of Breed winning bitch, Ch. Merry Song's Uppity Ms. From these lines and others, the legacy of Hang 'em High will continue for many years in the United States, as well as abroad. Hang 'em High was also the sire of US and UK Ch. Graadtres Hot Pursuit of Rossut who, in turn, sired Andrew Brace's British record-holder, Ch. Too Darn Hot for Tragband.

THE DOMINANT SIRE OF THE 1980s

On the East Coast, clearly the dominant sire of the 1980s was a Thirteen-inch dog called Ch. Teloca Patches Littl' Dickens, bred by Charles Grant and Marie Shuart. Dickens won the variety at the National Specialty three years in succession and became the foundation sire for the Lanbur kennel of Jon Woodring and Wade Burns. Dickens' influence on the American breed,

The famous little scene stealer, Am. Ch. Lanbur Miss Fleetwood, the 13 inch bitch who has become the top winning Beagle of all time in the USA. Bred by Wade Burns and Jon Woodring, she is by Am. Ch. Lanbur The Company Car out of Am Ch. Altar's Lanbur Lacy J., and was owned and handled by Eddie Dziuk. Photo: Kohler.

especially the Thirteen-inch variety, cannot be overestimated, as he was heavily used by the large breeding program of Lanbur as well as many other kennels. His get include Best in Show winner Ch. Meadow Crest's Fireside Chap out of Ch. Starbuck's Meadow Song, and at least three prolific sires. The first, Ch. Sureluv's Fran-Ray's Bandit was the 1989 Sire of the Year and produced the National Specialty winner, Ch. Lanbur The Company Car, sire of Ch. Lanbur Miss Fleetwood. The second, Ch. Lanbur Roshan Hi Fidelity, was the 1987 Sire of the Year and produced the Best in Show winners, Ch. Lanbur Formal Edition and Ch. Sureluv's Chasin' Rainbows. The last, Ch. Lanbur Sureluv's Kandee Man (a liver, no less), produced the beautiful bitch and National Specialty variety winner Ch. Fran-Ray's Lite-n-Lively. While Dickens did not always produce Thirteen-inch Beagles, it can be said that the Thirteens he did produce were true Thirteens, that is, hounds of proper proportion and balance in miniature, a difficult feat.

The importation of bloodstock from overseas has been very limited because much of the English and Australian lineage are, frankly, unattractive because of the larger size. The rigid discipline of the American height disqualification has prevented the creeping up of size that is occurring elsewhere. Conversely, the rigid quarantine restrictions and the extraordinary costs involved have limited exportation of American stock to English and Australasian shores. I understand that some of these restrictions may be soon up for review, allowing for a more global mixing of the gene pools, with hopefully a blend of the best of each.

Is the American Beagle better off now than it was twenty years ago? I would have to say a definite yes. A lot of the credit is due to the Supporting Membership of the National Beagle Club, which works hard to educate judges on Beagle type and to share information on genetic problems. This program is spearheaded by Judy Musladin of The Whim's Beagles. After all is said and done, the dedication of the supporting membership is creating a better Beagle in the United States. I would invite all our overseas visitors to come to the National Specialty for a first-hand look."

AMERICAN BEAGLE BREEDERS TODAY

The visit to the 1995 National Specialty left us British Beaglers admiring greatly the consistency of the American dogs, and their obvious compactness, and yet it resulted in a determination to preserve the forehand construction which we still have, as this is where some of the American dogs obviously fall down. It is my contention that there is much room for co-operation

between the like-minded among the British and American breeders and, perhaps, a greater exchange of breeding stock may help to narrow the gap that is obviously being created between the breeds in the two countries.

By way of presenting a profile of presently active American Beagle breeders, I have chosen to include details of a cross-section of kennels which are enjoying a high level of success. Some of these are longer-established than others, but they are indicative of the fact that in the USA, as in Great Britain, successful kennels range from small Beagle households to large-scale breeding establishments.

BEOWULF

Terri Giannetti established her Beowulf kennel when she bought her first show Beagle, Am. Ch. Bridal Vale Beowulf Moody Blue. Beowulf began small in the Boston area while, at the same time, Ted Swedalla was setting about establishing his Temateki kennel on Long Island. As Moody Blue was a son of Am. Ch. Chrisette's Macho Man, Terri got her foundation bitch from Sandy Robichaud's Chrisette's kennel in the form of Am. Ch. Chrisette's Beowulf Kashmir. The breeding of Kashmir to Blue proved significant for Beowulf in that it produced one of their most important bitches, the 13 inch Am. Ch. Beowulf Days of Wine and Roses. Meanwhile Ted had acquired a 15 inch bitch from Garland and Karen Moore's Buglair kennel called Am. Ch. Buglair Belle of Temateki. This bitch was renowned for her phenomenal side gait and when she won Best of Variety under Frank Sabella at six months of age, in the company of Best in Show winning Champions, Frank commented "Finally someone brings me a Beagle that looks like a Beagle!" Terri Giannetti had a high regard for this bitch

ABOVE: Am. Ch. Beowulf Mass In C Minor, a 13 inch son of Am. Ch. White Acres Designer Label and Am. Ch. Beowulf Days of Wine and Roses. Photo: Booth.

LEFT: Am. Ch. Beowulf Running On Faith, the 15 inch son of Am. Ch. Beowulf Sharp Dressed Man and Am. Ch. Buglair Belle of Temateki.

and tried desperately to buy her. Various alternative arrangements were suggested by both parties, including exchanging Wine and Roses for Belle, but to no avail, and there is some conjecture that Terri and Ted's interest in each other's bitches played no small part in their eventual marriage!

The third major bloodline which helped to create Beowulf is White Acres, now owned by Ed and Carol Tyte. Days of Wine and Roses was bred to Am. Ch. White Acres Designer Label which resulted in five Champions, notably Am. Ch. Beowulf Sharp Dressed Man, Am. Ch. Beowulf Mass In C Minor and Am. Ch. Beowulf Lipstick Sunset. Sharp Dressed Man was then used on Am. Ch. Buglair Belle of Temateki to produce the prolific winning Am. Ch. Beowulf Running On Faith, a

lovely-headed dog who has enjoyed a great career as a special. When Belle was bred to Mass In C Minor, four young Champions emerged including Am. Ch. Beowulf Serenade For Winds. Currently Beowulf has bred over 25 Champions, and in addition there have been more than 20 Champions sired by Mass In C Minor to outside bitches. Says Terri: "Our priorities in a Beagle are often heard to revolve around the words 'pretty' and 'fancy'. This is, by no means, to the exclusion of correct movement, as we are looking continually to improve those areas. However, a nice moving hound that is plain or common would find itself in lonesome company at Beowulf because of the threat that it would create in regard to loss of breed type. The current Standard places more importance on the head and the sum of the parts than it does on movement. Although I believe moving well is an element in the hound's ability to do an honest day's work in the field, I don't feel that it is crucial that said hound move like an Afghan to do so."

FULMONT

William and Julie Fulkerson whelped their first litter of Beagles in 1962 in the hills of Tennessee. The foundations of the Fulmont Beagles were rooted in the CS, SK, DoMor and Renoca lines. Combining their original stock with dogs from Carroll Diaz's (then Gordon) Page Mill kennel brought excellent results. Am. Ch. Fulmont's Megan had been bred to both Am. Ch. Page Mill Stagehand and Am. Ch. Page Mill Trademark. A Stagehand son (Am. Ch. Fulmont's Pub Crawler) was subsequently bred to his half-sister, the Trademark daughter (Am. Ch. Fulmont's Fable) to produce Ch. Fulmont's Flash Cube, a 13 inch male who became the first red and white Beagle of either size to win a Best in Show. In due course Flash Cube sired the Am. Ch. Page Mill On the Road Again, a stud dog who has been influential for many

kennels, including the Fulkersons' own. Two of his sons, Am. Ch. Swan Lake Fail Safe and Am. Ch. D'Capri's Tribute, have also helped in the Fulmont breeding program. Breeding on a small scale, the Fulmonts breed just one or two litters a year. Says Julie Fulkerson: "We concentrate on correct angulation and movement, and type in which elegance is balanced with substance."

MEADOW CREST

Didier's kennel began with the purchase of Am. Ch. Starbuck's Meadow Song. Her first litter was whelped in 1979 and contained Am. Can. Ch. Meadow Crest's Grand Slam, Am. Can. Ch. Meadow Crest's Top O' The Ninth and Ch. Starbuck's Full Count. These were sired by Am. Ch. Hickorynut's Hangman. While Meadow Song was a daughter of Am. Ch. The Whim's Buckeye, Hangman was by the legendary producing Buckeye son, Am. Ch. Starbuck's Hang 'em High. Meadow Song was also bred to Am. Ch. Sunbriar Lucky Star, which tightened up the Starbuck line, and to the outcross Am. Can. Ch. Teloca Patches Littl' Dickens. These combinations

Am. Ch. Fulmont's Flashcube, a 13 inch male who became the first red and white of either size to win Best in Show.

Photo: Twomey.

A major influence on the Fulmont breeding program was Am. Ch. D'Capri's Tribute, owned by Julie Fulkerson and Sharon Clark.

Photo: Alverson.

168

Am. Can. Ch. Meadow Crest's Grand Slam, a 15 inch son of Am. Ch. Hickorynut's Hangman and Annette Didier's foundation bitch, Am. Can. Ch. Starbuck's Meadow Song. Photo courtesy: Didier.

Annette Didier's home-bred 15 inch male, Am. Ch. Meadow Crest's Fireside Chap, a son of Am. Can. Ch. Teloca Patches Littl' Dickens and Am. Can. Ch. Starbuck's Meadow Song. Photo: Booth.

served to lay the foundation from which Meadow Crest still draws to maintain its type, structure and movement. More recently introduced bloodlines to the Meadow Crest base are Buglair, Validay and White Acres in addition to Sergeant Pepper (Netherlands) and Red Baron (Germany). Meadow Song produced 12 Champions in all and five Hound Group winners. Her son, Grand Slam, sired 19 Champions including Am. Ch. Starbuck's Fair Warning who was the top winning Beagle in the USA for 1983. In Meadow Song's fourth litter came Am. Ch. Meadow Crest's Fireside Chap, the kennel's first all breeds Best in Show winner. Both Am. Ch. Meadow Crest's Masterpiece and Am. Ch. Meadow Crest's Winjammer, from Song's second litter to Hangman, were Best of Variety winners at Specialty shows, with Masterpiece taking several Bests. Annette Didier's priorities in a Beagle include type, soundness, temperament, substance and balance. She continues: "Though each of these elements is imperative for the 'complete' Beagle, one is not more

important than the other. All elements must be in harmony, one affecting the other, for the 'proper' Beagle. A Beagle can be of beautiful type – however, without proper structure, adequate substance and balance, it cannot function properly. A well-structured and correct moving dog is of little value if the Beagle's temperament and type fall short of that desired. This is what determines a Beagle as a Beagle – aside from all other breeds."

SHADOWLAND
Born of the combination of Ralph C. Barger's Shadowrock and Andrea C. Bradford's Crackerland, Shadowland is the kennel name now used by the partners. Andrea Bradford admits that her first venture into breeding Beagles was none too auspicious. In 1984 she bred a litter of six puppies – all males with three testicles between them, and not two on the same dog! So she started over, buying a new foundation bitch in Am. Ch. Swan Lake Kelly Girl from Sharon Clark. From this bitch, the breeding program at Shadowland

Am. Ch. Shadowland I Say Again, a 15 inch male owned by Andrea Bradford and Ralph Barger.   Photo: Earl Graham.

has incorporated Page Mill and Fulmont bloodlines to good effect. To date the kennel has produced 26 Champions. Typical of these is the well known red and white 15 inch male, Am. Ch. Shadowland I Say Again, who was campaigned to many notable wins by Sharon Clark. Shadowland was the home for many years to Am. Ch. Fulmont's Fire Cracker, co-owned with Julie Fulkerson, and he was a great companion to Andrea Bradford. As regards her priorities in the breed, Andrea Bradford says: "My major priorities in a Beagle would have to be movement and overall type. A dog designed to spend his days in the field must be able to cover ground and last the day. I'm not sure the movement in some show Beagles can meet these requirements, but the type in the field dogs is frequently appalling."

SHAW'S
John and Peggy Shaw have now owned or bred some 78 Champions. They acquired their first show Beagle in 1974, Am. Ch. Timeric's I've Got Dibbs, a 13 inch bitch who was ranked Number 6. In 1975 they bought another 13 inch bitch, Am. Ch.

Timeric's Hilda and these two bitches served as the kennel's foundation. They were mostly of Busch's breeding and they were duly bred to Busch's males. The first litter consisted of one puppy, Am. Ch. Shaw's I've Got Charm, by Am. Ch. Busch's Ranch Hand out of Dibbs. Charm was later bred to a grandson of Hilda, Am. Ch. Shaw's Watch Out for Hermie, and from this start John and Peggy began to develop what they considered to be a very sound and consistent producing bitch line; however, they were not producing the type of male they really wanted. In 1985 they acquired Am. Ch. Kamelot and Shawe's Kome Lately, a 15 inch son of Am. Ch. Starbuck's Hang 'em High and a grandson of Am. Ch. Plain and Fancy Clover. This male, used on Hermie daughters, proved a highly successful outcross. The breeding of Kome Lately to Am. Ch. Shaw's Ado Annie produced the male line the Shaws were trying to develop, and resulted in Am. Ch. Shaw's Mikey Likes It, a National Beagle Club sire of the year who has produced more than 25 Champions. The kennel then brought in Am. Ch. Echo Run Kindred

Am. Ch. Shaw's Share The Spirit, a 13 inch bitch. She is full sister to Am. Ch. Shaw's Spirit of the Chase, being by Am. Ch. Shaw's Mikey Likes It out of Am. Ch. Echo Run Kindred Spirit.   Photo: Booth.

Spirit who was something of an outcross but did pick up on the Hang 'em High line. Owner-handled, this bitch did remarkably well in the show ring, taking several Groups and Specialty Bests as well as an Award of Merit at the National Beagle Club. When she was bred to Mikey Likes It, she produced Am. Ch. Shaw's Spirit of the Chase, Best of Winners at the 1994 National, Am. Ch. Shaw's Share the Spirit, winner of several Specialty Bests of Breed, and Am. Ch. Shaw's Esprit de Corps, also a Best of Variety winner at Specialty level. Both Am. Ch. Shaw's Friendly Ghost and Am. Ch. Shaw's Maser Shaw took Best of Winners at the National Beagle Club Specialty shows. The Shaws aim to breed sound, typical Beagles with correct movement, intelligence and outgoing personalities.

Am. Ch. Skyline Special Effects, a 13 inch daughter of Am. Ch. Meadow Crest's To The Point and Skyline's Private Collection.
Photo: Ashbey.

SKYLINE

Kathy and Judy Forbes bred their first Beagle litter in 1985, having originally started as a Basset Hound kennel in 1961. Kathy began in Beagles with Am. Ch. Merry Song's Husker in 1984, since which time Skyline has finished some 32 Champions, all but four of these being home-bred or sired by one of their stud dogs. Most of them have been handled by Kathy. The kennel is essentially founded on The Whim's, Meadow Crest and Merry Song bloodlines. The first Champion was Am. Ch. Skyline's Thief Of Hearts who finished by going Best of Winners at her first National Beagle Club Specialty in 1986. Later Am. Ch. Meadow Crest's To The Point was bought in and has subsequently proved a valuable influence on the breeding program. In 1992 Am. Ch. Wishing Well's Love Song was acquired and she has acquitted herself well, winning several Specialty Bests. The Forbes are keen to produce good sound Beagles with good type and correct movement coming and going as well as in side gait. They aim for a balanced dog with proper size and proportion and, says Kathy, "We also concentrate on remedying any health problems and temperament problems that are common in the breed."

TELOCA

While Marie Shuart originally bred Beagles under the Robin's name, she is best known as being Teloca. Breeding her first litter in 1966, her kennel was based on Kings Creek lines. Am. Ch. Robin's Red of Honey Hill CD became the first Champion and also won the kennel's first Obedience title. She was a top producer, and since her time there have been some 150 Teloca Champions. Of these the best known has to be Am. Ch. Teloca Patches Littl' Dickens, the Number One Hound for several years and subsequently the top producing hound. He won many Bests in Show at both Specialty and all breed Shows. The owner of the Telocas enjoys both conformation and obedience competition with her Beagles and consequently places great emphasis on the ideal temperament.

Three of Marie Shuart's original Beagles, all with Obedience titles: (left to right) Am. Ch. Robin's Red of Honey Hill CD, Lady Susan of Camelot CD and Am. Ch. Robin's Luv CD.

Photo courtesy: Stuart.

THE WHIM'S

The Whim's Beagle kennel was founded by Dr and Mrs Tony Musladin with the birth of its first litter in 1965. Am. Ch. Page Mill Wildfire, a 13 inch bitch, had been bought as a three month old puppy from Art and Carroll Gordon (now Diaz). Upon completion of her show career, this lovely bitch was bred to Am. Ch. Page Mill Trademark and produced four puppies. One of these, Am. Ch. The Whim's Firecracker, was mated back to her maternal grandsire, Am. Ch. Wandering Wind, and produced very well. Puppies from this breeding found their way to Canada and Denmark, where they produced equally successfully, but the most important from this combination has to be Am. Ch. The Whim's Buckeye, a 13 inch male who was one of the Top Hounds of the 1970s. He

made yet further impact as a stud, siring 99 Champions, many of whom were Best in Show winners at all breed and Specialty level. He also had the ability to produce the producers. Indeed, his son, Am. Ch. Starbuck's Hang 'em High, outdid his sire with both his show and stud record. Buckeye influenced the British Beagle to an extent, as Ch. Am. Ch. Graadtres Hot Pursuit of Rossut was by a Buckeye son out of a Buckeye grand-daughter. The Musladins have finished more than 70 Champions, and interestingly, by their own admission, their tightly-bred line proved stronger in males than in bitches, with a few exceptions. Am. Ch. The Whim's Cock of the Walk was a 13 inch male of interesting breeding. He was sired by Buckeye out of Am. Ch. The Whim's Chatterbox. Chatterbox was out of Am.

Tony and Judy Musladin's Am. Ch. The Whim's Buckeye, an exceptional 13 inch male who was a multiple Best in Show winner with 44 Group Firsts to his credit. He was the Top Beagle in the US for 1970, 1971 and 1972 and went on to sire 99 Champions. He influenced the breed in Britain to a degree, as the imported Ch. Am. Ch. Graadtres Hot Pursuit of Rossut was by a Buckeye son out of a Buckeye grand-daughter. *Photo courtesy: Musladin.*

Ch. The Whim's Priscilla Mullins, full sister to Buckeye, by Am. Ch. Seven Hills Black Gold, the dog who was to influence the breed so much in Denmark. Cock of the Walk sired 42 Champions, among them many Best in Show winners at Specialty and all breed level. Temperament is first in the Musladins' list of priorities, followed by balance and soundness. Says Judy Musladin: "A sweet expression is very important as well as a level topline."

WHISKEY CREEK
Although Michelle Sager acquired her first show Beagle in the early 1960s she and partner Tony Castellano did not breed their first litter until 1976. They began what they consider to be their current breeding program in the early 80s, with the acquisition of Whiskey Creek's Pretender from Robert Felty. She was a daughter of Am. Ch. Meadow Crest Grand Slam and really the foundation bitch of Whiskey Creek. Bred to Am. Ch. Meadow Crest Beau of Temateki she produced, among others, Am. Ch. Whiskey Creek's Jokeman CD and Am. Ch. Whiskey Creek N'Erin's Maddy Hays, the two Beagles who have heavily influenced the Whiskey Creek breeding program over the past decade. These dogs and their offspring, with their heavy Meadow Crest pedigrees, combined with Bayou Oaks and White Acre bloodlines, make up most of the kennel's dogs today. Over the years, in a limited breeding program, Whiskey Creek has produced or owned 36 Champions. These include Am. Ch. Whiskey Creek's Glory Days, Best of Winners at the 1985 National Specialty, and Am. Ch. Whiskey Creek's Racer's Edge, the Best of Variety at Westminster in 1984. Jokeman is considered by Michelle Sager to be their most significant Beagle, as a producer, a companion and an example of what they

Am. Ch. Whiskey Creek's Headliner, a son of Am. Ch. White Acres I'm Heavenly Too and Am. Ch. Whiskey Creek N'Erin's Maddy Hays. He was bred by Michelle Sager and Tony Castellano. Photo: Ashbey.

consider to be good breed type. He has put his stamp on the offspring from bitches of varying bloodlines. Maddy Hays was bred to Am. Ch. White Acres I'm Heavenly Too in 1992 and produced Am. Ch. Whiskey Creek's Headliner who has become the kennel's biggest winner in the show ring today. (Interestingly he has mainly been handled by Mike Scott, son of Ray and Ginger Scott who owned the Kamelot Beagles which have influenced several other successful kennels to a marked degree.) Headliner is now making his mark as a producer. Says Michelle: "In developing our breeding program, we have focused on producing what we consider good type, a pretty head, free whelping bitches and a temperament that makes the Beagle a pleasure to live with. We don't hesitate to go out to other bloodlines if we think they might have something to contribute to ours. Sometimes we have been successful, sometimes not. By doing so, over the past several years we have also made improvements in the front end assembly and movement of our Beagles, and are looking forward to Beagling in the years to come."

CANADA

While there is a very keen interest in the Beagle as a sporting dog in Canada, with many flourishing field clubs established, the breed has been through something of a low ebb as far as a popular show dog is concerned, with many shows attracting fewer than ten Beagles. However there remain stalwarts of the breed whose kennels continue to produce top quality hounds which can win not only in Canada but also in the United States.

Back in the Sixties, breeders such as Phillip Jacobi (Jacobi Kennel) and Betty McKillop (Branchflower) had produced excellent stock on which others could build. Donna James' Briarpatch kennel was founded on Jacobi bloodlines and enjoyed great success through the 80s, her dogs generally being handled by her daughter, now Sue-Ellen Rempel, an accomplished judge in her own right. In the 70s, the Buttonwood's kennel of Dorothy and Roy

Hornbostel produced some excellent winners, while Dennis Somers' Densom kennel not only bred some great winners for the home kennel, but provided sound foundation stock for future breeders.

Gwen Marotte was born in Australia, and imported Beagles from her homeland after she had settled in Canada. Her Yarra-Belle kennel combined the lines of the English Rozavel and American Elsy's Beagles, later incorporating Whim's bloodlines. In 1979 David and Beryl Broadbent emigrated to Canada from Northern England, where they had already been introduced to showing Beagles by Ruth Brucker of Twinrivers fame. One of their early dogs was a son of the American import Rozavel Elsy's Diamond Jerry, and they subsequently incorporated Rossut, Pinewood, Saravere and Wembury lines into their breeding programme. Taking a Saravere brood bitch with them to Canada, they later brought in Densom lines, and those of the American-based Meadow Crest kennel, with some success.

Jane Lloyd's first Beagle came from the Jacobi kennel in 1957, but the current

Jane Lloyd's Am. Can. Ch. Terwillegar's Hit The Roof winning the Hound Group at the prestigious 1991 Show of Shows in Canada.
Photo: Mikron.

Shirley Winslow's Am. Can. Ch. Lenwin's Dan Dee Li'l Duffer .
Photo: Mikron.

174

Shirley Winslow's Can. Ch. Lenwin's Nifty Li'l Nipper.   Photo: Mikron.

Bill and Sue Gear's Am. Can. Ber. Ch. Pinedale's Clancy was a big Canadian winner of the 1980s.   Photo: Alex Smith.

breeding of her Terwillegar Beagles stems from the progeny of Yarrabelle's males and a Whim's bitch. US Can. Ch. Whim's Raise The Roof was a leading light in Canadian show ring circles for some time and, when mated to a Page Mill dog, she produced Am. Can. Ch. Terwillegar's Hit The Roof, who remained Number One Beagle in Canada for three years. Jane's kennel has dominated the breed in Western Canada for some fifteen years, and she is presently campaigning Am. Can. Ch. Terwillegar's Country Boy.

Bill and Shirley Winslow's interest in the breed began with the purchase of a

companion for their son in 1982. The first puppy they produced also became their first Champion, Lenwins Solo Flight and also proved a great success in Obedience competition. Participating in that kind of competition taught her both humility and perseverance, claims Shirley! Subsequently the Lenwins kennel has worked closely with John and Peggy Shaw of Illinois, whose Shaw's kennel has produced several generations of excellent Champions. Mating Birchwood Justa Nuff Lenwin to Am. Ch. Shaws Mikey Likes It resulted in Shirley's Can. Ch. Lenwin's Dan Dee Li'l Duffer, described by his owner as "the

Best of Breed under judge James L. Rice at the 1992 National Beagle Club of America Specialty was Bill and Sue Gear's Am. Can. Ch. Lenergie Clancy Lower The Boom.

Photo: Ashby.

The 1994 winner of the National Club of America Specialty was Bill and Sue Gear's Am. Can. Ch. Fircone County Cousin, one of several Canadian-based dogs to have won well in the United States for these enthusiasts. He was handled by Will Alexander and the judge was Anne Rogers Clark.   *Photo: Kohler.*

ultimate show dog", and with a record to prove it. Duffer produced well and, when used by the Shaws, sired Am. Ch. Shaw's Savanah Rose, who then joined Lenwin's and became the dam of one of the kennel's current stud dogs, Can. Ch. Lenwin's Nifty Li'l Nipper.

One of the most successful of Canadian Beagle kennels is Lenergie, owned by Bill and Sue Gear, who have been breeding for twenty-five years, originally working with

Densom foundation stock. They have achieved many top honours, their hounds usually being handled by Will Alexander, one of Canada's leading professional handlers. Such honours include twice Best of Breed at the American National Beagle Club Specialty – in 1992 with Am. Can. Ch. Lenergie Clancy Lower The Boom, and in 1994 with Am. Can. Ch. Fircone Country Cousin.